Police Visibility

Police Visibility

Privacy, Surveillance, and the False Promise of Body-Worn Cameras

Bryce Clayton Newell

UNIVERSITY OF CALIFORNIA PRESS

University of California Press
Oakland, California

Library of Congress Cataloging-in-Publication Data

Names: Newell, Bryce Clayton, author.
Title: Police visibility : privacy, surveillance, and the false promise of body-worn cameras / Bryce Clayton Newell.
Description: Oakland, California : University of California Press, [2021] | Includes bibliographical references and index.
Identifiers: LCCN 2020048858 (print) | LCCN 2020048859 (ebook) | ISBN 9780520382916 (hardback) | ISBN 9780520382909 (paperback) | ISBN 9780520382923 (ebook)
Subjects: LCSH: Video surveillance—Social aspects—Northwest, Pacific—21st century. | Wearable video devices in police work—Northwest, Pacific—21st century. | Police—Northwest, Pacific—21st century. | Social control. | Privacy, Right of.
Classification: LCC HV7936.T4 N484 2021 (print) | LCC HV7936.T4 (ebook) | DDC 363.2/32—dc23
LC record available at https://lccn.loc.gov/2020048858
LC ebook record available at https://lccn.loc.gov/2020048859

25 24 23 22 21
10 9 8 7 6 5 4 3 2 1

Contents

Acknowledgments

Many individuals have impacted me and my work throughout the process of developing this book. It is not possible to name and thank each of these individuals here (and I would likely inadvertently fail to include everyone who deserves to be in such a list), but I do want to specifically thank my editor, Maura Roessner, for her insights and excitement for the project; Sandra Braman, who provided encouragement and insightful comments on prior drafts of this manuscript; the anonymous reviewers of the book proposal and drafts of the full manuscript, whose comments have challenged me but have also forced me to improve the work; my former doctoral supervisor, Adam D. Moore; and faculty mentors Batya Friedman, Ricardo Gomez, Steve Herbert, Ryan Calo, Stephen Gardiner, and Bert-Jaap Koops, all of whom contributed to various aspects of this work and to my development as a scholar throughout this process. I also wish to thank Mike Katell and Chris Hubbles for valuable contributions to the fieldwork for this study.

Thank you to Coke and Cindy Newell (my parents) for always supporting and encouraging me and for starting me out in life in an environment that prioritized and emphasized the importance of education, expression, and creativity.

Thank you to Aprille and our children, Annalesa, Caden, Aspen, and Oliver. I love each of you and am so incredibly grateful for your love and support—and for reminding me on a daily basis of what's really important in life.

And in memoriam to two wonderful former teachers and mentors: Floyd F. Feeney, who challenged me to take my first police ride-along while I was student in his Criminal Procedure class at UC Davis School of Law; and Keith Aoki, for being gracious and willing to supervise the development of my first published article while I was still a law student of his at UC Davis. These two experiences ignited my interests in scholarship and the police and set me on the path that has led me to where I am today.

Note about Prior Publications

The initial narrative near the beginning of the introduction and some text in chapters 1 and 6, the conclusion, and the "Methodological Note" were previously published in "Collateral Visibility: A Socio-Legal Study of Police Body-Camera Adoption, Privacy, and Public Disclosure in Washington State," published by the *Indiana Law Journal* 92, no. 4 (2017): 1329–99.

Much of the text in chapter 3 was previously published in "Context, Visibility, and Control: Police Work and the Contested Objectivity of Bystander Video," published in *New Media & Society* 21, no. 1 (2019): 60–76.

Some of the text in the conclusion builds on earlier versions of my argument, and text, previously published in "Technopolicing, Surveillance, and Citizen Oversight: A Neorepublican Theory of Liberty and Information Control," *Government Information Quarterly* 31, no. 3 (2014): 421–31; and "The Massive Metadata Machine: Liberty, Power, and Secret Mass Surveillance in the U.S. and Europe," *I/S: A Journal of Law and Policy for the Information Society* 10, no. 2 (2014): 481–522.

Some text in chapters 1 and 2 and the conclusion comes from my doctoral dissertation, "Transparent Lives and the Surveillance State: Policing, New Visibility, and Information Policy" (PhD diss., University of Washington, 2015).

Various parts of this book also build on ideas from my article "Crossing Lenses: Policing's New Visibility and the Role of 'Smartphone Journalism' as a Form of Freedom-Preserving Reciprocal Surveillance," *Journal of Law, Technology & Policy* 2014, no. 1 (2014): 59–104.

Introduction

Body-worn videos are the new cat videos.

—Jerome, police department IT director

The camera is not mine. It is not my choice to record, it is a choice the city—society—has made. I am not the one recording, the government is.

—Justin, patrol officer, SPD, 2018

The mass adoption by police of body-worn cameras is a specific manifestation of a larger phenomenon in which police departments are driving and shaping local criminal justice, surveillance, and information policies in the absence of much directly applicable legal regulation of police surveillance in the United States. However, unlike their response to many police surveillance technologies, national civil liberties organizations have also sometimes supported body-worn camera adoption as a means to protect communities from police misconduct—or at least to document aberrant police behavior.[1] Thus, the media, the police, and civil society have helped construct an image of body cameras as something different than typical police surveillance technology—as something more desirable and empowering of democratic civilian oversight of the police.

This is a dangerous assumption. And in many cases it is *wrong*.

There are some similarities between police body-camera and bystander—or "citizen"—video practices, but there are also some major differences.[2] The damning video recorded by seventeen-year-old Darnella Frazier depicting Minneapolis police officer Derek Chauvin kneeling on George Floyd's neck, suffocating and ultimately killing Mr. Floyd, sparked international outrage and a series of anti-police, police-reform, and Black Lives Matter protests in 2020. Police body-camera video has also sparked outrage and has led to some police accountability. However, who controls the camera makes a difference. Police have significant power in society. Body-worn cameras often increase that power, even when pitched to the public as serving community aims of transparency and police accountability. The introduction of body-worn cameras within the two police organizations studied here also highlights internal power struggles—power struggles that are largely due to concerns about who controls information. Analyzing police officers' subjective concerns about these cameras reveals a sense of fragility or vulnerability that works to solidify destructive us/them mentalities and magnify the warrior mentality that has become infused in American policing. The introduction of body-worn cameras reveals and exacerbates underlying fissures in police-community relations and in the relationships between frontline patrol officers and their superiors, leading to further police-citizen divisions in society.

Many proponents of police adoption of body cameras have argued that the cameras will "oversee" the police, keeping them in line and civilizing their behavior, much like bystander recordings captured by smartphones. These pro-camera narratives surrounding body-worn camera adoption are often based on the assumption that body-worn camera footage can provide more objective evidence of police-civilian interactions (like that captured by bystander video, but with more consistent and pervasive coverage of police-citizen contacts). However, in practice, rather than simply serving as accountability and transparency tools to the benefit of the public, these cameras serve the coercive aims of the state. Indeed, "because police are administrative agents, civilians will never have direct control over the regulations, application, and enforcement of police body cameras."[3] Body-worn cameras are a state-supported, administrative response to bystander video and other forms of increasing police visibilities; as such, they support the police and legitimize official state narratives and the use of state police power. In so doing, they represent a form of power that the state can use to dominate its citizens.

In combination with footage of police activity filmed by bystanders, online social media platforms are becoming flooded with videos of police conduct, which the mass media also present to their audiences. Within law enforcement, these developments raise concerns about objectivity, documentation, behavior modification, and transparency—all of which manifest as elements of a broader, and transforming, politics of information within the police and across broader society. Indeed, police practices related to using video as evidence can be seen as a form of "media labor" in which they employ "repurposing techniques and technologies borrowed from the domain of creative media production in order to invest recorded video with *indexicality*, or a direct, empirical connection to material reality."[4] These evidentiary media practices are embedded within a system that also prioritizes constructing narratives about police work, crime and social disorder, and symbolic police authority.[5] Against this backdrop, and with the advent of the body-worn camera, we can see that modern police labor has become imbued with media work, and that "both police *work* and police *authority*" have become "embodied, technical, data-intensive, performative, interpretive, and mediated."[6]

Any value for the police in increased visibility is contingent "upon maintaining 'normal appearances' and delivering 'proper performances.'"[7] The possibility that misconduct might become more visible because of increased recording poses a serious problem for law enforcement image management. The recording of nonarrest, peacekeeping activities may also subject officers to oversight from a variety of sources that may diminish their ability to exercise discretion or "act alternatively" in situations where they might otherwise have chosen not to make an arrest—for example, to merely give a warning in a situation where an offense was not patently illegal.[8] In the case of officer-mounted cameras, however, the police fulfill a gatekeeper role that is not available when they are confronted with the lenses of bystander video. This gatekeeping potentially threatens the public's ability to conduct effective citizen oversight, especially when combined with certain efforts and laws that would restrict the ability of citizens to conduct reciprocal surveillance (or "sousveillance") by filming officers in public spaces or during other police-citizen interactions.[9]

In the pages that follow, I draw from existing literature and original findings from qualitative fieldwork with police officers in two municipal police agencies in the Pacific Northwest during their initial adoption of body-worn cameras, as well as interviews with local police transparency and privacy activists, police supervisors, and body-camera technology developers. In conducting this research, I spent many hours riding in patrol cars with officers, observing and asking questions about their work and how they perceive body cameras impacting what they do on a daily basis. It is worth remembering that the departments studied were largely white and overwhelmingly male, like many police agencies, and that this also has implications for my findings. Throughout this book,

I aim to challenge popular, simplistic conceptions of police body-worn cameras as a positive, transparent mechanism for overseeing the police and ensuring "good" police behavior without serious negative consequences. Along the way, I attempt to illustrate how the advent of police body-worn cameras may also destabilize and recalibrate existing forms of information politics around police power and inadvertently violate the privacy of bystanders, victims, witnesses, and suspects—individuals who are most often members of marginalized or minority populations, the homeless, those with mental illness, and others who exist outside discriminatory social boundaries often reinforced by the police.

Throughout this book I develop an argument, based in legal and political theory informed by empirical findings, for regulating the use of body-worn cameras and the visual records that these cameras create. This argument is largely about limiting the potential for body-worn cameras to increase police power while also enhancing the ability of communities to understand and control the power their local police agencies wield. Along the way, I argue for a robust public right to document and access information about how the police do the work we've entrusted to them, for privacy-based limits on broad public disclosure in some cases, and for a more forward-thinking approach to the regulation of police surveillance powers. In particular, we should regulate the police in ways that forestall their ability to establish de facto information and surveillance policies through the unregulated procurement and deployment of surveillance technologies prior to public deliberation, debate, and consent.

By looking at police body cameras as a site of information politics and understanding how these politics emerge within the policing organizations I studied, I am concerned with how the adoption of these cameras implicates the possibility for state domination and, in response, how we can design law and policy to mitigate this power in favor of citizens. In doing so, I draw from neorepublican theories of freedom and "antipower" as framed by Pettit.[10] In this view, if an act or policy arbitrarily dominates the will and autonomy of citizens, thus violating their ability to self-govern (as a collective body of citizens), then these acts or policies are unjustified. This power to remove the potential for domination is Pettit's notion of "antipower."[11] This proposition is part of a larger neorepublican research agenda based on three primary tenants: individual freedom (conceptualized as freedom as nondomination), limited government power over its citizens based on a mixture of constitutionalism and the rule of law, and a vigilant commitment by citizens to maintain the freedom-preserving structure and substance of their government through active democratic participation.[12] This argument is closely related to Roberts's position that, "members of a republican democracy can only realize the ideal of self-government, and be sure that they will enjoy conditions of non-domination, through active participation in the decision-making processes that generate—determine the nature and extent of—the norms that will regulate their conduct."[13]

The notion of *antipower* is particularly important to my analysis. Antipower may manifest as rights or activities that promote the ability of the public to interfere with the coercive workings of the state. For example, rights to access government information, including body-worn camera footage, or to record the police exemplify antipower. Antipower, then, essentially encompasses the conditions necessary and sufficient for freedom to exist. When these conditions obtain, people "[enjoy] the non-interference resiliently" because they are not dependent on the arbitrary use of power, precisely because they have the power to "command non-interference."[14] As such, they enjoy some greater measure of freedom.

In the sections that follow, I introduce some of the major themes that emerge throughout the rest of the book. I start at the beginning of my fieldwork in late summer 2014, shortly after the tragic police shooting of Michael Brown, an unarmed black teenager, by a white police officer in Ferguson, Missouri.[15] In the scene that follows, I describe one of my initial encounters with the subjects of my study while attending the introduction of the cameras within one of the agencies.

September 2014: Inside the headquarters of a municipal police department in Washington State

I sit against the wall in an overcrowded room as about two-dozen police officers pull small black cameras out of square white boxes. Most of them appear eager to see what is inside, and they begin to talk excitedly among themselves as they try to figure out how to attach the cameras to their uniforms. A representative from the camera manufacturer explains to the officers what to expect from their new body-worn cameras. As the trainer explains how to activate and deactivate the cameras, electronic beeps fill the room as a number of the officers initiate their first recordings. All the officers, except two, have volunteered to wear the cameras as part of the department's initial body-camera pilot program. The other two, like all other new recruits and lateral transfers into the department, are required to begin using a camera as soon as they begin work or complete their field training. The officers have a variety of reasons for volunteering to wear the cameras, but some claim they want to be able to document evidence and counter unfounded claims of misconduct. Others hope that the footage will show citizens just how mundane most police work actually is, and that most police officers are not hell-bent on violating people's rights.

As the trainer shows sample videos of officers using electronic control devices (e.g., TASERs) to subdue uncooperative suspects, officers express excitement about the video they see on the screen and ask how they should mount their own cameras to get a similar perspective. As they try out various mounting options, one officer turns to another and, as he struggles to get the camera situated on his uniform, says, "Don't look at me like I'm a monkey, I'm just bad with technology." Another officer turns to his neighbor and says, "I guess I won't say anything stupid, I'm sure at least one person in the room is recording right now."

The good humor in the room is evident as the officers play with the cameras for another few minutes. Eventually one officer asks jokingly, "Where's the direct-to-YouTube button?" The subsequent commentary makes it obvious that some of the officers feel that they should have the ability to post videos of citizens to YouTube, just as citizens have been doing (with videos of the police) for years. "If citizens can do it," another officer asks me after the training, "why can't we also benefit from the ability to record in public places?" This statement, like others I heard, highlights the vulnerability officers feel because of the potential their work will become more visible, but it also suggests that the power the police hold in society is sometimes invisible even to themselves.

Just days after this initial training meeting, the department (and others across the state) received a blanket request from an anonymous member of the public, under the state public records law, for all video footage generated by body-worn cameras or dashboard cameras mounted in patrol vehicles (for the text of this request, see the box).

Working from the city attorney's legal advice that almost all the footage must be disclosed without any form of redaction, the department struggled to process hundreds of hours of early footage, a lengthy process that—at the time—involved manually redacting footage on a frame-by-frame basis. Within a couple of months, the department had disclosed all the test videos created by the officers during their training meeting, along with many other videos recorded by the officers over the next few weeks as they interacted with civilians during their shifts. After the department disclosed the footage, the (then) anonymous requester uploaded it directly to his YouTube channel. Within weeks it became

Text of Public Records Request Received by Department in September 2014

This is a public records request for the police department.

I'm requesting all dash and body camera videos not involved in pending litigation.

I would like the requested videos to be uploaded to Youtube by the department at https://www.youtube.com/user/[redacted] or another channel. If the department doesn't want to upload them to its own Youtube account then I would like it to consider uploading it to Youtube via an account I create and maintain. If uninterested in doing that I would like it to consider uploading the videos to a website, FTP server or cloud storage system like Dropbox or Google Drive.

I would like the videos uploaded in installments beginning with the oldest.

Videos disclosed to this requester were posted to an anonymous YouTube channel at https://www.youtube.com/user/policevideorequests. The Seattle Police Department responded by holding a hackathon and ultimately hiring the person who had filed the original request (Tim Clemans).

clear that the state's freedom of information (FOI) law was functioning as a legally sanctioned direct-to-YouTube alternative for police body-camera footage, albeit pushed online by private actors and not the police officers themselves.

POLICE VISIBILITY

The police, traditionally the most visible face of modern criminal justice systems, have generally been visible only through direct interactions with citizens, either to those with whom they interact directly or to nearby bystanders. This primary and unmediated form of visibility also includes police uniforms and marked vehicles as markers of official authority and legitimacy. Primary visibility may hinder some aspects of police work while facilitating others and may have an impact on the way citizens interact with officers.[16] However, the development of mass media and the more recent digital revolution have led to myriad—and often technologically mediated—forms of visibility, from television news broadcasts of video captured by citizens' video cameras or CCTV footage to the increasing prevalence of YouTube and other social media channels dedicated to highlighting police (mis)conduct. These secondary forms of police visibility allow many individuals to access photographic and narrative materials documenting and describing these encounters and subsequently pass judgment, even when they are not physically present at the scene of the original interaction. Additionally, the police have long engaged in "image work"—that is, "all the activities in which police forces engage and which construct and project images and meanings of policing"—and have actively worked to produce and generate the social meanings of policing.[17]

With the advent of mass media, police-media relations became an increasingly important consideration when managing police visibility. As Mawby has argued, police image work has always been about "seeking and retaining legitimacy."[18] It is about informational power and meaning making. Bystander video and online social media have shifted some informational power to those outside police organizations, challenging police ability to frame and anchor narratives. The video of police officers beating Rodney King in Los Angeles in 1991, filmed by bystander George Holliday, provides a clear—and now famous—example of how citizen video can quickly generate considerable visibility for police officer conduct. The mass media played or described Holliday's footage repeatedly for quite some time, leading to large protests across the United States and internationally. More recently, the police-involved killings of George Floyd, Oscar Grant, Ian Tomlinson, Eric Garner, Walter Scott, and many others—all captured by citizens on cell-phone cameras and later made available on YouTube and other (including newspaper) websites—demonstrate the increasing power of these recordings to spread widely and influence public perception, mass protests, and media coverage of police-related events.[19]

Bystander video and the presence of large numbers of recording devices in many public spaces (especially in densely populated, urban areas) have increased the nature and amount of policing's secondary visibility as more and more police-civilian encounters are being recorded and broadcast over the internet to increasingly wider audiences around the world. This increase in secondary visibility has been termed policing's "new visibility."[20] These recordings, available on YouTube and many other online platforms, also include numerous videos recorded by police department cameras installed in patrol vehicles (dashcams) or worn on officers' uniforms (body cameras), obtained by citizens under public disclosure requests, and uploaded to the internet. Of course, information law has provided access to certain police records for years, and journalists, researchers, nongovernmental advocacy organizations, and concerned citizens have long made use of these provisions to cast light on government conduct. FOI requests operate as a form of reciprocal surveillance.[21] As body-worn cameras continue to become more widely adopted, officers and departments will increasingly need to confront existing public disclosure laws. Indeed, the prediction that such adoption will result in greater numbers of videos being uploaded to the internet is an obvious one: as more footage is captured, more will get released through existing channels and subsequently be uploaded to the internet.

Although the first police deployment of modern body-worn cameras occurred in England in 2006 (and the Dutch police had also trialed portable cameras as early as 1998), the cameras did not really become mainstream in the United States until around 2014, when public and political forces pushed them onto the national agenda following the police shooting of Michael Brown in Ferguson, Missouri. The advent of body-worn camera deployment within local police departments is pushing policing's new visibility to the extreme. Body-worn cameras represent a new, radical form of police visibility insofar as they record more consistently and capture a much more inclusive picture of police officers' working lives than prior forms of surveillance. However, the fact that they are pointed away from the officer's body also suggests that officers are not the only ones subjected to this expanded visibility; those with whom officers interact are also being subjected to heightened, collateral forms of visibility whenever the cameras are activated. Indeed, these cameras also record victims, witnesses, suspects, and uninvolved bystanders who just happen to be present when the police activate their cameras. In addition, since state laws may not always require officers to inform others that they are being recorded, many who interact with police may not be informed enough to take advantage of this visibility when they have been treated badly. Unfortunately, both sides frame their efforts to manage visibility, to engage in information politics, as an act of war. We have a "war on cameras"—propagated by the police against recording bystanders—and a reciprocal use of cell-phone cameras as "peaceful weapons of resistance."[22]

COLLATERAL VISIBILITY

Beyond just increasing police visibility, broad public access to police body-camera footage (as well as bystander video of police-public contacts) makes those who are contacted by the police—including victims, witnesses, and suspects of crime, or merely those subjected to a traffic stop—potentially much more visible as well. As such, the increasing or "new visibility" of the police, based on video recorded ostensibly for the purpose of making police work more transparent and accountable, is necessarily intertwined with the increasing, *collateral visibility* of bystanders, victims, suspects, and witnesses.[23] Thus, this surveillance is refractive, as observation of one party—the police, in this case—"can facilitate control over another party that is not the direct target of data collection."[24] Importantly, those (nonofficers) made visible by the recording of police work are often those who are contacted more frequently—and sometimes disproportionately—by the police: members of marginalized or minority populations, the homeless, and those with mental illness. Importantly, when state FOI law requires police departments to disclose this sort of footage under the guise of state transparency, as is currently the case in several US states, the increased visibility of private individuals can easily become the collateral damage of our (otherwise laudable) transparency regimes.

The increased visibility that body cameras and other forms of surveillance bring with them is uncomfortable, perhaps because it violates the "implicit historical assumption that people who do not want to be observed can shield themselves from observation relatively easily by withdrawing behind visual barriers (walls, curtains, clothes)."[25] Surveillance of this sort, especially when practiced by the state, with its coercive powers, can result in the "loss of autonomy in the watched."[26] Indeed, "if people move beyond visual barriers, they knowingly take the risk that others can see them, and they can adapt their behavior accordingly. However, when visibility leads to records, where an exact reproduction can be made of an otherwise transient image, the situation changes. The image after all is being recorded, it comes within the reach of others, can be multiplied or published. . . . The fact that a fleeting image is captured in a potentially durable record makes people more vulnerable."[27]

As I spent numerous hours riding with patrol officers over the course of my research, it became increasingly clear that the privacy and other concerns commonly expressed about body cameras have much more direct (and disparate) impact on the lives of certain disenfranchised and disadvantaged minority groups. On multiple occasions, I met the same people while riding with different officers on different days, often contacted by the police for similar reasons. The revolving doors between the streets and the local jails began to come into sharp focus as officers and I repeatedly hauled people off to jail for offenses that both parties knew would not result in anything but immediate "book-and-release," leaving the arrestees with the task of finding their own way home, back across town, often without money or other resources.

"Maybe What I Really Should Do Is Stop Drinking"

One winter evening, I find myself standing inside a couple's living room with two officers as the man and woman, separately, try to explain why the wife had called 911 and accused the husband of threatening violence. The husband is drunk—and drinking continuously while talking to the officer who is wearing a camera on his chest—and tells a rambling story about how much trouble his wife has caused him over the years. *Perhaps he should leave her and move on. Perhaps he loves her. On the other hand, she has caused him nothing but grief, and she makes his life miserable.*

Accepting the officer's "If you think that's what needs to be done, then what are you going to do about it?" as an affirmation of his tentative plan to leave his wife, the man says, "Now, don't try to force me into anything. . . . I see what you are trying to do here." Moments later, he says, "Maybe what I really should do is stop drinking," and he takes another sip from his beer can.

Turning to me, he asks, "Who are you?"

I have been in the room as long as the officer has been, about ten minutes at this point, but this is the first time the man has really noticed me standing a few feet to the officer's side. I'm wearing street clothes, including a collared shirt and jeans—certainly not police-officer blues.

He stares at me intently for a few moments.

"He's with us," the officer says, and then points to his body camera. "He's evaluating how we work while wearing these cameras."

"Oh, that's good," the man replies, and his attention moves back to the officer.

Even if he were sober, he probably would not realize that this conversation was possibly bound for YouTube and virtually unlimited visibility. If he did, would he or his wife (who was talking to a second officer in the far corner of the room) have let the police into their house in the first place? Would the wife even have called to report her husband's threats? It's a very sad, very personal, and intimate discussion with a police officer (and me), and it's not entirely private, especially due to the presence of the camera and the legal obligations that the department is under to release footage.

Because some individuals and communities are filmed by officers' body cameras much more frequently than other segments of their communities, their images, activities, and conversations are most likely to be disclosed under freedom of information laws and uploaded to the internet for virtually unlimited visibility. However, when asked, most of these individuals expressed some level of approval for police body cameras; as one arrestee told me in the booking area of the jail, "It protects him [the officer] and it protects me." This general sense of approval has also been noted in other studies, in which most arrestees as well as general members of the public have supported the idea of police officers wearing cameras.[28] However, several officers from my study did report privacy-related concerns about the recording or public disclosure of recordings depicting people in mental health crises or other vulnerable situations. For example, concerns about public disclosure of footage were heightened, for some officers, "when [members of the public] are in mental crisis, medical crisis, or the victim of a crime" (Joseph, lieutenant, SPD, 2018). In the end, body-worn cameras have been touted as a "technological fix" to problems of overpolicing, inappropriate uses of force, and discriminatory policing practices, but in reality, they raise serious privacy concerns that might not be worth the trade-off.[29]

THE TECHNO-REGULATION OF THE POLICE

The premise behind many arguments for body-worn camera adoption has been the notion that cameras will regulate officer and civilian behavior in positive ways—for example, by "civilizing" their behavior during moments of interaction—despite conflicting evidence about whether or how body-worn cameras reduce violence and conflict in police-public interactions. (However, it should be noted that the adoption of body-worn cameras in other countries, like the Netherlands, has often been motivated by different concerns, including protecting police officers and other public employees from *civilian* aggression.[30]) It is no secret that information and communication technologies (ICTs) have "revolutionized police practices" for decades, and the recent, widespread adoption of body-worn cameras by local police departments in the United States is no exception.[31] In just the past few years, a rapidly growing body of research has questioned whether and how the deployment of body-worn cameras within police agencies is or is not altering the behavior of police officers and the civilians with whom they interact.

Within this context, body-worn cameras can be seen as a *normative technology*—that is, a "technology with intentionally built-in mechanisms to influence people's behavior."[32] In doing so, body-worn cameras (and the attendant policies about officer discretion, camera activation, and access to footage) have become a popular tool for the *techno-regulation* of the police—that is, they represent a "deliberate or intentional use of technology to regulate human behavior."[33] This behavioral regulation represents the use of administrative and supervisory power over frontline police officers, and the information generated by these officers' use of body-worn cameras only exacerbates these internal tensions. Indeed, police departments clearly have an interest in regulating the visibility of the activities of their personnel, as negative media attention may have significant implications for department image management and efforts to build trust with local communities. Secrecy, despite certain legitimate justifications (e.g., not compromising an ongoing investigation) has become a familiar protective practice used by police leadership to avoid embarrassment and accountability.

If we separate routine police work into two types—law enforcement and keeping the peace—it is also clear that law enforcement activities, like arrests and warranted searches, have also traditionally been subject to more public visibility than other, peacekeeping activities. The recording of these peacekeeping activities with officer-worn body cameras may subject officers to new levels of oversight from a variety of sources. This new visibility promises greater possibilities for oversight, but it also potentially diminishes the ability of officers to act alternatively in situations that may not have traditionally resulted in formal, law enforcement outcomes. For example, officers may choose to give warnings in situations where the observed offense is not patently illegal, or where they feel a formal, punitive action would do more harm than good. However, if these decisions are recorded on camera and subject to scrutiny, officers may feel more inclined to initiate formal enforcement actions (e.g., arrests or citations), or they may choose not to engage in as many citizen contacts in the first place.[34] On the other hand, of course, restricting body-camera use and enacting broad public disclosure exemptions for body-camera footage both potentially threaten the public's ability to conduct effective oversight. Combined with widespread efforts in some jurisdictions to restrict the ability of citizens to record police conduct—in public spaces or during other police-citizen interactions—these concerns are significant.

The increasing visibility of police work directly affects human behavior, including the behavior of police officers. Along these lines, one patrol officer I surveyed stated:

> Right now (in the state of Washington) officers are making discretionary decisions to turn off the camera to protect the public's privacy (due to the freedom of information act). In reality, officers shouldn't be the ones having to make that decision. . . . If an officer decides to turn a camera off because they are taking a sexual assault case, there is going to be serious argument by the defense once it goes to trial. (Wade, patrol officer, SPD, 2015)

This refrain was echoed in several of my interviews with officers, especially during the first few months of deployment, when the anonymous public disclosure requests were fresh on the officers' minds. However, sadly, the concern for victim privacy echoed in this quote doesn't reflect the more dominant strain of responses I heard, which prioritized evidence gathering and officer privacy. More often than not, officers said they wouldn't stop recording because they needed to protect themselves if someone complained about their conduct.

Importantly, any behavioral change by frontline patrol officers will likely extend not only to their public performances, such as public interactions with members of their communities, but also to various backstage performances, such as writing internal reports. If so, body-worn camera deployment by public police agencies will likely affect the quality and nature of information generated on the front lines of policing—information that may often be relevant to criminal prosecutions, civil disputes, internal affairs investigations, and FOI requests from the media and members of the public. Additionally, the techno-regulatory effects of body-worn camera deployment will affect the information politics of documenting, sharing, and supervising police work throughout the stages of this information's life cycle, from initial recording by officers to its use in various downstream contexts.

The combination of legal ambiguity, questions about the long-term impacts the cameras will have on police practice and police-public interactions, and the privacy implications of public disclosure laws suggests the need for empirically grounded research and, potentially, evidence-driven policy reform. Although body-worn camera adoption in the United States may have been perceived initially as a response to officer-involved violence and a need to capture evidence of officer misconduct—or to deter such conduct in the first place—usage of the cameras may end up significantly impacting the nature of police-civilian interactions in ways not intended or even envisioned at the time the technology was deployed—and the wide public release of body-worn camera footage will likely contribute to these changes. Indeed, despite early empirical research indicating that the use of body cameras has resulted in decreased use of force by officers, subsequent research has found that this may only be true when officers are not allowed much discretion about when to turn cameras on, and that wearing a camera may—in some circumstances—also increase the risk of assaults on officers by civilians.[35]

However, although the normative aims embedded in desires to techno-regulate police conduct may guide some implementation programs, that is clearly only part of the story. Body-worn camera adoption is also largely about the state managing its image and controlling its visibility to the public. It is, in short, the practice of information politics.

INFORMATION POLITICS IN CONTEXT

Body-worn camera use; bystander video practice; and related questions of surveillance-related data collection, information ownership, information control, and public access to these recordings (and the other data they produce) speak directly to the idea of *information politics*—or the role that information plays in mediating power relationships—and the need for informed information policies to address these developments. Information politics has been described as "the manipulation of information access for political gain" and "the use of information and information processing as a decisive tool of power-making."[36] If by "information policy" we mean "to capture the decisions and actions and investments that occur to create and shape the environment in which information is made available," then information politics refers to the power-related dimensions of those decisions.[37] In a broad sense, then, information politics encompasses the collection, use, analysis, interpretation, and dissemination of information to enable or effectuate governance, regulate behavior, or implement information policies for normative purposes.

Information politics is constituted in the activities and processes that define and regulate information ownership, access, and control. Clearly, information politics is linked to power, but it must also be more than using, processing, or manipulating access to already existing information. Indeed, it is no coincidence that the concept of surveillance bears a striking resemblance to the concept of information politics. Vision, as one form of the surveillant gaze, has been described as "a sense of power," while "visibility is precisely the complex field where the visible and the articulable coexist."[38] Indeed, visibility has clear connections to exposure, recognition, subjectification, and objectification. Publicity, or the act of making visible, has been called the "governing concept of the information age," and the acts of concealment and disclosure as critical to democratic politics.[39] Thus, the acts and practices of surveillance and sousveillance are embodiments of the exercise of informational power and as such represent forms of information politics that are increasingly important to explore, question, and critique in the contemporary surveillance-saturated information society.

Body-worn cameras, in particular, provide several affordances to the individual officers and users of the cameras, their supervisors, and anyone else seeking to use the information generated by the cameras to prove an allegation or provide greater transparency and visibility to police work. In some circumstances, the ability of an officer to choose *not to record* a citizen contact may have significant (positive) implications for a citizen's privacy interests. However, officers may be hesitant to proactively cease recording to protect others' privacy interests. Officers expressed the concern to me that if they chose not to record an interaction, the media and the public would distrust their decision and assume the officer was acting badly. Additionally, by not recording, the officers will not capture potentially exculpatory evidence to ward off unfounded complaints of misconduct. The affordances of body cameras give rise to important questions about information control and access, privacy, transparency, visibility, social control and behavioral modification, and the potential for state domination—all questions of power and competing interests.

This, of course, is a rapidly changing landscape. As Braman has illustrated quite clearly, the past two centuries or so have seen a dramatic change in the extent to which governments engage with information policy as a form of governance and in the exercise of power.[40] The rapid development of ICTs and the growth of myriad forms of surveillance in recent decades have only added fuel to the fire. However, this reality cuts both ways: governments and citizens now both potentially have much greater access to information about the activities of the other than they have had in the past—and this information has the potential to produce and influence power on both sides. In some accounts, the growing ability of the citizenry (or those not typically empowered in panoptic structures) to watch the powerful may lead those in power to realize of their own visibility will lead them to "develop a self-interest in the politics of surveillance."[41] But this desire to publicize, to make information about state action visible or to force more transparent practices by the state, may also engender the depoliticizing communicative capitalism described by Dean, wherein "the deluge of screens and spectacles undermines political opportunity and efficacy" for many people.[42]

Visual media–based citizen journalism has been described in a variety of ways but is often framed as a form of witnessing and the citizens' cameras as "technologies of truthtelling."[43] It has also been framed as a form of inverse or reciprocal surveillance (or sousveillance), all forms of what Castells refers to as "counter-power."[44] A bystander's choice to record the police—for the purposes of making officers' actions visible or holding them accountable—exemplifies sousveillance as a form of information politics. Additionally, when bystander video is shared online, becoming visible to the masses, it allows a form of synoptic surveillance, empowering the public to scrutinize the conduct of the police.[45] Indeed, this "uncontrolled visibility diminishes [police] power, making the surveillance of others less possible at times and exposing them to disciplinary and legal liability. Visibility of less flattering or illegal practices challenges their operational 'sovereignty based in anonymity and observation.'"[46] This is exactly why the right of citizens to record and document police activity promotes antipower much more clearly than the adoption of police body-worn cameras does. After all, the accessibility and initial framing of body-camera footage is controlled, to a large extent, by the police themselves.

Within this context, we see that our information policies, or the "laws, regulations, and doctrinal positions . . . involving information creation, processing, flows, access, and use" greatly determine the relative power of those affected by those policies.[47] Braman, in her seminal work on information policy and power, refers to informational power as "the most important form of power in today's world," exercisable "only by those who can control power in its virtual form through ownership of the very processes by which information is created, processed, and used."[48] Wielding this informational power in certain ways implicates domination, as it allows those in power to exert control over other people's basic interests in making autonomous choices and acting independently from arbitrary interference by others.[49] Resisting this form of information-fueled domination by arranging relationships, policies, and institutional structures in ways that minimize the potential for the exercise of arbitrary power and grant some measure of antipower—the ability to command noninterference—to the citizenry has become vitally important to preserving individual and collective liberty in the contemporary surveillance age.[50]

THE WAY FORWARD

To achieve the objective set out here, my aims over the remaining chapters are fourfold: (1) to examine how the crossed lenses of police body cameras and bystander video cameras (including smartphones) are making both police and civilians more visible, (2) to question how these forms of surveillance (and their attendant visibilities) are changing the information politics at play within the police, (3) to interrogate how the adoption of body-worn cameras is changing police work on the ground (as a form of techno-regulation), and (4) to develop an argument for how we ought to balance privacy and transparency interests within this rapidly evolving context.

In chapter 1, I focus on the concepts of visibility and surveillance. Surveillance, law and regulation, and the technological regulation of human behavior all come together in ways that affect our privacy and, ultimately, our freedom. I outline how the affordances of surveillance-enabling technologies, such as body-worn cameras and smartphones, in combination with the affordances of new media platforms and liberal public disclosure laws, interact to create radical new forms of secondary visibility for the police as well as for those with whom they interact during their work. Finally, I emphasize the role that information plays in generating power, as well as the potential for domination.

In chapter 2, I address some of the overarching legal and political ideas that motivate my analysis, especially theories of privacy, freedom, free speech, and access to information. I link various legal and political theories to body-worn cameras and police surveillance more generally. I also set the stage for the arguments developed later in the book and set out explicitly in the conclusion. The recent proliferation of surveillance in society and its attendant questions about information access and control have important ramifications for how we think about political freedom. The reduction of arbitrary power (domination) clarifies roles and promotes individual and collective political freedom but does not necessarily reduce the ability of the government to protect its people. Achieving this balance while maintaining robust individual rights of privacy and free speech (including access to information) is no small task.

In chapter 3, I highlight the practices and legality of bystander video—that is, when members of the public record the police using their smartphones, camcorders, or other devices. I present a legal analysis of how the law protects this "right to record" by examining court decisions at both federal and state levels. In most cases, courts have held that the First Amendment to the US Constitution protects the right of citizens to record the police, and this finding is reflected in the law of Washington State (the site of my fieldwork). Moving from the law to empirical findings, the remainder of the chapter analyzes how police officers perceive and understand bystander video and its impact on their work.

In chapter 4, I focus directly on officer perceptions of, and attitudes toward, body-worn cameras over time. Based largely on my interview and survey data, I outline officers' concerns as well as what they find useful about the cameras. My analysis also shows that despite their initial fears, officers became much more positive about the cameras over time, especially as they perceived them as primarily growing into evidence-gathering tools within the department that would support criminal prosecution of civilians and also exonerate officers in cases of alleged misconduct. However, officers continued to have concerns related to how their footage would be interpreted by those who might wish to hold them accountable.

In chapter 5, I focus on various ways in which law and technology regulate police work or police officer behavior. I examine how various legal questions arose throughout the fieldwork, from camera activation to the public disclosure of footage, and then question how body-worn cameras may work to "civilize" the police who wear them and the community members with whom they interact.

In chapter 6, I focus directly on issues of public disclosure. I highlight how the unintended increase in the visibility of ordinary citizens due to a combination of body-camera usage and liberal public disclosure laws has become an important variable to consider when developing law or public policy in this area. Body-worn cameras are often adopted for the stated purpose of making police officers more accountable and amenable to oversight, but we should remember that these cameras point away from the officers' bodies, and their lenses are primarily focused on those with whom the officers interact. These are often not regular middle- or upper-class members of the community, but people who are experiencing difficult and painful circumstances and/or who suffer from mental illness or homelessness, or those who are members of other communities that receive heightened police attention, for whatever reason (including race, religion, etc.).

In the conclusion, I come back to the conceptual themes that animate much of the normative argument in this book: the need to develop information policies and regulatory frameworks that ensure state surveillance does not become a dominating source of state power and is counterbalanced by effective forms of antipower. Body-worn cameras must not only serve state surveillance interests, and our laws and information policies must allow the citizenry robust opportunities to keep its government in check and document its activities. My argument begins by focusing on the importance of ensuring citizens have the right to access government information and document how police do their work in society. I argue that because the people are sovereign, they should presumptively retain the right to access and document information about how their government conducts the activities and duties they entrust to it. Next, I outline how and why the privacy of individuals captured in government surveillance records (like body-worn camera footage) should, in appropriate cases, overcome this initial presumption. Individuals' basic privacy interests, and their visibility to both the state and the public, should not become the collateral damage of a transparency regime that doesn't properly balance access, oversight, and speech, on the one hand, and privacy, on the other.

Throughout the chapters to come, I examine a variety of findings, often presented in narrative form, that help us understand the impact that body-worn cameras have on actual police practice, how officers perceive and use the cameras, and how the use of these cameras—and public disclosure policies—impact privacy and other important civil liberties of civilians within the communities served by these agencies. The big-picture questions that motivate much of this work revolve around how our communities and elected representatives should navigate the tensions between privacy and transparency—and information access and control—implicated by police body cameras, access to information laws, and the growing First Amendment right of citizens to record police officers carrying out their official duties. Lines need to be drawn that not only have practical applicability in the law enforcement community but also aim to reconstruct what it means to *police* our communities in the first place. These lines must respect long-standing free speech and (evolving) privacy rights but also have relevance in the context of mobile, wearable camera deployment by law enforcement officers across the nation.

We need an information policy that allows for balanced oversight but also avoids making personal privacy a part of the collateral damage of our transparency policies. In developing this information policy at local, state, and national levels, we must focus our energy on crafting policies that limit the possibility of arbitrary interference by the state—or state agents—with individuals' choices and promote the ability of the people to engage in democratic deliberation and active civic participation (the aims of nondomination). As framed by Vitale, "We don't need empty police reforms; we need a robust democracy that gives people the capacity to demand of their government and themselves real, nonpunitive solutions to their problems."[51] In short, we need police and information-policy reforms that generate "antipower," the ability of individuals and communities to command noninterference and resist domination.[52]

I draw from my empirical research with the aim of outlining an information policy that is defensible and practical enough to speak to law. In the end, the trustworthiness of my normative conclusions, of course, depends on my development of defensible arguments. In the chapters that follow, I seek to outline and defend these arguments, concluding the book with a consolidated argument for how we ought to rethink our existing information policies.

CHAPTER 1

Visibility, Surveillance, and the Police

"DOPER RADAR"

It was a clear but chilly afternoon in midwinter. It was also slow, as few calls for service had been placed in the last few hours—something I eventually realized was quite common, despite frequent apologetic comments from officers to the effect that "it's strangely slow today, usually there is more to do." (Of course, officer statements about slow shifts might be connected to the fact that they are more keenly aware of, or interested in, the pace of their work while entertaining a rider.) A slow day for the police is, of course, not necessarily a bad thing, at least insofar as it means less crime and violence has been occurring in the community, but it does alter the way they go about their work. On this particular day, we were just driving into an older neighborhood identified by the department's predictive policing (CompStat) system as an area of concern due to the number of prior crimes perpetrated in the area. These "hot spots" often hung around in the officers' computer-aided dispatch lists as low priority calls, and when officers really got bored, they would sometimes assign themselves to the designated area (rather than patrol elsewhere) just to fill time.

As we approached the area designated by the CompStat algorithm as a problem area, I asked a simple question that led to one of the more uncomfortable moments of my fieldwork. "How do you decide who to stop and contact?" I asked the officer as we turned off the main drag and onto a quiet residential street lined with older single-family homes. The officer responded that, as a police officer, you developed an ability to sense and identify possible suspects, something he called "doper radar." Just a few moments later, the officer pointed to a disheveled man in a black trench coat walking toward us on the sidewalk. "Here we go," the officer said as he pulled the patrol car to the curb and placed it quickly into park. I followed the officer's lead as he exited the car and quickly stepped onto the sidewalk about fifty feet from the man in the trench coat. The "suspect," who had been approaching us, stepped off the sidewalk, walked up to the front door of a modest white house, and knocked on the front door to get the attention of someone inside. By this time, I could see he was also wearing a backpack with what looked like large bolt cutters sticking out of its partially unzipped main compartment. He was white, looked to be in his early thirties, and had dirty blond hair that hung to his shoulders.

"Excuse me," the officer called loudly from about fifty feet away. "Can I speak to you for a moment?"

The man, looking agitated, stared straight ahead at the closed door of the house, refusing to make eye contact with the officer, who was still standing on the sidewalk. "I don't need police assistance!" he called back loudly—a phrase he repeated each time the officer continued his attempt to convince the man to talk.

"Whose house is that?" the officer asked.

"I don't need police assistance!" the man repeated again, while still standing on the small concrete porch and staring intently at the closed door in front of him.

At this point, the officer and I returned to his vehicle. As we sat down, while keeping watch on the man on the porch, the officer told me it was a shame that "we can't legally stop and detain him," even though the officer was convinced he had been up to something illegal. The officer opened his laptop and entered a few names into the system, trying to figure out who this man might be and whether, for example, he might have any outstanding warrants that would justify police intervention. Unsuccessful in his attempt to identify the man, he sat back and waited. Soon the man left the porch and walked back down the sidewalk, moving away from us in the direction from which he had come. "Here we go," stated the officer, as he put the patrol car in gear and slowly followed the man down the street. We followed the suspect around the corner at the next intersection, then quickly turned right again to follow him into the alley behind the row of houses where we had first encountered him.

As we entered the alley, we saw the man disappear into what appeared to be the backyard of the white house he had visited earlier. As we pulled up to the rear driveway of the home, we saw a few other men and one woman standing in the backyard or sitting on the back steps of the house, but the man we had been following was nowhere to be seen. The officer recognized one of the men and, as we exited the car, he tried to strike up a conversation. He introduced himself to the others as well and asked about the man we had been following. The men confirmed that he had just entered the house through the rear door. "What is his name?" the officer asked them. "Does he have any outstanding warrants?" After a bit of back and forth that lasted for about five or six minutes (it was apparent they didn't want to identify their acquaintance), one of the men finally offered up a first name. The officer then walked back to his car and searched through the department's database using the name he was given. In just a few minutes he located information about and a photograph of the man. The officer confirmed that—indeed—the man had an outstanding warrant, and he then used his radio to call for backup. Within minutes another officer arrived and waved at us over the fence from the front yard, indicating that he would be monitoring the front door in case the suspect exited at the front in an attempt to evade being taken into custody.

Returning to the backyard from his car in the alley, the officer told the other individuals present that the man inside the house had an outstanding warrant and asked if they would be willing to talk him into coming outside. When they insisted that the suspect would not be willing to come outside, the officer asked the other men if they would be willing to show him their IDs. They all agreed to do so. As one young man (who appeared to be in his early to midtwenties) handed over his driver's license, he admitted to the officer that he had an outstanding warrant as well, for a failure to appear in court in response to a previous infraction. The officer took each of the IDs back to his car, entered the information into his system, and returned after a few minutes. Having confirmed that the young man's confession was accurate, he informed him that he would be arrested and taken for booking at the local jail. The young arrestee informed the woman present, who we learned was his wife, that he would likely be out of jail later that day after being booked and processed (something the officer confirmed), and that she should try to arrange transportation for him to get back home. This, it appeared, would not be a simple task. Meanwhile, as this arrest was occurring, we were informed that the initial suspect had been apprehended in the front yard after exiting the house through the front door.

Afterward, the officer turned to me and asked, "What did you think of my actions, as a member of the community?" Because of my role as a researcher, I struggled to express a point of view that could be regarded as neutral, exhibiting some small level of surprise at various aspects of the events I had watched unfold but not taking a strong position one way or the other. However, I was deeply conflicted about what I had seen. I was not necessarily concerned that the officer had overstepped constitutional boundaries in his procedure, but I was somewhat unnerved by the persistence his actions displayed and his focus on one individual despite there having been no clear indications (to me) of criminality at the outset. I couldn't help but notice that he was asking me to judge his actions and the outcome of his persistence, in this case, as one who was witness to it. At the same time, I wondered whether my question, "How do you decide who to stop and contact?" or my mere presence as a rider had provoked any of what I had witnessed. My perception of this officer was that he had a desire to portray the specialized nature of police work, as well as his own prowess—the way he was able to use his power to enforce the law. The scene I had watched unfold was motivated by the officer's desire to demonstrate the efficacy of his own "doper radar."

There were not many cameras present during this incident. At least one of the men in the backyard was holding a cell phone, but it was not immediately apparent to me that it was ever used to record (at least it was never overtly pointed at the officer or myself). If the officer had not been wearing a body camera, I doubt any of the encounter would have been documented except by the officer himself in his own written report. However, this encounter also exemplifies how new forms of vision and visibility are being interjected into police work. The officer's primary visibility here was limited to visual observation by those physically at the scene (me and the others in the backyard). There was the potential for bystander recording, although that potential was not obviously realized. However, the officer was subjected to secondary visibility by the mere fact that he was using a body camera throughout the incident. Afterward, the recording was likely subject to public disclosure under the state's public records law, and the footage was certainly visible to the officer's supervisors at the police department if they ever chose to watch it.

Whether my presence had provoked anything that would not otherwise have happened, or caused the officer to perform differently in any way, was not clear. In this specific case, the officer appeared to be very confident he had performed well. His actions, initiated as a means of demonstrating his intuition and skill at his craft to an outsider, had resulted in two arrests and vindicated his claims of having proficient perception and instinct. This was the sort of visibility he apparently wanted, or at least wasn't the sort he feared. Later in the shift I asked him how he felt about being observed or recorded by others as he worked. He responded, "I do things cleanly and appropriately, so I don't care if people see what I do some of the time, but nobody is perfect, and we all have bad days too."

VIEWING THE POLICE

Liberal legal frameworks generally view the police as necessary and fundamentally beneficial to modern society. However, there is a substantial, and rapidly growing, body of research and activism (including the Black Lives Matter movement) that challenges this notion head on. Regardless of how one views the police, we should not ignore this wealth of critical perspectives or the argument that police, as an institution, is inseparably linked to state violence, domination, and exclusion. Many social actors, including many supportive of body-worn cameras, have long argued for police reform; indeed, body cameras are seen by some as moving that agenda forward.[1] For some, police reform itself is seen as nothing more than "the science of police legitimation accomplished through the art of euphemism": a project of maintaining existing social and economic structures (including social marginalization and control) and reinforcing state power. Others argue that the police cannot—and should not—be recuperated but instead must be abolished.[2]

Throughout this book, I attempt to stake out a (sometimes uncomfortable) middle ground. I feel it necessary to be explicit about my own views here, as these undoubtedly color my interpretation of my findings throughout this book. However, my goal in this book is not to set forth a broad argument for police reform; rather, my aim here is much more limited. I focus on issues of surveillance, privacy, access to information, and the empirical evidence we do have about how technology (and visibility) are impacting the way the police do the work we have currently assigned them to do. In the pages that follow, I argue for a robust public right to document and access information about how the police do the work we've entrusted them with, for privacy-based limits on broad public disclosure in some cases, and for a more forward-thinking approach to the regulation of police surveillance powers. In particular, we should regulate the police in ways that forestall their ability to establish de facto information and surveillance policies through the unregulated procurement and deployment of surveillance technologies prior to public deliberation and debate.

I also recognize that many of the perspectives offered from my data are those of the police. My data give voice to the perspectives of police officers, often reflective of what Correia and Wall refer to as "copspeak."[3] Epistemologically, I believe it is important to understand the perspectives of police officers within this context, as this may help us understand, for example, the impact that technology adoption or other information policies might have on how police officers police the way they do, or how they change their practices based on the adoption of some form of new technology. From this place, we might better understand their perspectives and how our information policies might impact our communities, but also be positioned to see how these perspectives fit into the broader rhetoric and legitimizing language of the police. I hope that my inclusion of numerous quotations from my police respondents throughout this book is seen in that light—as balancing the police perspective with its vulnerability to critique—rather than simply as an attempt at apologizing for the police.

I argue that society has a strong interest in promoting *some forms* of effective and efficient police work. However, the work we give the police to do ought to change. My views on police reform generally track those expressed by Vitale: "Any effort to make policing more just must address the problems of excessive force, overpolicing, and disrespect for the public" (especially disregard for people of color and members of other disenfranchised groups).[4] This is alternative to mainstream ideas about police reform that do not challenge police violence head on. After all, mainstream, politically accepted narratives about reforming the police—including arguments in favor of "arming" officers with body-worn cameras—are institutionalized means by "which the state manages and justifies its claim to a monopoly on violence."[5] We must question whether American policing is broken, or whether "it works exactly as designed."[6] This project will require us to think more broadly about the roles our leaders should ask the police to play in our communities and the range of social problems they task the police with addressing (the overpolicing thesis).[7]

At the outset of this project, my perspective was highly pro-privacy and anti–police surveillance; I was skeptical of police power, yet I was certainly not a police abolitionist. As a white male raised in a middle-class family in an assortment of middle-class, almost exclusively white communities in Colorado and Utah, I had few encounters with on-duty police officers. The encounters I did have were limited to a few moments in which I was pulled over for traffic infractions (and generally let go with a warning, even when I argued with the officer about the legitimacy of the stop). However, as my fieldwork progressed, my perspective became more pointed, more nuanced. I was highly troubled by some of my experiences with the police, while in others I became more acutely aware that police officers themselves are only human; many are very friendly and thoughtful (including critical) in their discussion of their profession. The distinction between the institution (and its institutionalized practices) and many of the individuals who enact those practices on a daily basis as part of their jobs is an important one.

While riding with and observing officers during my research, I encountered officers, situations, and patterns of conduct that alarmed me, as well as some that made me feel quite reassured. During my very first ride-along, in the early fall of 2014, an officer invited me into his home and introduced me to his wife and children. At the end of the ride, at about 3:00 a.m., we stopped by a small doughnut shop, where the officer bought a dozen fresh doughnuts from a local baker and offered one to me. (I have no doubt that some officers tried to sugarcoat things for me, on occasion, because I was observing them with the intention of writing about what I saw and heard, but I'm also convinced that some of the officers were genuinely decent and friendly people who went to work hoping to be a positive force in their communities.) In other circumstances, however, I was confronted with officers who introduced themselves to me as the type that "likes to break bones first and ask questions later." Many officers also spoke of their perception that they needed to be direct and even downright rude, including using coarse language, to certain "segments of the population," who they thought were incapable of understanding or responding appropriately to more polite, civilized forms of communication.

As we have seen in the many recent examples of police officers using their power to limit the ability of bystanders to record, or "watch back," the police often do "actively fabricate social order by eradicating anything [they deem] a threat."[8] The ability of the police to "provide basic citizen security" (if, indeed, that is what the aims of having police *should* be) often hinges on public trust. Such trust is fragile, as recent movements for police reform in the United States have clearly shown, yet the "extent and very existence" of this trust "depends upon a range of factors both within and outside police control."[9] Neocleous and others argue that the liberal, Western obsession with security, which pervades current approaches to state policing, subverts other freedoms.[10] And these efforts are not without discriminatory consequences. Indeed, the police are a central institution within a "criminal justice system that profoundly discriminates against non-whites and especially Blacks."[11] According to Brucato, this "system was devised primarily to administer slavery, then adapted to manage segregation. Today, U.S. police maintains *the color line* in an officially *color-blind* polity."[12]

The police have also developed a "'warrior' problem."[13] This has become a uniquely American problem in many ways. Indeed, "there is no question that American police use their weapons more than police in any other developed democracy."[14] *Enforcement* of criminal law has become the dominant mode of policing, while peacekeeping often gets neglected.[15] Police training and tactics overwhelmingly reinforce the warrior mindset, to the detriment of police-community relations, and the idealization of "police warriors" threatens to "prevent or undermine efforts to improve public perceptions of police legitimacy."[16] Armed with military-grade weaponry, police often use force too quickly, under the "belief that entire communities are disorderly, dangerous, suspicious, and ultimately criminal."[17]

These ideas are clearly reflected in my findings. Officers often told me that, for example, "people don't understand the job and how ugly the world is through our eyes" (Bond, senior patrol officer, SPD, 2018), and "our job is ugly" (John, detective, SPD, 2014). Often framed in us-versus-them terms, officers' statements frequently indicated that civilians were not to be trusted. Generally, this sentiment was reason enough for officers to support the adoption of body-worn cameras and the recording of all police-public encounters to protect themselves—for example, to "record them all because in America's current climate our judgement is not trusted" (Hale, patrol officer, SPD, 2018). For others, these same concerns led to the opposite conclusion about the benefits of cameras, as the public were viewed as standing ready to "condemn a single misspoken sentence as though we are murderers" (Hugh, detective, SPD, 2018), and "no other career path takes so much flak. The only thing to fix is stupid people [referring to certain members of the public], not the response to them" (Conrad, senior patrol officer, SPD, 2016).

The warrior ethos became particularly clear to me during a ride-along in late 2014. We were called to a home where a domestic disturbance had been reported by a neighbor. When we arrived, along with a few other officers, it became apparent that the man inside the home was suffering through some sort of mental health crisis. He was carrying a large knife and was yelling loudly into the yard at the police. As officers pulled rifles from their vehicles, we watched him barricade the home, placing furniture behind the front door and an upstairs window. One of the officers also reported seeing other people inside the home. The officers called in a negotiator and their emergency response (SWAT) unit, assuming things had turned into a hostage situation. They also began to yell into the house at the man, trying to get him to talk to them. At various moments he would appear in the upstairs window, knife dangling from his hand, urging the police to kill him, screaming "shoot me!" repeatedly. By this time I was sitting in the passenger seat of the officer's SUV, which was parked in the middle of the front yard, and—by request—was aiming one of the vehicle's spotlights at the window. A short time later I was asked to leave the scene, and another officer was assigned to drive me back to the station. As I walked toward the officer's car, I watched as the department's armored SWAT vehicle rolled slowly up to the curb in front of the house and officers with shields and riot gear emerged, taking position on the lawn.

Seven months later, on the other side of the state, I spent the night riding with an officer assigned to the graveyard patrol shift. In the early morning hours, just as the sun was coming up, we received a report of gunshots at an all-night party in a residential neighborhood. When we arrived on scene, we parked alongside a few other squad cars at the end of the street, blocking the road as it exited the neighborhood. As I emerged from the passenger compartment and stepped into the street, I noticed that officers already had their guns drawn. A sergeant had his rifle pointed down the street, roughly in the direction of a young man who was stumbling slowly toward the blockade. The officers presumed he might be the suspect, who was reportedly armed. As he drew near, two things became clear: first, he was not armed; and second, his face was covered in blood. After he was taken into custody, we walked up the street to the location of the party, where we found a large group of young people standing around, many obviously intoxicated. While the officer interviewed the crowd, I searched the pavement for the spent round, which, we were told, had been fired into the air right there in the street after an argument, just before the gunman had sped off in his car. Someone in the group showed the officer the perpetrator's Facebook profile. I found the spent round in the grass just at the edge of the pavement.

A few minutes later, after leaving in our SUV, we received a report that the perpetrator's vehicle had been spotted leaving the neighborhood. We quickly drove to the nearest overpass, parked, and watched traffic move quickly below us. After about two minutes, we saw a vehicle matching the description headed north on the freeway. We quickly merged onto the freeway and, quickly surpassing the speed limit, caught up to and followed the vehicle off at the next ramp and into a Denny's parking lot. We parked about twenty feet away from the suspect's car, which had been parked at the curb outside the restaurant. The officer got out and immediately pulled his gun. While shouting loudly at the passengers in the vehicle to "get out of the vehicle with your hands up!," the officer kept his attention on the vehicle. After a few moments, several people stuck their hands and arms out of the car's windows. Two other officers arrived along with a county sheriff's deputy. To me, standing behind a police SUV and between four armed officers, handguns and rifles were seemingly everywhere. The sheriff's deputy and sergeant had rifles. The other two officers had handguns. All were pointed at an angle, downward, but generally in the direction of the suspects' vehicle (and the restaurant window behind it). Within a few moments, each of the passengers exited the car and, at the command of the officers (and at gunpoint), held their hands up, pulled up their shirts, turned up their collars, and rotated in a circle. Each was handcuffed and detained. The officers confirmed that none of them was the alleged shooter; they had simply left the party to get breakfast. Without probable cause to hold them, the officers questioned them about the shooting and then let them go.

Fortunately, officers did not fire their weapons in either of these incidents. In both cases, the suspects were white, and the officers were white. (Indeed, the demographics of these communities are not very diverse and, by a large margin, the encounters I witnessed most frequently involved both white officers and white suspects.) However, as countless incidents around the country have shown, this is not always the case, especially in cases involving Black, homeless, or mentally ill individuals.

SURVEILLANCE IN THEORY AND PRACTICE

Surveillance, or the "focused, systematic and routine attention to personal details for purposes of influence, management, protection or direction," has clear, explicit ties to social control.[18] It's not just about watching. In fact, much of the rhetoric surrounding increased body-camera adoption after the shooting death of Michael Brown in Ferguson,

Missouri, in 2014 was based on claims that the cameras would modify both officer and civilian behavior and reduce violent police-civilian interactions. The basis for this surveillance lies not only in documenting and recording the conduct of the other (or the self) but also in modifying behavior (a form of social control) through the mere presence of the recording device itself and/or the attendant visibility of the resulting footage. As such, popular demands for outfitting officers with body cameras have included direct calls for "the collection and analysis of information about populations in order to govern their activities."[19]

Policing and criminal justice have long played prominent roles in how surveillance is conceptualized. When we hear that a person is "under surveillance," we generally link that surveillance to a supposed law enforcement purpose.[20] Indeed, police have long utilized various forms of surveillance to make spaces—and the inhabitants thereof—more visible to the state, from naked-eye observation on Victorian streets to the use of high-tech devices for undercover police work, stingrays (cell site simulators), license plate scanners, facial recognition and other biometric identification technologies, large-scale CCTV networks, and body-worn cameras.[21] In US law, spatial considerations play a large role in determining whether privacy rights can be attached to conduct in various spaces. Public spaces are generally seen as less, or not at all, private—thus surveillance is broadly allowed—while the interiors of homes or other more private or enclosed spaces attract greater (privacy) protection from the state's intruding surveillant gaze. This surveillance of public spaces also likely affects some categories of citizens disproportionately, with the potential for increasing stigmatization and more frequent criminalization of those members of society who are already more visible.[22]

In contrast to *surveillance* (which originates from the French word *surveiller*, meaning to watch over something, and is typically associated with governments or corporations watching individuals), *sousveillance* generally refers to the act of an individual watching from below as a form of inverse surveillance. The term was coined by Steve Mann, an academic and inventor, who derived the term from the French *sous* (under) and *veillance* (to watch). Sousveillance may refer to the ability of an individual person or group of persons to observe or record the actions of authorities or to the ability of individuals to watch each other. Regardless, forms of inverted surveillance are still forms of surveillance, especially when bystander recording is framed as people attempting to hold the state accountable for its conduct.

Links between totalitarian surveillance—of the sort envisioned by George Orwell in his conceptualization of Big Brother in *Nineteen Eighty-Four*—and modern liberal democracies has been a common theme in academic surveillance theory.[23] Despite the fact that ancient states also maintained records on citizens, the modern bureaucratic state's routine and sophisticated expansion of record keeping and monitoring has magnified potential threats to individual liberty. The history of the police, with its roots in managing poverty and preserving white interests, also cannot be ignored here. State surveillance does not generally focus on all, or even a large part, of society. Indeed, very early on in my rides with officers, what critical police scholars have been saying for decades became clear: officers interact primarily with a small subset of society, primarily the poor, the undocumented, those living on the streets, those with mental health challenges and/or substance abuse problems, and those who are living in violent domestic relationships. Precisely because *on-officer* cameras point away from the officers who wear them, these *civilians are the primary subjects* of body-camera surveillance. Of course these same individuals are also more likely than most to be recorded during sensitive or embarrassing moments and are probably the least able to contest the recording itself, the subsequent disclosure of footage under FOI laws, or the posting of the footage to YouTube, Facebook, or elsewhere online.

The "panopticon," Jeremy Bentham's famous architectural design idea, developed as a metaphorical landmark of power and social control by French philosopher Michel Foucault, has become a leading model and metaphor for surveillance.[24] In the panoptic design, an agent in power has the ability to watch others without their knowledge and—because of shades or other privacy mechanisms—can do so without the risk that the others will watch back. Although this metaphor may have been more or less true at various points in time, critics have argued that prioritizing the panoptic model to symbolize surveillance only provides a one-sided account that ignores the realities of modern surveillance, including the prevalence of surveillance conducted in the other direction—citizen video of police conduct, for example—or horizontally between peers. As such, the panoptic model has perhaps been overextended at the direct expense of other important aspects of surveillance.[25]

Foucauldian panopticism also omits the role of the media (either the mass media or social media).[26] Mathiesen's concepts of the "synopticon" and the "spectacle" attempt to bring this missing element back into the equation.[27] Mathiesen focused primarily on the role of the mass media in shifting society from one in which the few watched the many—the panoptic model—to one in which "*the many . . . see and contemplate the few*, so that the tendency for the few to see and supervise the many is contextualized by a highly significant counterpart."[28] However, this synoptic view can easily be extended beyond just the role of the mass media. Scholars have presented notions such as "inverse surveillance" or "sousveillance," "counter-surveillance," and the "panspectron."[29] While *inverse surveillance* generally refers to reversing the panoptic gaze by empowering individuals to watch those in power through the use of technology or other means, *countersurveillance*—as defined by Monahan—refers to "intentional, tactical uses, or disruptions of surveillance technologies to challenge institutional power asymmetries" more akin to resistance.[30] The *panspectron* refers to widespread data collection from a variety of *nonoptical* sensors and the resulting storage of data in massive databases that can be queried at will to bring subjects into focus. Combining data collected through combinations of optical and nonoptical surveillance results in the creation of abstracted "surveillant assemblages" and "data doubles" of real people, who are visible in the system only as represented by their "digital dossiers."[31]

Marx also distinguishes between symmetrical and asymmetrical surveillance, explicitly recognizing the role of freedom of information requests as a form of surveillance from underneath—that is, as a means for the many to watch the few:

> Surveillance that is reciprocal may be asymmetrical or symmetrical with respect to means and goals. Thus in a democratic society citizens and government engage in reciprocal but distinct forms of mutual surveillance. For example citizens can watch government through Freedom of Information Requests, open hearings and meetings, and conflict of interest and other disclosures required as a condition for running for office. But citizens cannot legally wiretap, carry out Fourth Amendment searches or see others' tax returns. In bounded settings such as a protest demonstration, there may be greater equivalence with respect to particular means e.g., police and demonstrators videotaping each other.[32]

Likewise, the panoptic possibility of the watcher being able to watch others without being visible to them may not be inclusive enough to fully explain the cases of police body-cameras or civilian video, as these phenomena include both elements of surveillance (in a panoptic sense) as well as aspects of sousveillance (or watching back). In some respects, each of these forms of surveillance relies not only on documenting and recording the conduct of the other or the self but also on modifying behavior (a form of social control) through the mere presence of the recording device itself. This finding is not necessarily inconsistent with panoptic theories of surveillance, but a focus merely on surveillance as directed from state to citizen may not be broad enough to capture and explain the broader dynamics inherent in inverted or reciprocal surveillance that often occur in this context. Likewise, Haggerty and Ericson's concept of the "surveillant assemblage" directs our focus to the "disconnected and semi-coordinated character of surveillance" in modern times.[33] Surveillance is disconnected because it is not all organized and instituted by one single entity. However, when institutional actors coordinate and share information, they can harness a great deal of power.

Some evidence suggests that despite their limited effects on crime rates, video surveillance systems may reduce antisocial and undesirable behavior in certain cases, although more research is likely necessary to draw firm conclusions.[34] However, some researchers report that surveillance may be used to discriminate against certain groups by limiting their access to public spaces through targeted monitoring and coordinated officer interventions.[35] This phenomenon of discrimination through surveillance technologies has been referred to as the "purification" or "commercialization" of public spaces, or "surveillance as social sorting."[36] This desire to "purify" public spaces and—in the commercial space—to not "put customers off" means, in practice, "excluding 'undesirables.'"[37] Similar observational research has documented that security operators more often than not "single out and target" individuals based on appearance alone, rather than behavior.[38] The actual or potential discriminatory effects of surveillance technologies have been documented or discussed in a variety of settings.[39] These include

public streets, transportation centers, and shopping malls;[40]
the workplace;[41]
use of electronic identity cards;[42]
intelligent transportation systems;[43]
genetic testing;[44] and
"racializing" of medical research.[45]

In an observational study of various video surveillance control rooms in Scandinavia, for example, researchers have reported various patterns of discriminatory enforcement by private security firms, instituted through coordinated monitoring and officer intervention.[46]

The accumulation of large amounts of information from multiple sites of surveillance results in surveillance agents mining for documentary traces and examining the data doubles of both the weak and the powerful members of society.[47] However, those in society without the means to exploit these surveillance potentialities—generally those who are both poorer and more frequently the target of state observation—are often left without the recourse available to the more economically well-off members of society.[48] Additionally, our perceptions about surveillance may also be linked to our exposure to surveillance, by potentially leading to lack of concern on the part of those who are not confronted with intense or obtrusive police surveillance on a regular basis. However, despite continuing inequities, we have also seen the proliferation of social visibility, in which "more people from more walks of life are now monitored."[49] Freedom of information laws and processes, as well as the right to record public officials, are powerful and important tools for the citizenry to wield in the name of inverting visibility, further increasing social visibility at all levels, and calling government actors to account. This sort of inverse surveillance is much more democratic than Mathiesen's mass media–based *synopticon*—and is potentially much more powerful.

Body-worn cameras, when worn by the police, clearly represent a form of state surveillance. However, the rhetoric surrounding their mass adoption in the United States since 2014 indicates a broad consensus that officers should be subject to heightened levels of formal accountability for their actions. We should not assume that surveillance itself is necessarily good or bad, but the recognition that body-camera technologies do constitute top-down, state-controlled surveillance systems—with the potential to invade the most private precincts of citizens' (or immigrants') lives—should provoke thoughtful and critical policy development *prior to* the adoption of these tools. These policies should also be responsive to findings that emerge from empirical research. Significant value conflicts should restrain our normative conclusions about surveillance, including its emancipatory or reforming potential, prior to some deeper analysis of the particular aims and dynamics of specific surveillance projects and the sociopolitical contexts in which they arise.[50]

Foucault's argument that visibility would encourage "soul training" as a disciplinary function to nudge inmates toward self-reflection and behavioral change has resonance with claims made by proponents of body-worn camera adoption. These proponents claim that body-camera usage by police officers will affect the behavior of the officers as well as the citizens with whom they interact.[51] These claims may actually play out in practice to some extent. In my rides with officers during this study, a number of officers admitted that wearing a camera made them more cognizant of how they interact with civilians—many noting that they try to swear less because the camera may be listening—and that they believe the cameras may have diffused confrontational situations:

> I previously wore one through my old department, and it helped negate complaints. Once people know you have a camera, it changes their behavior. [Body cameras] will help officers tremendously. (Dominic, patrol officer, SPD, 2014)

On the other hand, some officers also hope that the public will be able to see how badly citizens behave on camera as well:

> The portion of the population we typically deal with often believe they will not be held to any standard of behavior. At the same time, the public at large is unaware of the lowly behavior of these people and don't believe it unless they can see it for themselves. (Travis, sergeant, SPD, 2015)

The recent media and political clamor for speedy body-camera adoption among local police departments across the United States demonstrates how popular perceptions about some forms of surveillance can vary dramatically from others; for example, we accept and encourage body-camera adoption, but we abhor mass surveillance of our emails or phone calls. As such, some of Foucault's ideas about producing "docile bodies" and critiquing "vision" as playing a role in state domination are indeed still relevant.[52] However, a strict panoptic analysis would ignore the fact that the social control imagined by wearable and handheld surveillance cameras cuts both ways: it applies to both those in power (the police) and those who are not (the civilians). The social control and "soul training" that may be present in the prison may not be the sole (or primary) functions of new forms of surveillance, such as body cameras and bystander video. These cameras are also strongly oriented toward the evidentiary value of recordings. Despite the need to look beyond the panopticon, however, it may be best "to accept the panoptic presence, even if only as the ghost lurking within the post-panoptic world."[53] Surveillance theory cannot ignore panoptic theory, but it must move beyond it.[54]

NEW VISIBILITIES

Policing's new, increasing visibility can be carved into at least three different forms: transparency (disclosure of agency records, e.g., footage or reports, initiated proactively by the officer or the agency), external visibility (primary visibility, or secondary visibility due to recording by outsiders), or hybrid forms (e.g., FOI, in which agency records are disclosed pursuant to a request by an outsider and then made visible to external audiences, generally online). Until relatively recently, the police have mostly been subjected to *primary* forms of visibility, being visible only to those directly involved in, or within sight of, actual police-citizen interactions.[55] However, the various technologies that police officers have used to "conduct surveillance of others" for decades are now also being "used for surveillance of their own work," a reality exacerbated by the affordances of new media platforms and increasingly affordable surveillance-enabling technologies (e.g., smartphones and cameras).[56] The mounting ubiquity of handheld video recording devices and growing public and media interest in documenting police activities in recent decades has driven a rapid proliferation of user-generated video of police (mis)conduct on sites like YouTube, Facebook, and other social media platforms, as well as the development of smartphone apps designed specifically to enable covert recording of the police.[57] These forms of *secondary visibility*, enabled by the development of new media, reach well beyond the barriers of proximity and timing and, along with the rapid adoption of body-worn cameras, have transformed police work into a "high visibility" career.[58]

These developments, along with the adoption of body-worn cameras, are driving changes in the information politics of the police. Many commentators view inverse or reciprocal surveillance (forms of sousveillance) as shifting power to the public and away from the police. Many also see the adoption of body cameras as serving a similar purpose. Indeed, after the tragic events in Ferguson, Missouri, in the summer of 2014, calls for police adoption of body-worn cameras became intense in the United States. Between 2013 and 2016, reported rates of adoption (or plans to adopt) by local police agencies across the country increased significantly.[59] The Barack Obama administration pledged millions of dollars toward equipping local police forces with body cameras.[60] The American Civil Liberties Union (ACLU) came out in support of police body-camera adoption.[61] Fan argues that, despite the perils of body-camera adoption, including those to privacy, "the next frontier [in police oversight efforts] is using audiovisual big data and predictive analytics for improved police regulation, civil rights and civil liberties protections, and violence protection in law enforcement encounters."[62] Recording police officers and analyzing the "audiovisual big data . . can generate ways to better avert harm; promote officer and public wellness; and protect civil rights."[63]

However, these techno-utopian forecasts—especially when tied to the promotion of police adoption of surveillance technologies like body cameras—mask the tremendous, invasive realities of state surveillance and the serious threats to privacy and other civil liberties that these technologies enable. Of course, recording the police will uncover acts of misconduct that otherwise would have been hidden, but these reforms do nothing to fundamentally alter the underlying problems with American policing. In Vitale's words, "body cameras . . . reinforce a false sense of police legitimacy and expand the reach of the police into communities and private lives."[64] As, I would add, do other technologies that enable the police to collect and analyze large amounts of data on the individuals in their communities. The promotion of these efforts reflects a liberal and legalistic approach to police reform that has been failing for decades in its efforts to make policing more just. If the primary purpose of body cameras and other technologies with the ability to "watch" the police is to ensure police accountability and protect civil rights, "perhaps the footage should be under the control of an independent body and not the police."[65] In the absence of broader police reforms, the cameras may offer a Band-Aid (and this is no doubt helpful), but they do not promise a cure.

The concepts of reciprocal or inverse surveillance do play a role in helping us understand how to better conceptualize visibility in a post-panoptic environment, despite all simply being forms of surveillance themselves. The connections between visibility and surveillance have historical roots in the idea that the watchers are watching because they do not trust the watched. Of course surveillance is not necessarily detrimental; it can be deployed for purposes that provide care or empowerment. However, "particularly in asymmetric situations, visual observation can easily imply a loss of autonomy in the watched."[66] And for those who don't trust, whether an employer, police officer, or citizen, visibility can turn bodies into something "to be observed and tested."[67]

This increased visibility, of both states and citizens, has been driven (at least in part) by advancements in technology and the methods of surveillance that such technological change has enabled. The consequences of these developments, and our society's legal, technological, and political responses, have important ramifications for individual freedom, and highlight tensions between individual interests in free speech, privacy, and security. The use of surveillance technologies, such as body-worn cameras, might be viewed as only abstractly linked to the stated police purposes of social control, "based on symbols (that which is hidden must be revealed), theories (surveillance deters) or faith (technology works; it will work here as well)."[68] These assumptions play on our society's increasing reliance on and trust in technology to mediate power relationships and protect us from actual physical harms. Whether these assumptions are correct in any set of cases is a question of great practical, philosophical, and empirical import.

COLLATERAL VISIBILITY

Police visibility not only shines sunlight on the police. In many cases, it may also expose those with whom the police interact to high levels of visibility—whether collateral or intended. In this context, police body cameras and bystander video, both deployed to make the police more transparent and accountable, are prime examples of what Levy and Barocas have called *refractive surveillance*, in which "monitoring of one party can facilitate control over another party that is not the direct target of data collection."[69] If sensitive personal information about victims, witnesses, suspects, or bystanders is recorded and disseminated online (in the case of body cameras, disclosed under legal FOI requirements), this information could easily contribute to violations of individual privacy. Under some existing regulatory frameworks, the visibility of individual citizens (innocent, presumed innocent, or guilty) is inextricably tied to the visibility of the state.

Indeed, just months after police agencies in Washington State began using body-worn cameras in 2014, sensitive video footage of interviews with alleged prostitutes in hotel rooms and other officer-citizen interactions and arrests began to be posted to YouTube after the agencies were required to disclose every recording made by the cameras under broad state FOI law. When personally identifying information captured by an officer's body-worn camera is subject to public disclosure under FOI laws designed to keep government power in check, violations of individual privacy become part of the unintended collateral damage of these desired ends of transparency and accountability. The combination of police use of body-worn cameras and broad public disclosure rules and agency disclosure practices is making, or has the potential to make, civilians increasingly visible (and their interactions with the police less obscure) in the process of routine police work. As such, collateral visibility is a direct result of police technology adoption within a social context devoid of adequate ex ante legal regulation—that is, when the adoption and deployment of technology works as a form of policy making by procurement on the part of the local police departments.[70]

Transparency and visibility here are not synonymous. Statements about visibility are generally descriptive, about empirical evidence, encompassing both the availability and accessibility of information.[71] Transparency is a normative concept, laden with ideological baggage, that "has been largely conceived as a trust-building alternative to secrecy."[72] It is appealing from a public relations standpoint because of "its promise to circumvent the need for, and usurp the role of other forms of disclosure such as scandal, gossip, and conspiracy theories."[73] Transparency practices by the police are, for example, elements of their own image management strategies; they are acts of information politics. The visibility of the police, however, is a function of how available information about the police is and how accessible it is to external audiences (e.g., the public and the media), including how access to information law and informational gatekeepers regulate such accessibility. Importantly, visibility and transparency do not always correlate. Making the police more visible by, for example, equipping them with body-worn cameras, does not necessarily lead to increased police transparency to the public. Indeed, in some states, body-camera adoption led directly to legislative exemptions for body-worn camera footage in state FOI laws that directly prohibit police transparency or at least give the police (blanket) power to act as informational gatekeepers.[74]

Managing their own image has become a contested activity for the police, filled with political choices about sharing or withholding information. It is also an exercise in police power. Body-worn camera adoption has been so rapid, at least in part, because it provides a response to the host of image management problems and recent surge in media attention to police-involved violence generated by the rise of bystander video.[75] Relatedly, as noted by Wall and Linnemann, "even if police didn't actively destroy cameras wielded by unauthorized photographers, police power remains animated by the interplay between coercion and consent and leans towards the excessive."[76]

Police departments have "a clear interest in how their personnel and activities become visible to others and in what is revealed as a result to outsiders."[77] For example, the Seattle Police Department engaged in a series of lawsuits wherein it objected to the release of dash-camera footage to local news organizations, attorneys, and private citizens.[78] On their face, these refusals were based on interpretations of state privacy laws, out of concern for invading the privacy of innocent bystanders captured on tape. The SPD also initially claimed the ability to seal footage for three years unless it is relevant to current litigation and then to destroy footage at that point (the expiration of the statute of limitations), effectively exempting footage from public disclosure except in certain narrow circumstances.

Secrecy, despite certain legitimate justifications (e.g., not compromising an ongoing, legitimate investigation), has been a "familiar protective practice" used by police to avoid "public embarrassment and formal accountability," and any allowances for secrecy ought to be accompanied with clear sunset provisions to force disclosure when the justification has been exhausted.[79] Thus, it would be naïve to believe police officers and institutions would (1) record all encounters judiciously, (2) preserve all recordings properly, and (3) properly release all footage related to public requests under state disclosure laws (especially when the footage is damning, and even when the law requires disclosure), unless strict laws, regulations, or other transparency measures were in place—including, ideally, forms of independent oversight. Additionally, the recent changes in state public records laws around the country that largely exempt police body-camera footage from public disclosure are evidence that the information politics of body-worn cameras extends well beyond police institutions, finding fertile, police-friendly ground in state legislatures and other lawmaking bodies.

INFORMATIONAL POWER

Informational power is everywhere. But the ability to wield this power effectively, in ways that have the capacity to evoke democratic change, has often been limited to those who already had social or political power. In recent decades, however, the miniaturization and decreasing cost of camera technologies have empowered citizens to record matters of public interest, including the actions of police officers and other public officials, and hold the powerful to account. YouTube and Facebook (and others) are replete with images and video of police officers interacting with civilians and provide platforms for the secondary visibility of police (mis)conduct. In this view, information is, or can be, "a constitutive force in society"—and wielded this way, informational power has the potential to institute, establish, or enact change.[80] On the other hand, these same technological developments have also led to increased information acquisition about individual persons by states (vertical surveillance) as well as by other civilians (horizontal surveillance). In some ways, access to information has increased dramatically in recent decades; in others, political implementation of information policies has created an "information politics," including "the manipulation of information access for political gain."[81] Indeed, in our present informational state, where "the mutual transparency between the individual and the state has been destroyed," the proliferation of body-worn cameras is likely to cast greater light on individual civilians than on the state.[82]

Braman has defined *informational power* as a fourth major type of power, alongside instrumental, structural, and symbolic forms: "Informational power shapes human behavior by manipulating the informational bases of instrumental, structural, and symbolic power. Informational power dominates power in the other forms, changes how they are exercised, and alters the nature of their effects. Informational power can be described as 'genetic,' because it appears at the genesis—the informational origins—of the materials, social structures, and symbols that are the stuff of power in its other forms."[83]

Following Braman's lead, however, we might conceptualize informational power as an overlay that is related to, and that affects, the underlying types—much as we might conceptualize informational privacy as an overlay for other forms of privacy.[84]

Bystander and body-worn camera recordings are records with constitutive potential. Each can be used to force the visibility of police officer (mis)conduct by providing audiovisual evidence. The informational power they make possible is often symbolic. But frequently the exercise of such power is aimed at making structural change. Ultimately, the interplay between the right of citizens to record police in public/private spaces, police filming citizens on the streets and in their homes, and the visibility provided to both parties through the public disclosure process raises important questions about privacy, accountability, and transparency. When technology advances rapidly, law written in decades past often loses relevance. As surveillance methodologies become more sophisticated, less expensive, and mobile (wearable), states and individuals each have the power to collect increasingly large amounts of information about the activities of the other. Indeed, Wexler forecasts a future in which body-worn cameras contribute to a state of affairs wherein a police officer is, essentially, "a walking sponge, indiscriminately absorbing information from the environment" (including inside private homes).[85]

In the United States, the rights of citizens to document government action and access public records have a strong foundation in First

Amendment (free expression) principles, but states, under existing structures and mandates, also have legitimate interests in collecting certain types of information to promote efficiency, public safety, and law enforcement. These interests are also regulated by constitutional law (e.g., the Fourth Amendment) and personal privacy rights, and often, what statutes and/or courts define as "public" or "private" is dependent on spatial and property-based considerations. As state surveillance continues to capture more and more potentially sensitive personal information about individual citizens (or noncitizen residents and others), broad FOI laws and other transparency initiatives, and the gatekeeping practices enabled by these pieces of legislation, may come into significant tension with individual privacy rights when they would require states to disclose sensitive personal information about individual citizens simply because the information happens to be included within a government record.[86]

Additionally, as police officers are outfitted with mobile surveillance devices, such as body-worn cameras, which are not constrained by proprietary or spatial limitations (i.e., they can be worn into private residences, onto private property, or anywhere else the officer chooses to be), the tensions between privacy, state surveillance, and public access become increasingly escalated. Sensitive personal information captured in video footage from officers' cameras has already begun to hit YouTube, Facebook, and other online repositories due to access-prioritizing FOI law in some states, and particularly in Washington State, where these tensions have been felt acutely since late 2014. Breakdowns between law and policy, on the one hand, and technological development, on the other, require us to rethink our information policies: From a legal and regulatory standpoint, how should we balance information access and information control in a way that properly balances public access to records and democratic oversight with personal privacy and an effective criminal justice system?

Despite long-standing tensions between government power and citizen oversight, public record keeping is a relatively recent phenomenon that largely emerged in the twentieth century.[87] As part of the recent expansion "in the extent to which governments deliberately, explicitly, and consistently control information creation, processing, flows, and use to exercise power," this shift—what Braman refers to as a "change of state"—has important ramifications for democratic governance.[88] Public access to information is often a prerequisite to citizens exercising power or seeking redress for potential rights violations stemming from secret (or not highly visible) activities of others.[89] As such, an imbalance in information access between a people and their government can tip the scales of power and limit the ability of the people to exercise democratic oversight and control over those they have put in power to represent them.[90] FOI laws often provide a great deal of access to government records and serve as a powerful and effective means for empowering oversight by journalists and ordinary citizens. In a very real sense, these laws provide a legal mechanism for citizen-initiated surveillance from underneath: a form of sousveillance, inverse surveillance, or reciprocal surveillance that grants citizens greater power to check government abuse and force even greater informational visibility.[91]

CHAPTER 2

Privacy, Speech, and Access to Information

Police and civilians often "cross lenses" in their attempts to record the actions of the other. These surveillance practices implicate many areas of law. In the pages that follow, I focus on how body-camera adoption and bystander video recording intersect with privacy, free speech, and access to information concerns, from both legal and philosophical perspectives. Police use of body-worn cameras implicates privacy interests both by recording police interactions with civilians and by the subsequent use and/or public disclosure of the resulting footage, which raises sharp tensions between these privacy interests and access to government information for oversight or transparency purposes. The rights of citizens to document government action and access public records have a strong foundation in free speech (e.g., First Amendment) and broader democratic principles. States also have legitimate interests in collecting certain types of information about citizens to promote efficiency, public safety, and law enforcement. The tensions between these competing—and legitimate—aims are substantial. In the context of police use of wearable camera systems, limiting the scope of law enforcement data collection and retention to protect citizen privacy might also (over-) protect the privacy of the police officers using these systems, as disclosure of the resultant footage to the public under FOI laws can allow citizens to scrutinize the conduct of individual officers, especially if the systems are always on. Thus, wearable cameras become a useful means of watching the officers themselves.

In this context, the more recognizable tensions between protecting privacy and ensuring efficacious policing are compounded by a direct tension between privacy interests and interests in freedom of information as an important form of freedom-preserving reciprocal surveillance and citizen oversight. This form of checking government power resists the reification of potential domination. However, the refractive aspects of this surveillance, in conjunction with broad public disclosure requirements, can increase the collateral visibility of individual citizens. In effect, the visibility of individual citizens (innocent, presumed innocent, guilty, or uninvolved) is inextricably tied to the visibility of state actors such as the police. One possible response would be to limit public access to footage. This would protect the privacy of innocent individuals *and* police officers, but at the cost of limiting the public's ability to conduct a certain form of oversight.

When sensitive personal information is captured on body-camera recordings and then disclosed by the police under FOI requirements, this information can easily contribute to violations of individual privacy interests. These concerns have arisen in other contexts in the past, as the release of public records has long implicated personal privacy interests. The concept of "practical obscurity," which gained recognition in US case law surrounding FOI disputes, is based on the presumption that the disclosure of certain public records in aggregated form "could reasonably be expected to constitute an unwarranted invasion of personal privacy."[1] In 1989, the US Supreme Court stated that "the issue here is whether the compilation of otherwise hard-to-obtain information alters the privacy interest implicated by disclosure of that information. Plainly there is a vast difference between the public records that might be found after a diligent search of courthouse files, county archives, and local police stations throughout the country and a computerized summary located in a single clearinghouse of information."[2]

As Hartzog and Stutzman have put it, "The Supreme Court found a privacy interest in information that was technically available to the public, but could only be found by spending a burdensome and unrealistic amount of time and effort in obtaining it."[3] In that sense, the personal information contained in the otherwise disclosable public records was "practically obscure because of the . . . low likelihood of the information being compiled by the public."[4]

On the other hand, the collateral social consequences of criminal justice involvement in various social processes have been documented in a variety of contexts.[5] These so-called collateral consequences "refer to the negative effects of criminal justice involvement that typically manifest outside of the traditional sentencing framework. Rather than being imposed by the decision of a sentencing court, these effects occur by default through associated social processes."[6] Police officers frequently cause negative social consequences within the communities in which they work. Body-worn cameras may exacerbate some of these injustices, especially when sensitive personal information captured in video footage from officers' cameras is published on YouTube, Facebook, and other online repositories due to access-prioritizing FOI law.

The two police departments with whom I worked over the course of this research were directly confronted with the realities and intricacies of Washington State's broad public disclosure law from the very beginning of their body-worn camera pilot programs. Importantly, prior to June 2016, Washington's Public Records Act (PRA) did not include any exemptions specific to body-worn camera footage. Certain provisions, based on protecting personal privacy in some circumstances, were enacted and took effect in mid-2016, almost two years after the agencies began deploying body cameras. These provisions provided a (much-needed) legal basis for denying public requests for body-camera footage "to the extent nondisclosure is essential for the protection of any person's right to privacy," as defined by state law.

Washington State has a very broad and inclusive public disclosure law. Body-worn camera footage is generally subject to disclosure under the PRA although, since 2016, the state legislature has enacted several important exemptions. Even despite these considerable new grounds for redacting parts of video recordings, many of the exemptions to the PRA are unlikely to apply to body-worn camera footage on a routine basis. Agency personnel responsible for responding to public disclosure requests are required to review (and redact, when needed) both the video and audio of recorded body-worn camera footage prior to disclosure, and this process takes a tremendous amount of time and agency resources.

In early 2016, the state legislature adopted several new provisions, each establishing a presumption that certain body-camera footage was exempt from disclosure. The legislature expanded these exemptions somewhat in 2018 and made them permanent and applicable to a broader number of police agencies in the state.[7] The updated provisions exempt all "body worn camera recordings to the extent nondisclosure is essential for the protection of any person's right to privacy," a test met by recordings that are considered "highly offensive to a reasonable person." The new exemption also made disclosure of certain footage presumptively "highly offensive to a reasonable person" when it depicted (1) parts of medical, counseling, or therapy facilities where patients receive or wait for treatment or where health care information is shared with patients; (2) protected health information; (3) the "interior of a place of residence where a person has a reasonable expectation of privacy"; (4) an intimate image (as defined in state law); (5) a minor; (6) the body of a deceased person; (7) the identity of or communications from a victim or witness of an incident involving domestic violence or sexual assault; or (8) the identifiable location information of a community-based domestic violence program or emergency shelter.[8] In 2018, the legislature also exempted aural and visual recordings of "child forensic interviews" conducted during child abuse investigations and made all of the existing exemptions permanent by removing the 2019 end-date clause.[9]

Despite the presumption against disclosure of videos that meet one of the categories just noted, the law allowed requesters to overcome the presumption of nondisclosure by providing "specific evidence in individual cases" that would refute the expectations of privacy regarding particular recordings. The law also required requesters to provide specific types of information about the recording sought, including the name of a person involved in the recorded incident; the case number assigned to the incident; the date, time, and location of the incident; or the name or identity of a police officer involved in the incident. Additionally, in a radical departure from the historic openness of the Washington PRA, the new law also imposed potentially substantial fees for most requesters, requiring them to "pay the reasonable costs of redacting, altering, distorting, pixelating, suppressing, or otherwise obscuring any portion of the body worn camera recording prior to disclosure . . . to the extent necessary to comply with the exemptions."[10] The new provisions also enabled agencies to require identification from requesters who requested fee waivers to ensure they are eligible under the act to receive recordings under such conditions. On the other hand, the act also required agencies to "use redaction technology that provides the least costly commercially available method of redacting body worn camera recordings, to the extent possible and reasonable."[11]

Such provisions provide significant limits on the public disclosure of body-camera recordings, compared with the state of the law in 2014 when my study began. The increasing limits on body-worn video disclosure in Washington is reminiscent of similar anti-disclosure developments in other jurisdictions as well.[12] Interestingly, many of these limits are consistent with the opinions expressed by the police officers I interviewed and surveyed throughout this study.

FREE SPEECH

The First Amendment to the Constitution of the United States declares, in part, "Congress shall make no law . . . abridging the freedom of speech." Just as privacy is subject to numerous definitions and overarching theoretical accounts, the theoretical basis for a right to free speech and expression (and broader First Amendment rights, such as the rights of assembly, association, and belief) has also been much debated. There are, of course, quite a few different consequentialist and nonconsequentialist theories for why we might want to protect freedom of expression. Of these, a few consequentialist justifications are particularly relevant to my approach to understanding the proper role of the First Amendment's free speech guarantee—specifically, those based on the ideals of truth discovery, checks on abuse of power, and democratic deliberation.

The basic consequentialist justification for free speech is the importance of *truth discovery* and sustaining the marketplace of ideas. This justification holds importance to both liberal and republican conceptions of free speech. The idea that an open marketplace of ideas, in which individuals have the ability to present ideas without risk of censure, may stimulate debate, critical thought, and the eventual collective discovery of truth, is obviously important, regardless of whether or not we ought to limit the protected sphere to only those ideas related to collective self-governance (and whether or not "truth" always rises to the top). John Stuart Mill, for one, was concerned with the potential for governments to suppress communication and to make us dependent on them, undermining self-government, because even attempts to suppress "false" information may well also capture true or partly true information and would hamper the development of the open marketplace of ideas. To a great extent, this viewpoint has been captured by the liberal tradition, and Volokh's passionate defense of free speech in the face of potential privacy restrictions (which he largely sees as unwarranted and dangerous) pushes this justification close to its limits.[13]

To others, speech of merely private concern that does not implicate or further efforts to effectuate democratic self-governance may be appropriately limited. This view (or views, as there are many) also relies heavily on the truth discovery justification for free speech, but it places limits on the types of speech that ought to fall within constitutional protections. For example, Meiklejohn differentiates between "communication" and "speech" (which, as a subset of communication, impacts self-government).[14] Meiklejohn's conceptualization allows us to protect speech (communication that impacts self-governance) but doesn't negate the ability to regulate or limit communication—for example, based on privacy grounds. Others have differentiated between high- and low-value speech.

Closely connected to, and potentially contained within, the truth discovery rationale is a second line of reasoning: that free speech provides a check on abuses of (especially government) authority. This checking power extends beyond checking abuse, however; it also rests on the assumption that the First Amendment should support the exposure of wrongdoing—which implicates the right to gather and access information as a predicate for actual speech. This theory also has ties to the democratic governance theories described in the following paragraphs.

The idea that free speech contributes to the development and maintenance of democratic rule has also been very influential. Some of these theories can appropriately be termed republican in nature. Sunstein focuses on the connections between James Madison's conception of American sovereignty (in the People) and the right of free speech. This right to "freely examin[e] public characters and measures, and of free communication among the people thereon" is "the only effectual guardian of every other right."[15] In Sunstein's view, current First Amendment jurisprudence "protect[s] speech that should not be protected" because its theoretical basis is "off the mark" and even threatens democratic efforts of the people to self-govern. Likewise, Meiklejohn argued that "the First Amendment does not protect a 'freedom to speak,'" rather, "it protects the freedom of those activities of thought and communication by which we 'govern.'"[16] Thus, the First Amendment right to free speech concerns "a public power [and] governmental responsibility" rather than "a private right."[17] Meiklejohn was primarily concerned with the power, and obligation, of the people to vote, but also found that "people do need novels and dramas and paintings and poems, 'because they will be called upon to vote.'"[18]

In a similar vein, Justice Louis Brandeis, in the 1927 US Supreme Court case *Whitney v. California*, stated forcefully:

> Those who won our independence believed that the final end of the State was to make men free to develop their faculties, and that, in its government, the deliberative forces should prevail over the arbitrary. They valued liberty

> both as an end, and as a means . . . that, without free speech and assembly, discussion would be futile; that, with them, discussion affords ordinarily adequate protection against the dissemination of noxious doctrine; that the greatest menace to freedom is an inert people; that public discussion is a political duty, and that this should be a fundamental principle of the American government.

Balkin argues that the First Amendment's free speech principle is about more than just democracy (qua voting), and he would extend it to encompass what he calls "democratic culture," meaning "a culture in which ordinary people can participate, both collectively and individually, in the creation and elaboration of cultural meanings that constitute them as individuals."[19] I read this claim as related to, and potentially consistent with, Meiklejohn's extension of free speech rights to the creation of novels, dramas, paintings, and poems, which Meiklejohn believes are necessary to educated and informed voting and political participation. According to Balkin, democratic culture is "about individual liberty as well as collective self-governance."[20] However, if we extend free speech rights to democratic culture, which I think we should to some extent, rather than just democratic political participation, we also run the risk of having speech interests butt up against privacy more frequently—and we may have to create a more complicated balancing mechanism.

Reddish has recently provided another democratic theory for the mix, sharply criticizing the prior accounts as being too focused on collectivist cooperation rather than on protecting individual self-interest.[21] Reddish advocates an individualistic account of the purposes of the First Amendment that specifically promotes the individual right to speech and organize in a person's own self-interest as a way to incentivize political participation. Meiklejohn and Post, on the other hand, promote more collectivist and cooperative democratic participation, with differing emphases on voting and individuals recognizing themselves as self-governing, respectively, as the ends to be achieved.

Democratic theories of free speech that focus on prioritizing expression that enables democratic participation provide one way to claim that personal privacy interests should be overridden by the right to free speech only when the speech furthers the democratic project and pertains to self-governance. Information privacy (defined as the right to control access to and uses of personal information) can be squared with the First Amendment rights of speech, association, and belief in a couple of primary ways:

First, the First Amendment itself protects certain privacy interests, including the right to speak anonymously, the freedom of assembly, freedom of thought, and to some extent, the right to gather information. All these First Amendment protected activities implicate privacy in various ways and also help to limit the potential for domination of individual citizens or groups by states or other actors.

Second, conceptualizing free speech as primarily protecting communication that promotes or impacts democratic self-governance allows for stronger personal privacy rights to control personal information than some broad theories that prioritize speech would permit. For example, if the government is restricted from regulating or prohibiting strictly private speech (e.g., if it cannot limit the right to publish intimate personal details about another person, even when this information is not connected to self-governance), protecting a robust right to control access to and use of our own personal information becomes much more difficult. It would essentially equate privacy with absolute secrecy. However, under a democratic theory of free speech, the government could legitimately provide legal avenues of redress for such invasions of privacy.

In my view, the First Amendment is inextricably tied up in notions of self-government, truth discovery (at least when restricted to matters related to governing or, if not, those that do not invade another person's privacy), checking potential government abuse or domination, and—to some extent—allowing individuals to participate in the creation of culture and meaning within society. That said, we should recognize robust rights to gather information, to withdraw and contemplate or discuss openly and debate ideas in public, to think and believe as each individual sees fit, and to assemble for these purposes, insofar as such activity does not violate another person's rights (including the right to privacy). However, speech that does not promote, facilitate, or relate to self-government may need to give way to privacy rights. As we increase transparency and the visibility of the state (e.g., by instituting or liberalizing access to information laws) while also maintaining or increasing surveillance and information seeking by government agencies (e.g., by allowing or requiring police officers to wear body cameras), we also increase the visibility of individual citizens who, importantly, may incur significant privacy costs.

In later chapters, I apply these ideas within the contexts of bystanders recording police conduct, accessing police body-camera footage through the accordances of information law, and disseminating police video online, especially via social media platforms that provide widespread access to the recordings.

PRIVACY

Police use of body-worn cameras implicates a number of privacy concerns, despite also having the potential to promote oversight and police accountability. These privacy concerns can be divided into two main areas: (1) privacy violations stemming from the surveillance activities of the state, including the collection of evidence via body-worn camera recordings and the nature of consent or notice required for such recording to occur in the first place, and (2) privacy violations occurring as a consequence of subsequent access to the recordings, including the public disclosure of body-worn camera footage and the dissemination of those recordings online.

Privacy has been defined in a multitude of ways, both normatively and descriptively. Some scholars go so far as to claim that defining privacy is a fruitless task because, like liberty, privacy means so many things to different people.[22] As stated succinctly by Cohen, "privacy has an image problem."[23] We might understand privacy as an umbrella term, encompassing what it is and how it should be valued as well as a narrower right to privacy that outlines the extent to which privacy is protected by the law or other rule-like systems. Privacy has been conceptualized in reductionist (privacy as an element of another more fundamental right) and nonreductionist (privacy as a distinct right in itself) terms.[24] Scholars have also identified several different types of privacy and privacy harms.[25] In response to the existing ambiguity surrounding how to define privacy, colleagues and I defined a typology of eight basic types of privacy (bodily, spatial, communicational, proprietary, intellectual, decisional, associational, and behavioral), with the concept of *informational privacy* existing essentially as an overlay that touches each of the underlying types but is not a type itself.[26] For present purposes, I consider *informational privacy* as such an overlay, defined as the right to control access to and uses of personal information. This normative definition includes the right to control both initial and subsequent uses of personal information across privacy types (e.g., a person may consent to the use of the personal information for certain purposes by specified entities but may object to further sharing and subsequent use for additional purposes outside the scope of the original consent). This definition, despite its clear connections to liberal individualist and libertarian thinking, also resonates with aspects of both liberal communitarian and republican thought.

Privacy is valuable, in part, because it shields the individual from domination and is a necessary condition for human flourishing.[27] Privacy promotes human flourishing and antipower by making individuals less visible (more obscure), creating "breathing room to engage in the processes of boundary management that enable and constitute self-development," as described by Cohen, and is an important and instrumental means of supporting the goal of maintaining individual liberty from government intrusion, interference, and/or domination.[28] Privacy is a "core value that limits the forces of oppression."[29] This conception of privacy is consistent with the claims that privacy has objective moral value, though its contours might be relative to culture, religion, time, and place. Conceptualizing privacy as a necessary and freedom-preserving right protects individuals from intrusions well beyond the basic privacy interests in territoriality and a need for space away from overcrowding. Privacy rights should also be protected against expression to a greater extent than US law currently suggests. As stated by Westin, "the achievement of privacy for individuals, families, and groups in modern society has become a matter of freedom rather than the product of necessity."[30] Like Cohen, I also argue that "freedom from surveillance, whether public or private, is foundational to the practice of informed and reflective citizenship" and that "privacy . . . is an indispensable structural feature of liberal democratic political systems."[31]

As Westin explained, humanity may share some basic universal need for privacy—although it may surface differently in various cultural contexts—and this might also extend to other animal species as well. It may well exist as an independent human value that ought to be protected by law—for example, as a fundamental human right. However, this need for some basic level of privacy protections may be more limited than some modern conceptions of privacy, and it is likely to be at least partially related to physical privacy concerns. In modern society, "our contemporary norms of privacy are 'modern' and 'advanced' values largely absent from primitive societies of the past and present."[32] These "advanced" values are more likely embedded in the "socio-political realm" and, I would argue, privacy's instrumental connection to political liberty is important for human flourishing but not necessarily indicative that all of this privacy is reducible to liberty.[33] This characterization allows us to agree on a possible core, universal, right to privacy (which humans may share across different cultures, and even with other animals), while recognizing that some privacy interests are also culturally and individually distinct choices about values.

Robust privacy rights should be promoted by democratic civic participation, self-governance by the people, and the promotion of liberty—or nondomination—buttressed by constitutional guarantees of equality, due process, and limits on pure majoritarian decision-making to preserve minority rights. Roberts has recently provided the first explicitly "republican" modern theory of privacy, though other writers like Cohen and Etzioni have also provided alternatives to privacy theories based in liberal individualism. According to Roberts, "the value of privacy for republicans lies in its capacity to shield individuals from the threat of domination. A consequence of loss of one's privacy is that others may acquire dominating power—the capacity to interfere in one's decisions on an arbitrary basis."[34]

Cohen's concept of *semantic discontinuity* resonates with much of the broader republican theory of privacy and access to information I argue for here. Cohen developed the concept of semantic discontinuity as an important component of her broader theory of personal freedom and human flourishing.[35] Ultimately, Cohen elaborates three key ideas necessary for human flourishing: "Information law and policy should foster institutional and technical structures that promote access to knowledge, that create operational transparency, and that preserve room for the play of everyday practice."[36] Semantic discontinuity itself refers to "gaps and inconsistencies within systems of meaning, and to a resulting interstitial complexity that leaves room for the play of everyday practice."[37] Balkin takes this to mean that "although Cohen initially states this idea in terms of meanings, it soon becomes clear that she is talking about gaps in enforcement and in systems of surveillance and control."[38]

These "gaps and imperfections in systems of control and surveillance"—also referred to as "disorganization"—make space for the play of everyday practice to occur.[39] This also requires legal and institutional mechanisms that would avert the "perfect preventive state," implicating tensions with efficiency and accuracy in criminal justice and law enforcement.[40] Of course, beyond limiting (more) perfect surveillance, this might also encompass creating gaps in rules about access to information to protect individuals' privacy interests. Cohen also advocates that "the politics of 'access to knowledge' should include a commitment to privacy."[41]

Privacy law should be reactive to subjective experience to the extent that it can generalize such experience in a way that can apply fairly to a broad citizenry with drastically divergent life experiences. Cognitive and behavioral sciences are undoubtedly important to ensuring privacy laws act in ways that support human flourishing, but the law cannot cater to the subjectivity of myriad selfhoods. What we need is an arrangement that allows individuals to autonomously enact their own projects (to play as part of their own everyday practice, in Cohen's terms), based on their own subjectivity but limited by the rights of others, without the risk of domination. A theory of antipower that accounts for both privacy and access to information ought to be a sufficient condition to achieve this outcome. Indeed, it is exactly the premise of the republican theory of privacy that greater visibility (access) or use of this personal information directly implicates domination. As such, "the loss of privacy we suffer when others watch or acquire information about us is harmful to the extent that it provides others with power to interfere in our decisions that we do not control—the power to remove, replace or misrepresent options that would be available to us had we not suffered a loss of privacy. This harm arises whether or not we are aware that others are watching or acquiring information about us."[42]

Likewise, Solove has argued that the primary problem state or commercial databases of personal information create "emerges from subjecting personal information to the bureaucratic process with little intelligent control or limitation, resulting in a lack of meaningful participation in decisions about our information," which also "foster[s] a state of powerlessness and vulnerability."[43] The existence of these expansive databases of information about individuals increases civilian visibility, defeats obscurity, and violates the concept of semantic discontinuity. Specifically, it exhibits the characteristics of *domination* and calls for an increase in *antipower*.

LIBERTY, DOMINATION, AND "ANTIPOWER"

Under the republican conceptualization of liberty, privacy, speech, and access to information can all be said to be valuable—at least in part—because of their ability to limit the actual interference and domination experienced by individuals. That is, they are each distinctly valuable as independent rights, and their instrumental potential to effectuate and preserve liberty is particularly important because freedom from domination is a vitally important component of, and necessary condition for, human flourishing. The benefits of protecting these individual rights are directly tied to the structural institutions and processes that allow for self-governance by the people and, ultimately, render government action nonarbitrary (or at least less arbitrary). Privacy rights, free speech protections, and access to information laws are much less meaningful if, for example, the public has no ability to command noninterference in the first place (i.e., government could alter these rights on a whim without fear that the people could overrule the government action).

Discussing the domination of some by others may lead us to question what we can or ought to do to diminish or remove the subjugation. Reversing roles would not solve the problem; it would merely relocate it. Fairly allocating power to both sides, however, would not merely equalize the subjugation; if both sides—say the people and their government—may interfere with the other's affairs, then neither may act with impunity, since the other may exact something in return. Thus, "neither dominates the other."[44] This is an exemplification of antipower—that is, "what comes into being as the power of some over others—the power of some over others in the sense associated with domination—is actively reduced and eliminated."[45] Antipower, then, subjugates power and, as a form of power itself, allows persons to control the nature of their own destiny; in this sense it functions much like *rights* do more generally. This makes sense when antipower essentially encompasses the conditions necessary and sufficient for freedom to exist. When these conditions obtain, people "enjoy the noninterference resiliently" because they are not dependent on the arbitrary use of power, precisely because they have the power to "command noninterference."[46] As such, they enjoy some measure of freedom.

Much of this work can be accomplished by instituting legal frameworks that insist on equal rights, due process, and fair application of law, but I think the neorepublican philosophy can help provide reasons and direction in support of these ends. In the cases of police body cameras and bystander video, the ability to document and access information about government action and government surveillance programs can act as a form of antipower, reducing domination. However, the release of some personal information as part of these transparency processes may also deter active disclosure requests, at least by those with something to lose by disclosure, or shift dominating power to external (i.e., nongovernment) entities.

ACCESS TO INFORMATION

Information policy encompasses a wide terrain, from enabling (or limiting) access to government information, to allowing or prohibiting governments from accessing information about their citizens, facilitating

First Amendment guarantees of free speech, and defining intellectual property policy. All these instantiations of information policy have significant implications for democracy. However, the rights of the citizenry to document or access information about how their representative government carries out its duties stand out as particularly important, especially in the pursuit of nondomination. Limiting access to government records not only limits the ability of the public at large to oversee government activity, it also hinders journalists and the news media, as well as academic researchers and librarians, from effectively carrying out their broader social functions, limiting our ability to understand what and how the government is carrying out its delegated authority.

Democracy and political liberty should be predicated on the presumption that the public is sufficiently informed—or has the effective ability to become informed—and able to participate in political life, including having the capability to engage in oversight of government action, regardless of whether a preferred political theory claims civic virtue is inherently or instrumentally valuable. It is also clear that "without access to adequate and appropriate information related to governance, such informed participation and deliberation are impossible."[47] Ideally, the nature of representative government would dispel the idea that governments and citizens stand opposed to each other. Indeed, much government surveillance is ostensibly conducted for the good of the citizenry writ large (to protect against crime and terrorism or provide evidence of unwanted and illegal conduct, among other things), and governments are generally far from monolithic entities with singular purposes standing opposed to public access to information. But the ongoing collection of massive amounts of information by state bodies does reify the coercive power of government. Without similar expansion in the people's right to access information about and document government action through forms of reciprocal surveillance, the people may lose their ability to conduct oversight and ensure government acts in a nondominating fashion.

However, as previously noted, this same public access to information (which plays a significant part in ensuring transparency and holding government accountable to its citizens) may also potentially threaten the viability and effectiveness of such methods to achieve socially desirable outcomes and may also violate individual rights to privacy when personal information collected by the surveillance systems is disclosed or disseminated to third parties—including the public—under FOI laws. Privacy, in this context, is needed to limit broad access to the "digital dossiers" of ordinary citizens who happen, for whatever reason, to be caught up in widespread government data-collection programs. These risks have been highlighted by the public disclosure and secondary publication (via YouTube, Facebook, and various blogs and online news outlets) of sensitive personal information contained in government records, including body-worn camera and dash-camera video footage, ALPR databases, gun-permit registries, and campaign contributions in support of controversial political endeavors, among others.

It is clear we need an information policy that strikes a better balance while still retaining a robust system of information access. It is also clear that democracy is predicated on the presumption that the public is sufficiently informed (or has the ability to become informed) and able to intelligently participate in political life, regardless of whether a preferred political theory claims civic virtue is inherently or instrumentally valuable; "without access to adequate and appropriate information related to governance, such informed participation and deliberation are impossible."[48]

VISIBILITY, SUBJECTIVITY, AND POLICE POWER

If policing is a means to an end—a means to create social order through the application of power—then the addition of wearable cameras to the officer's toolkit must be examined for its potential to quell or instigate various forms of violence.[49] Information, seen as some "thing" that facilitates knowledge and grants power to its holder over the information subject, can enable power of some over others.[50] Through vertical surveillance, police gain evidentiary information (as "knowledge") about civilians.[51] And through public disclosure of footage in which other civilians are the primary subjects, citizens can engage in increasingly revealing forms of horizontal surveillance, potentially generating shifts in power relationships among ordinary people.

The use of wearable cameras also has the potential to alter or disrupt the nature of nonreported, "peacekeeping" aspects of policing and the attendant discretion that officers have historically enjoyed in their activities not resulting in arrests. Wearable cameras may serve to exacerbate the compromised position of the patrol officer, who is often under the "dual pressure[s] to 'be right' and to 'do something,'" even in stressful or dangerous situations.[52] The use of body-worn cameras can be a two-edged sword. It promises some benefits but also poses important problems. The use of such systems is not necessarily inimical to freedom (and its attendant privacy and speech concerns), but significant checks need to be employed to ensure against the possibility of arbitrary interference and the improper use of power generated through the accumulation of information and potential intimidation implicit in these surveillance practices.

The proper role of officer-mounted wearable cameras is also informed by an understanding of some of the power dynamics implicated by police-citizen encounters. Herbert provides a useful articulation of three dynamics that structure police efforts to legitimize themselves to the citizenry they serve: subservience, separation, and generativity.[53] This three-pronged analysis provides an important theoretical basis for critiquing and exploring the risks and benefits of implementing these systems in actual police practice, as well as police officers' reactions to being surveilled themselves (whether by citizens or through the use of these wearable systems or dash-cam systems).

First, democratic government institutions must be subservient to the public to some degree.[54] As such, police must be responsive to citizen oversight.[55] Wearable cameras and civilian video both plainly hold the promise of exposing wrongful action (one purpose of oversight). However, as previously stated, police have a clear interest in controlling the extent of their visibility in this regard. Because of this, there is a direct tension between police subservience to the citizenry and the second dynamic, separation. The dynamic of separation may also help explain why officers often react negatively to citizens recording their public activities. For the police to deliver "proper performances," they require control over the choices that guide collection (camera-activation policies, officer discretion) as well as dissemination of, and access to, the resulting recordings (supervisory review policies, public access, public relations–related disclosure).[56] The nature of dissemination, whether online or internally within the police agency, is also an important consideration.

Third, Herbert problematizes the idea that state and society are separate and argues that in some respects, society is generated by the state. In reality, the police may not actually do much, if anything, to reduce crime or alter structural conditions in society that affect their communities. As such, the "police's generation of society is largely limited to the epistemology they mobilize and the moral architectures they construct."[57] This point is particularly important to my reasons for explaining and unpacking so many subjective police concerns about body-worn cameras and bystander video throughout this book. Indeed, understanding police officers' perceptions of the technology and its role in their work can reveal quite a lot about police power in society. "Officers create the social reality that they police" by "filtering information . . . sifted through officers' screening mechanisms," including information from the citizenry in their local communities.[58] Thus, by understanding this social reality, as projected by the police themselves, alongside their information practices, we gain an understanding of how body-worn camera adoption is generative of information politics within the police and how this may impact the way they work in their communities. As Manning has argued, "the environment in which officers act is one they largely project, act in accord with, and reify."[59] Indeed, my findings suggest that this projection flows from a sense of fragility or vulnerability and that this sense works to solidify destructive us/them mentalities. Body-worn cameras exacerbate preexisting police-society tensions related to subservience and separation, possibly forcing the police and society further apart rather than healing wounds and bridging rifts.

In each of these areas (subservience, separation, and generativity), there are conflicting interests in controlling informational power. Frontline police officers may not be able to affect laws or even internal departmental policies regarding activation, supervision, or access. However, they exert their power in how they enact the use of the cameras in their daily work—that is, in the choices they make about when and what to record, or how and whether to regulate their conduct in certain ways while the cameras are recording.

Many of the proposed benefits of body cameras, as well as significant causes for concern, are tied to the concept of police visibility (with its potential to change the dynamics of police-citizen encounters, to either exonerate or implicate officers in wrongdoing, or to provide evidence of citizen misconduct). Left to their own devices, the chance that the police would move toward secrecy is obviously a strong possibility. The use of body-worn cameras documents more encounters, which can then serve as evidence for or against officer or citizen misconduct. However, too much reliance on audiovisual evidence could also possibly decontextualize events and possibly diminish the recognition given by the public and courts to the realities that confront police officers on the ground. In short, it might lead to judgments about the wrongness/rightness of police action based on small windows of reality that ignore relevant context. This may also affect policing by further diminishing the amount of discretion available to officers. Indeed, police have historically kept few records of procedures that do not involve making arrests, and the nature of their work has unavoidably led to officers having a great deal of discretionary freedom.[60] These facts, combined with the reality that police work has long been divided into both law enforcement and peacekeeping activities (which involves officer discretion outside the domain of making arrests), suggest that wearable cameras (especially those operating under policies that require frequent or constant recording) might begin to document wide swaths of police conduct that have heretofore been largely left to the officers themselves.

Thus, in the context of skid-row policing investigated by Bittner, the fact that officers use force to effectuate arrests on the basis of risk (considered in the aggregate for the area) and personal knowledge, rather than mere individual culpability, may be antithetical to the wider public's notions about legitimate police work. "When arrests are made, there exist, at least in the ideal, certain criteria by reference to which the arrest can be judged as having been made more or less properly, and there are some persons who, in the natural course of events, actually judge the performance. But for actions not resulting in arrest there are no such criteria and no such judges."[61]

However, with the rise in the number of cameras present in public and the advent of the officer-mounted wearable cameras, these nonarrest situations are becoming increasingly documented, and as a consequence, there are potentially numerous judges (police administrators, elected officials, the media, or the public) and a variety of criteria against which individual officer conduct may be judged. Indeed, this reality lies behind the concerns that officers frequently expressed about "Monday morning quarterbacking" and being judged by evidence that is taken out of context or that fails to capture the officer's subjective experience of a situation. These realities are exacerbated by the ease of uploading footage to the internet and the availability of police records under public records laws. The resultant footage can be viewed, searched, and analyzed by superiors, and when accessible to the public under state disclosure laws, it provides very broad-ranging access to records of such police work. This reality also suggests that what it means to do a good job "keeping the peace" could be defined more by outside forces than by the officers themselves. This will likely create tensions between the officers' self-perception as separate and distinct skilled practitioners and the public's preferred perception of police as subservient to society.[62]

Some argue that wearable cameras promise to document police abuse and preserve evidence to exonerate officers falsely accused of improper conduct. A transparent monitoring system, this argument suggests, would encourage proper behavior on both sides and restore trust in policing.

Others argue that police will only behave more appropriately under surveillance if they know someone is actually going to watch what their cameras record (i.e., active monitoring/oversight) and that wearable cameras shouldn't replace written reports, including legal justifications for officer actions.

As the empirical findings presented in subsequent chapters show, officers may not be strongly opposed to all forms of public disclosure and public accountability, but they do appear to maintain an interest in their own *practical obscurity*. This desire may be rooted both in capturing audiovisual evidence that can provide more context to a contested police-citizen interaction and in retaining power to control their image and how they are made visible to outsiders. That is, they disapprove of policies and legal requirements that would make their day-to-day work activities much more directly visible to the public (e.g., liberal public access to recordings and proactive disclosure to YouTube), but they don't generally object to visibility in all its forms—for example, they often approve of limited disclosure to persons depicted in the recordings.

These findings reflect the officers' conception of themselves as skilled practitioners who ought to be shielded from unnecessary outside meddling. Here, this concern is one of information politics. Limiting public disclosure of certain body-worn camera recordings because of the ease of discovery and vast nature of potential visibility does make both the officers and the civilians they encounter more practically obscure. Indeed, the recordings can act as gaps or inconsistencies in these systems of surveillance. In that regard, recent legislative action to exempt certain types of body-camera footage from public disclosure is a positive step forward. However, the legislative choice to limit the applicability of the new law to body-worn camera recordings, rather than applying it to all forms of police video, is an unfortunate one, as it fails to adequately address future developments—or even current use of dashboard cameras, drones, or other recording devices that may also generate recordings of the type prohibited if the camera is worn on an officer's body.

Relatedly, preserving the rights of citizens to conduct reciprocal surveillance is also important. Significant questions remain about whether, and to what extent, police body cameras could also be used to intimidate or chill legitimate speech and other protected activities or even whether individuals will be less likely to report crime or call the police for assistance because of the additional collateral visibility that would be foisted upon them due to a liberal public disclosure regime, or simply the *presence* of an activated camera. Additionally, long-term storage and archiving of police footage could pose a threat to privacy interests of innocent citizens, as the release of such footage under state disclosure laws threatens to embarrass innocent bystanders caught on tape or individuals who ask police for help in sensitive circumstances. Indeed, the storage of large amounts of body-worn camera footage by police agencies (largely facilitated by commercial data storage services provided by body-camera companies like Axon) can act as one node in a broader surveillant assemblage, and these data can potentially be connected to data in other databases, providing state or commercial interests with highly "valuable" information about people's private lives.

Footage from a body camera, if it had existed, may well have provided better evidence of what transpired between Michael Brown and Officer Darren Wilson in Ferguson, Missouri, than what was available from conflicting eyewitness testimonies and after-the-fact bystander video. However, the potential for police body cameras to increase transparency and accountability needs to be considered side by side with a consideration of the privacy risks inherent in the use of such technologies, as well as the inherent limitations of the technology itself to stand in as a neutral observer (which is highly questionable) and the underlying regulatory regime that, if it exists, guides police use and implementation of surveillance technologies.

When technologies touted as tools to make law enforcement officers more visible in cases where alleged misconduct occurs also lead to drastic increases in civilian visibility, we need to think critically about how to regulate the use of these systems of surveillance. When personally identifying information contained in government records, such as body-camera footage, is subject to public disclosure under FOI laws designed to keep government power in check, violations of individual privacy can occur. We cannot ignore the unintended consequences—such as the collateral visibility and horizontal surveillance of and between civilians enabled by public disclosure—that make our lives more transparent, not just to government agents but also to our neighbors and the world at large. If we do, we may find that the walls of our homes become transparent to the world anytime we invite a police officer through the front door.

CHAPTER 3

Bystander Video and "the Right to Record"

I don't like the 24/7 pop-culture world I have seen develop. Anything can be made to look bad on YouTube with editing.

—Ray, patrol officer, SPD

BYSTANDER VIDEO AND ONLINE SOCIAL MEDIA

Sitting in the passenger seat of a police sergeant's patrol car in the Pacific Northwest one evening in the fall of 2014, it becomes clear to me that this officer, like many others in the department, is frustrated by the way bystander video can, as he puts it, decontextualize the events (and officer conduct) it depicts. His impression is that the video gets "sliced up" before it ends up on sites like YouTube.com, and much of the context, or the events leading up to the "interesting" part of the video, get lost—whether purposefully or not. Instead of a longer string of events, he says, we see only a fistfight and an officer punching a citizen in the face. We don't see the events that preceded the violent altercation, events that would, in the officer's opinion, place the officer's conduct in a different (more understandable and justifiable) light.

Later, on the other side of the state, in another patrol car with a different officer, I hear something similar. As we drive around the city center looking for persons or activity of interest, this officer, who has spent considerable time patrolling the downtown parts of the city, admits that he sometimes thinks twice before engaging in certain situations out of concern that dozens of people are likely to record his actions. Intervening in a disturbance at a crowded downtown bar, for example, he states calmly, is certain to result in his intervention being recorded and uploaded to YouTube by multiple people. Everybody has a camera, and—in his opinion—they are all too eager to post what they film online.

Indeed, it is not hard to find copious amounts of bystander video, dashboard camera video, and body-worn camera video of on-duty police officers online. In many cases, it is easy to find multiple videos of single events, filmed by multiple bystanders or the combination of police and bystander cameras at the scene. Many of these videos depict death and killing, and they can be shocking and difficult to watch. For example, the video that Keith Lamont Scott's wife, Rakeyia, recorded with her cell phone of Keith's fatal encounter with police in a parking lot outside his apartment in Charlotte, North Carolina, on September 20, 2016, is particularly fraught with emotion.[1]

Initially, Rakeyia starts recording as officers are trying to get Keith to exit his vehicle. As she walks closer to the scene, she says repeatedly, "*Don't' shoot him. . . . He has no weapon.*"

Then we hear officers yell, "*Gun! Gun!*" "*Drop the gun! Drop the fucking gun!*," followed by the sound of multiple gunshots in the background.

"*Did you shoot him? Did you shoot him?*" she yells as she runs toward where the officers are standing around her husband as he lies face down and bleeding in the middle of the parking lot.

"*He better not be fucking dead!*" she says, her voice turning from panic to anger. "*I know that much. He better not be dead!*"

As she approaches, an officer seems to tell her to back off. "*I'm not gonna come near you,*" she replies. "*I'm gonna record though! I'm not coming near you, I'm gonna record though. He better be alive, 'cause I. . . . He better live. I swear, he better live.*"

These videos are often seen by many people, all around the world. Clearly the capture of these scenes is an act of information politics by the bystanders and others who do it, as are their efforts to disseminate and promote the videos on platforms like YouTube, Facebook, Instagram, and Twitter. They challenge the power of traditional police image work. But we see the police engaging in information politics in these scenes as well, from ordering bystanders to stop recording or confiscating cameras to simply not engaging as actively out of visibility-related concerns. Where activists aim to construct a police-oversight framework of "regulation by information," the police are "acutely aware that the image is a dynamic social force working in and against the interests of the state."[2] Unpacking the subjective concerns and attitudes held by officers is important here, as doing so shines a light on the generative nature of police responses to increased visibility and bystander video practices.

And particularly in the case of bystander video, this visibility highlights the vulnerability and loss of informational power felt by officers who are caught between the image-work politics of their agencies (which partly motivated body-worn camera adoption) and the narratives driven by community members and others on social media platforms.

THE RIGHT TO RECORD

Bystanders recording the police, as a form of inverted surveillance, is a social practice that can range, on the one hand, from the "passive or hidden observation" or "spontaneous image capture" that characterized George Holliday's recording of the Rodney King beating at the hands of four Los Angeles Police Department officers in 1991 to, on the other hand, premeditated and targeted, overt, and (sometimes) obstructionist activism engaged in as "a form of civic engagement or duty."[3] Holliday's recording was not premeditated, but a spontaneous response to witnessing a violent police-public encounter. However, for present purposes, the importance of the King recording, which has been described as "a pivotal moment in the rise of citizen journalism," lies in the confluence of factors that made its subsequent visibility, and the reaction to it, so extreme: the (then) recent advent of affordable "point-and-shoot" camcorders and the wide distribution of the video on national television networks.[4] As with the King video, many of the highly publicized bystander videos of police-involved violence in recent years have been captured by individuals who just happened to be present when a violent encounter began to unfold—such as Darnella Frazier's recording of George Floyd's death in Minneapolis in 2020. However, in the years following the aftermath of the King video going viral on national television in 1991, including the resulting riots and national outcry against police brutality, organized cop watching has also emerged.

Bystander video and the affordances of new media platforms are significantly impacting contemporary police work, from enabling new forms of media and information politics to altering on-the-ground policing practices as officers adjust their behavior due to visibility- and accountability-related concerns. Evidence from multiple studies suggests that "the routine presence of cameras is changing the dynamics of policing on the ground."[5] In the past few decades, bystander video has had a powerful impact on public perceptions of police legitimacy, as evident from examples ranging from the beating of Rodney King to the police-involved killings of George Floyd, Oscar Grant, Eric Garner, Walter Scott, and Keith Lamont

Scott—among numerous others—in more recent years. This has led to "record everything to know the truth" becoming "the mantra" for police reform and calls for greater police accountability.[6]

Video filmed by bystanders has found its way into the popular discourse about accountability in policing and government, and millions have witnessed shocking events of alleged police misconduct via online video-sharing websites, the websites of traditional media and press outlets, blogs, and other social media. Conflicts between police officers and civilian journalists leading to police arresting civilians for violations of state laws in some states are not uncommon, even in recent years. Reports of these occurrences have continued to come to light even in some jurisdictions where police departments have explicitly promulgated department policies that recognize that citizens have constitutional rights to film officers and that have instituted or increased officer training on that point.[7]

Consequently, state and federal courts have begun to weigh in on the legal rights of civilians to document police action and the constitutionality of the state eavesdropping laws that prohibit such conduct. In the United States, a string of federal appellate court decisions has largely legitimized bystander video of police conduct by recognizing legitimate First Amendment interests in documenting government conduct as a form of—or as predicate to the exercise of—protected speech. However, despite these emerging legal protections, the issue has been—and presumably will continue to be—contentious on the ground for years, due in part to the fact that even within these jurisdictions, courts have frequently found that such a right was not yet "clearly established" at the time the police interfered with the bystanders' ability to record, thus finding that officers were immune to prosecution for civil rights violations under the doctrine of "qualified immunity." Even in circuits without "right-to-record" decisions, some federal trial courts and state courts have also begun to rule in favor of the right to record.[8]

In about a dozen US states, wiretapping or eavesdropping statutes prohibit civilians from making audio or audiovisual recordings of conversations without getting consent from all parties to the recorded conversations. These state laws vary in their scope but have been used frequently in recent years to arrest, detain, and harass photographers, including civilians and members of the credentialed press. Officers may at times invoke these statutes to stop civilians from recording encounters with police officers and restrict subsequent disclosure of information that might subject an officer to possible censure. Most of the statutes only apply to the recording of private conversations, although a prior version of the Illinois eavesdropping statute had applied to all conversations—regardless of the existence of any expectations of privacy—prior to being struck down in the courts as being unconstitutional for being overly broad. Some of these laws may have made recordings of conversations between civilians and police officers illegal and some civilians have been prosecuted for recording officers under these provisions. Elsewhere, in the United Kingdom an antiterrorism law similarly used by police officers to detain and question photographers was held to be in violation of the European Convention for Human Rights and Fundamental Freedoms.[9]

Because of the overlap and potential inconsistency between state eavesdropping laws and judicial interpretations of the First Amendment, at least in the states that criminalize the recording of conversations without the consent of all parties to those conversations, the production and practice of bystander video—whether covert or not—raises interesting and important legal issues. Federal appeals courts faced with the issue have generally recognized a constitutional First Amendment right to film police in public spaces. However, the continued proliferation of smartphone applications designed to allow civilians to *covertly* record encounters with police officers in efforts to hold public officials accountable may place some users (perhaps even unwittingly) at serious legal risk. Indeed, activists and organizations such as the New York Civil Liberties Union and the American Civil Liberties Union of New Jersey have in recent years distributed smartphone applications designed to allow civilians to covertly record encounters with police officers as part of law enforcement accountability programs, while also actively pursuing litigation—along with other organizations like the National Press Photographers Association—on behalf of photographers and civilian journalists arrested for recording officers.

There is a small but growing body of qualitative social research examining how police officers understand and perceive the impact of bystander video on their work. The remainder of this chapter seeks to contribute to that body of research by addressing how the law regulates practices of bystander recording and how police officers understand and perceive the impact of bystander video on their work.

The Present State of the Law

As of early 2020, six federal appellate courts—the First, Third, Fifth, Seventh, Ninth, and Eleventh Circuits—have handed down decisions in favor of the right to record. Importantly, no federal appellate court has held to the contrary. All but one of these decisions directly addressed the rights of bystanders to record police conduct, while the Ninth Circuit's decision held more broadly that bystanders could not be arrested under state law for recording conversations made in public spaces. In the earliest of these cases, *Smith v. City of Cumming*, the 11th Circuit affirmed a lower court's holding that the First Amendment protects the right to "photograph or videotape police conduct," but that this right was "subject to reasonable time, manner and place restrictions."[10] The court found it persuasive that a number of other decisions around the country had previously upheld First Amendment rights to film public meetings or matters of public interest and had held that the press generally should not have any greater right to document or access information than members of the general public.[11] Likewise, in *Fordyce v. City of Seattle*, the Ninth Circuit held that the Washington State eavesdropping law—requiring consent of all parties prior to recording a private conversation—could not be used to prosecute a person for recording conversations made in a public place, as those conversations were not "private" under the law.

After several intervening years of relative judicial silence on the issue, at least at the federal appellate level, the First Circuit decided *Glik v. Cunniffe* in 2011. The decision was heralded as a landmark for the burgeoning right to record the police. In *Glik*, the First Circuit held that the First Amendment clearly gave citizens the right to record police officers and other public officials while they were performing their official duties in public spaces, at least insofar as the citizens did not interfere with the police officer's legitimate work and made the recordings overtly, not secretly. The decision arose in a civil rights lawsuit brought by a Boston attorney, Simon Glik, after he was arrested for recording officers making an arrest in Boston Common. When he saw officers using what he thought was unnecessary force to affect the arrest, Glik pulled out his smartphone and made a video recording of the incident. When one of the officers approached and asked whether he was taking photographs, Glik indicated that he was recording video and audio of the events. Subsequently, the officers arrested Glik and charged him with several crimes, including violation of the Massachusetts state wiretapping statute. Ultimately, the court found that the right of individuals to film public officials in public spaces was a "fundamental and virtually self-evident" right under the First Amendment.[12] According to the court, "though not unqualified, a citizen's right to film government officials, including law enforcement officers, in the discharge of their duties in a public space is a basic, vital, and well established liberty safeguarded by the First Amendment."[13] After the court handed down its decision, the City of Boston paid Glik $170,000 in settlement to close his case.

A year after *Glik*, the Seventh Circuit preemptively enjoined the Cook County state's attorney from using the Illinois wiretapping law to arrest members of the ACLU while recording police officers as part of a police accountability program. The Illinois statute, as it existed at the time, prohibited making audio recordings even when officers did not maintain any expectation of privacy in their conversations and carried steep criminal penalties as a class 1 felony—equivalent to sexual offenses such as rape. In that case, *ACLU of Illinois v. Alvarez*, the Seventh Circuit held that the statute, as written and applied to the facts of the case, "likely violates the First Amendment's free-speech and free-press guarantees" and remanded the case to the district court.[14] Several state courts likewise held the statute to be unconstitutionally broad, and the Illinois legislature has since amended the statute, limiting its applicability to the recording of "private" conversations.

Elsewhere, in 2014 the City of Baltimore agreed to a $250,000 settlement with a man named Christopher Sharp after the police seized and deleted video recordings from his phone before giving it back to him after he filmed officers arresting one of his friends. Prior to the settlement in that case, the US Department of Justice (DOJ) had filed an unprecedented Statement of Interest with the trial court, stating that "the right to record police officers while performing duties in a public place, as well as the right to be protected from the warrantless seizure and destruction of those recordings, are not only required by the Constitution. They are consistent with our fundamental notions of liberty, promote the accountability of our governmental officers, and instill public confidence in the police officers who serve us daily."[15]

The DOJ also wrote a letter to the Baltimore Police Department in advance of a settlement conference in which it reiterated the DOJ's position in favor of the First Amendment right to record police conduct. The Baltimore Police Department subsequently instituted a formal policy recognizing the First Amendment right of citizens to "record, photograph, and/or audio record [Baltimore Police Department] Members while [Baltimore Police Department] Members are conducting official business or while acting in an official capacity in any public space, unless such recordings interfere with police activity."

In 2014 the First Circuit, which had decided *Glik* three years prior, decided *Gericke v. Begin*, in which it held that video recording a traffic stop was protected by the First Amendment and that the right to record was a clearly established constitutional right.[16] Also in 2014, the Eleventh Circuit, which had decided *Smith*, reiterated its prior holding that "the First Amendment protects the right to gather information about what public officials do on public property" in *Bowens v. Superintendent of Miami South Beach Police Dept.*, a case in which a photojournalist was arrested at gunpoint for recording the arrest of another person.[17]

In 2017 the Fifth Circuit decided *Turner v. Lieutenant Driver* and the Third Circuit decided *Fields v. Philadelphia*. In both cases, the right to record was upheld but was found to not be clearly established at the time the of the arrests in question, thus, allowing the officers protection under the qualified immunity doctrine. In *Turner*, the Fifth Circuit held that "a First Amendment right to record the police does exist, subject only to reasonable time, place, and manner restrictions." The court also stated that "the principles underlying the First Amendment support the particular right to film the police. . . . Filming the police contributes to the public's ability to hold the police accountable, ensure that police officers are not abusing their power, and make informed decisions about police policy. Filming the police also frequently helps officers; for example, a citizen's recording might corroborate a probable cause finding or might even exonerate an officer charged with wrongdoing."

In *Fields*, just a few months later, the Third Circuit held that "under the First Amendment's right of access to information the public has the commensurate right to record—photograph, film, or audio record—police officers conducting official police activity in public areas." Elaborating, the court noted that "to record what there is the right for the eye to see or the ear to hear corroborates or lays aside subjective impressions for objective facts. Hence to record is to see and hear more accurately. Recordings also facilitate discussion because of the ease in which they can be widely distributed via different forms of media."[18]

The court held that the right to record is subject to place, time, and manner restrictions, although "in public places these restrictions are restrained."[19] The court also found that "bystander videos provide different perspectives than police and dashboard cameras, portraying circumstances and surroundings that police videos often do not capture," "fills the gaps created when police choose not to record video or withhold their footage from the public," and "complements the role of the news media."[20] What's more, the court continued,

> the proliferation of bystander videos has spurred action at all levels of government to address police misconduct and to protect civil rights. These videos have helped police departments identify and discipline problem officers. They

> have also assisted civil rights investigations and aided in the Department of Justice's work with local police departments. And just the act of recording, regardless what is recorded, may improve policing. Important to police is that these recordings help them carry out their work. They, every bit as much as we, are concerned with gathering facts that support further investigation or confirm a dead-end. And of particular personal concern to police is that bystander recordings can exonerate an officer charged with wrongdoing.[21]

A few other court decisions around the country have also protected the public's right to record officers in public. In 2017 the Supreme Court of Hawaii upheld the constitutional right to record, under both state and federal constitutional law.[22] The Federal District Court for the Southern District of New York likewise expressed support in 2017 for the argument that the right to record encompasses expressive conduct protect by the First Amendment.[23] However, reports of officers arresting photographers on eavesdropping charges continue to occur—in some cases, even in jurisdictions where police department orders have expressly stated that officers should not arrest civilians for recording. In one case, a civilian recorded a conversation with an official while making a public records request; when the civilian brought the recording to the department's attention, claiming the recording showed that his request was inappropriately handled, the police department arrested him for violating the eavesdropping law.[24] Civilians have also frequently been arrested for filming their encounters with police during traffic stops or while witnessing arrests in a variety of situations.

Clearly the right to record is slowly establishing itself as an integral component of First Amendment protections, although work still remains in some parts of the country to ensure the right is enjoyed more broadly. In some jurisdictions, courts have limited the rights of civilians to record in various settings, for example, finding no First Amendment right to record courtroom proceedings or security officials in airports.[25] Courts have also found officers immune from prosecution in a variety of situations—for example, where it was still not "clearly established" under prior case law that filming officers during a "tense active arrest situation with crowd control concerns would not be viewed as subject to some reasonable restrictions."[26] As recently as 2018, the Tenth Circuit held that it was not yet "clearly established that police officers violate the First Amendment when they prevent a person who is subject to police action from filming police activities."[27]

As noted earlier, courts have come to differing conclusions about whether the right to film officers while they are on duty is a clearly established First Amendment right to record within their circuits, with several courts holding that officers were entitled to qualified immunity for confiscating cameras or arresting or detaining bystanders for recording. Within the Third Circuit, a few cases stand out. First, in *Kelly v. Borough of Carlisle*, the court held that, on the facts in that case, there was "insufficient case law establishing a right to videotape police officers during a traffic stop to put a reasonably competent officer on 'fair notice' that seizing a camera or arresting an individual for videotaping police during the stop would violate the First Amendment."[28]

The *Kelly* court put significant weight on the fact that "traffic stops [are] especially fraught with danger to police officers."[29] This allowed the *Kelly* court to distinguish its case from that in the Eleventh Circuit decision in *Smith v. City of Cumming* and a prior district court decision in the Third Circuit, *Robinson v. Fetterman*. In *Robinson*, the district court had held that the plaintiff had a First Amendment right to film state troopers when his filming did not interfere with the officers' truck inspections on a public roadway, when he filmed from private property and remained at least twenty feet away from the officers.

More recently, in *Fleck v. Trustees of University of Pennsylvania* a district court in Pennsylvania held that an officer was entitled to qualified immunity when she seized a preacher's camera after he refused to move the camera away from her face as she questioned him as he was "impeding the flow of congregants into [a] mosque" while preaching loudly about how Islam was a "destructive religion."[30] The court held that the officer's actions were justified because the plaintiff had "ignored repeated police requests to move from the mosque doorway" and because the court found that "there was then no clearly-established First Amendment right in our Circuit to film police activity where, as here, the plaintiffs actively impeded efforts to restore public order." However, the court did state, in a footnote, that subsequently issued Philadelphia Police Department guidelines affirming the right to record might have made that issue "ripe for reconsideration in [the Third] Circuit."

The State of the Law in Washington

In Washington State, where I conducted my fieldwork, bystanders have benefited from earlier and more continuous recognition of their right to record the police than in most parts of the country. The legal status of the right to record in Washington is particularly important to unpack for present purposes, as it is the law that applied—to bystanders and police officers—in the context of my fieldwork. In possible tension with the right to record, the state's eavesdropping law makes it unlawful for any individual to record any private conversation "without first obtaining the consent of all the participants in the communication." Applying this provision requires an understanding of what the law meant by the term "private conversation," what it required in terms of "consent," and whether any other relevant exceptions existed at the time. I address each of these questions, in turn, in the paragraphs below.

Private conversation. Washington courts have looked to a variety of factors to determine whether a recorded conversation was private or not for purposes of the eavesdropping law. These decisions have included three primary inquiries: (1) location (e.g., was the bystander recording occurring on a public roadway or inside a private residence?), (2) whether third parties are present, and (3) the nature of the conversation itself (e.g., was the conversation between a civilian and police officer or between private parties?). The Supreme Court of Washington elaborated on the appropriate test for determining whether a conversation is private: "In determining whether a communication is private, we consider the subjective intention of the parties and may also consider other factors that bear on the reasonableness of the participants' expectations, such as the duration and subject matter of the communication, the location of the communication, and the presence of potential third parties. We will generally presume that conversations between two parties are intended to be private."[31]

However, conversations held in public spaces—and especially if held in front of third parties—will generally not be considered private.[32] In *State v. Flora*, the Washington Court of Appeals held that an arrestee's covert recording of a conversation between him and "public officers performing an official function on a public thoroughfare in the presence of a third party and within the sight and hearing of passersby" was not restricted by the statute because, in such a situation, the police officers could not "enjoy a privacy interest which they may assert under the statute."[33] In that case, Flora had covertly recorded his arrest by police officers using a tape recorder hidden inside a pile of papers. The court concluded, in line with prior state court decisions, that the word "private" in the state eavesdropping statute meant "secret," "intended only for the persons involved (a conversation)," "holding a confidential relationship to something," "a secret message: a private communication," or "secretly; not open or in public." In conclusion, the *Flora* court held: "Because the exchange was not private, its recording could not violate [the state eavesdropping statute] which applies to private conversations only. We decline the State's invitation to transform the privacy act into a sword available for use against individuals by public officers acting in their official capacity."[34]

In a series of later cases, Washington courts and federal courts deciding cases arising under Washington law have repeatedly maintained this interpretation of state privacy law.[35] These courts have held that "[d]etermining whether a particular conversation is private is a question of fact," but that "where the pertinent facts are undisputed and reasonable minds could not differ on the subject, the issue of whether a particular conversation is private may be determined as a matter of law."[36]

Following the *Flora* case, several additional decisions have affirmed the general holding in that case, that conversations with the police cannot be "private conversations" for purposes of state law. For example, in *Alford v. Haner*, the Ninth Circuit held that it was clearly established in Washington law, based on the decision in *Flora*, that "tape recording officers conducting a traffic stop is not a crime in Washington."[37] Likewise, in *Johnson v. Hawe*, the Ninth Circuit held that police radio communications audible outside an officer's vehicle were not private because the officer had "knowingly expose[d] them to the public" by virtue of having been listening to his radio with his vehicle windows down near a public skate park.[38]

Similarly, a 2014 opinion by the Washington attorney general, issued just after both agencies in this study began using body cameras, stated that all conversations between on-duty police officers and members of the public are "public" conversations, not subject to the state eavesdropping law; thus, both officers and bystanders/suspects can record their encounters without fear of violating state law.

Consent. Under the state's eavesdropping provisions, consent to record a conversation by all parties was required to record private conversations. Consent may be either explicit or implied. Implied consent to recording exists whenever any party to a conversation "knows that the recording is taking place."[39] The relevant provision of state privacy law states: "Where consent by all parties is needed pursuant to this chapter, consent shall be considered obtained whenever one party has announced to all other parties engaged in the communication or conversation, in any reasonably effective manner, that such communication or conversation is about to be recorded or transmitted: PROVIDED, That if the conversation is to be recorded that said announcement shall also be recorded."[40]

Courts have upheld this sort of implied-consent-by-virtue-of-knowledge conclusion in cases where a party has intercepted telephone conversations, emails, and voicemail messages when the complaining party had reason to know the communications were being intercepted.[41] Additionally, employees of a "regularly published newspaper, magazine, wire service, radio station, or television station" engaged in "bona fide news gathering" must meet a low threshold for consent purposes; specifically, the journalist exception requires only that, if consent is not explicitly given, "the recording or transmitting device" used by the journalist "is readily apparent or obvious to the speakers."

Other exceptions. In other cases, when the conversations at issue contain requests to commit murder, convey "threats of extortion, blackmail, bodily harm," or make other unlawful requests or demands, only the consent of one party is required.[42] Single-party consent is also required to record emergency calls to police and fire stations, communications "which occur anonymously or repeatedly or at an extremely inconvenient hour," and communications related to hostage takers or barricaded persons.[43]

BYSTANDER VIDEO AND THE POLICE

In reaction to bystander video (and other new forms of secondary visibility), the police have begun to "develop a self-interest in the politics of surveillance."[44] This has been at least partly motivated by police perceptions of the act of bystander recording as antagonistic. The ability of bystanders to (mis)interpret or (mis)represent officers' recorded conduct and to make the officers visible is an example of what Goodwin has referred to as "contested vision"; that is, by separating the interpretation from the experience and "professional vision" of the police, bystander video can contest the "socially organized ways" that police see and understand the recorded events.[45]

Similarly, bystander recordings impede "the police's ability to control the accounts of what happened on the street."[46] This "account ability" means "the capacity to provide a record of activities that explains them in a credible manner so that they appear to satisfy the rights and obligations of *accountability*."[47] If we see account ability as a matter of "negotiating control," the perceived loss of control that officers report due to the documentation, framing, dissemination, and interpretation of bystander recordings—as opposed to the potentially greater control they have regarding their own body-camera recordings—decreases officers' ability to explain and anchor the narrative surrounding their conduct (e.g., in their own written reports).[48] Thus, in some cases, officers may "pull[] back from doing their jobs" because they don't want to have an altercation recorded by a bystander.[49] This is a clear example of information politics impacting real-life police work.

Indeed, in a number of cases, police officers have targeted civilians or video activists, detaining or arresting them for recording in violation of local laws and ordinances and, in some cases, even breaking or confiscating cameras in the "war on cameras" as a "preemptive security" measure.[50] This resistance to bystander recording, an expression of (informational) power, may also be understood as a byproduct of the "security–photography encounter," wherein police officers perceive the bystander wielding a camera as "the subject of security" who is "contingent, continually changing, and possibly becoming dangerous."[51]

PRIOR WORK ON OFFICER ATTITUDES TOWARD BYSTANDER VIDEO

A few recent studies have examined officer attitudes toward bystander video, and their findings largely track my own. Sandhu and Haggerty found that officers "display . . . nuanced and apparently contradictory views" toward cameras, organizing officers' responses about policing on camera into three categories, reflecting the orientation of the response: "(1) camera shy; (2) habituated; and (3) strategic advantage."[52] The first orientation, *camera shy*, is characterized by "a series of anxieties about the risks and annoyances of working in an environment where officers . . . have the realistic prospect of being recorded." Officers were concerned about cameras (and the bystanders wielding them) interfering with or altering the dynamics of their work, damaging their reputations, and not accurately and objectively depicting the reality of what had occurred or what assumptions officers were working under during an encounter. They also expressed concerns about citizens "consciously manipulating their recordings" and intentionally broadcasting images that placed the officers in a negative light.[53] Accordingly, the authors found that "officers were attuned to how an image's depiction of reality is contingent" on a variety of variables beyond the officers' control and that "the public was quick to judge but did not have the knowledge required to fairly interpret recordings of police actions."[54]

The second orientation, *habituated*, points to responses indicating that officers have become accustomed to the presence of the cameras to the point that the cameras tend to blend into the background. Officers see the risks but feel it is unlikely they will be impacted personally in any career-defining or career-ending way. Despite overwhelming consensus that bystander video could easily misrepresent police action and that the public is ill-equipped to interpret such visual evidence, habituated officers generally stated that "when explained correctly and viewed by unbiased audiences, [bystander video] will ultimately support an officer's interpretation of a situation and exonerate them from accusations of wrongdoing."[55] The third orientation, *strategic advantage*, is characterized by officers who recognize the benefits that come from being on camera, including bystander video. This feeling was often tied to the evidentiary value of visual recordings and the likelihood that such recordings would be shared with the police to help investigate a case or to exonerate an officer and deter "bogus complaints."

In another recent study, Farmer interviewed a small sample of police officers to better understand the "anxieties" officers had regarding "how cameras and recordings can alter the dynamics of policing."[56] Respondents felt that bystander recording was distracting or posed safety concerns (both to the officer as well as to the person recording), especially when bystanders got too close and risked interfering with police work, baited officers, or otherwise tried to verbally engage with or escalate a police-civilian encounter. Like Sandhu and Haggerty, Farmer and Sun found evidence that officers had become accustomed to being recorded by bystanders, but they also reported that some officers perceived the act of recording as a form of "subtle defiance" and "passive resistance" and that bystanders were less likely to obey officers' commands while recording and were more likely to be confrontational.[57] Officers also felt that bystander video, with its perceived focus on capturing "something exciting," had generally decreased community trust in law enforcement.

Drawing from data collected through surveys and a set of twenty interviews with officers in two major Canadian police agencies, Brown investigated officers' self-reported judgments about how cameras had driven changes in their use-of-force-related behaviors.[58] Brown found that "the awareness and concern that their conduct could be video-recorded by a citizen was something that was *always present* in their consciousness."[59] Relatedly, most respondents reported that the (possible) presence of cameras had affected their use-of-force behavior, including their willingness to "tune up" "the odd bad guy who desperately deserved a punch in the head."[60] Interestingly, 86 percent of Brown's respondents reported that the dissemination of bystander video influenced "their decision to moderate violence" as much or more than their concerns about the physical presence of cameras.

In an earlier study, Huey et al. examined the experiences and motivations of members of a "Cop Watch" group based in Vancouver, British Columbia.[61] Based on interviews with several Vancouver police officers, they highlight concerns about the "anti-police values" of the cop watchers and the perception that officers are "pulling back from doing their jobs" because they don't want to have an altercation recorded by a bystander.[62] The police reported that cop watchers were interrupting police contacts and attempting to provoke officers while someone else was recording the interaction. From these officers' point of view, these intrusions impacted their ability to "establish a safety perimeter," something they are trained to do to protect themselves and others at a scene. Officers also expressed concern that having a camera follow them around limited their discretion to let a suspect off with a warning.

POLICE OFFICER ATTITUDES TOWARD BYSTANDER VIDEO

Across my surveys, a relatively small number of officers reported not having concerns about bystander video (10% in the 2015 survey, 8% in 2016, and 14% in 2017). These responses were generally explained as a consequence of officers becoming accustomed (or habituated) to frequently being recorded. For example, officers expressed sentiments like the following: "we are on camera all the time" (Kendrick, sergeant, SPD) and "civilians have been filming us for years" (Rachel, patrol officer, SPD). Some officers also qualified these responses, suggesting that if civilians are not interfering and keep a safe distance, they are not perceived as a problem. The refrain, "I don't mind being recorded, but stay out of my way" (Maynard, crime scene investigator, BPD, 2016) was common, as was something like the following:

> Being recorded does not bother me on its own. Where I have the issue is how the citizen is going to manipulate and then use the recording. It is also an officer safety issue, when citizens believe their right to video tape us trumps our safety. (Lois, sergeant/detective, BPD, 2015)

These concerns were generally directed toward the overlapping issues of accountability; visibility; and a perceived loss of control over the documentation, framing, dissemination, and interpretation of visual recordings of the officers' encounters with civilians. Many of these concerns were also reflected in the reported perceptions officers had about their own use of body-worn cameras. However, in terms of accountability, while officers saw body cameras as also increasing their potential exposure and visibility (to supervisors, the media, and the public), they also appreciated the ability to document evidence to counter claims of misconduct. This protective element was not present in the case of bystander video, and this exacerbated officers' sense that they could not control the consequences stemming from bystander video as compared to their own body cameras. Additionally, when officers talked about their perceptions of bystander video, they frequently began by noting how accustomed to it they had become (or by suggesting that officers who still complained about being recorded were being unrealistic). Some freely related personal anecdotes, but they often focused on controversy sparked by bystander recordings of other officers (including high-profile recordings in other cities, e.g., the recordings of Eric Garner and Walter Scott being killed by police).

Across surveys, between 70 and 80 percent of officers reported being "very comfortable" or "somewhat comfortable" with civilians recording them while they worked, and this was generally the sentiment expressed by officers during ride-alongs as well. Contrasted against the numerous concerns officers expressed, this reported level of comfort may be surprising. However, data collected during interviews suggest that officers have learned to live with being recorded and that they do not frequently experience adverse consequences, but that they recognize that such consequences could potentially occur (or had occurred to others).

Overall, the concerns officers expressed generally fell into two categories: (1) those about losing control of the immediate physical interaction and incident response (e.g., in cases of bystanders recording and getting too close or interjecting themselves into a crime scene or police-civilian contact) and (2) those involving the framing and disclosure of the subsequent recordings of the incident online. The first concern is connected to fears about safety and the ability to do their jobs (by restricting interference, obstruction, or distraction), while the second is about visibility, tied up in ambiguities about the motivations of the recording bystanders, the loss or misrepresentation of context, and the potential for heightened visibility through online dissemination. The first of these concerns is predominantly present in responses to questions about bystander video (although some officers also feel that the presence of their own body-worn cameras may also lessen the amount of discretion they are able to exert during a contact), while the second concern is connected more broadly to both bystander video and body-worn cameras.

The concerns officers expressed about physical safety and controlling their interactions with suspects and bystanders have also been raised in several of the right-to-record decisions discussed earlier. For example, in *State v. Russo*, the state argued that officers' attempts to conduct crowd control, including by asking bystanders to "step back" and "cease interfering," should be recognized as legitimate time, place, and manner restrictions on the bystander's First Amendment right to record.[63] The *Russo* court relied on the reasoning of the First Circuit, in *Gericke v. Begin*, finding that such restrictions are constitutional "only if the officer can reasonably conclude that the filming itself is interfering, or is about to interfere, with [the officer's] duties."[64]

The Physical Use of Cameras

Officers were concerned about the physical use of cameras by bystanders for a variety of reasons. However, the most commonly cited reasons relate to bystander interference (e.g., distracting an officer's attention) or the obstruction of police work. Distraction is frequently tied to safety-related concerns, ranging from having attention pulled away from a possibly threatening situation, to having "black metal objects pointed at me while I am in tense and rapidly evolving circumstances" (Russ, patrol officer, BPD, 2016), to the somewhat more extreme concern regarding "weapons disguised as a camera" (Roger, patrol officer, SPD, 2015). Most commonly, officers report being concerned about distraction simply because it is inconvenient and frustrating to have bystanders interfere with their work:

> I find that during a tense call for service my attention can be distracted by persons filming, especially if they are near enough to pose a threat or possibly prevent me from physically doing my job. (Shane, detective, BPD, 2015)

Others expressed more general concerns about being under constant surveillance or being recorded while working. During the limited pilot phase of deployment, officers frequently stated that other officers were not always happy to see a camera arrive on scene and wanted to be informed whenever a camera was activated. In response, some officers developed hand signals to signify to other officers that their body cameras were recording, while others simply announced their cameras to other officers when they arrived on scene—and when that didn't happen, officers often asked.

In terms of obstruction, some officers expressed concern about the more premeditated and targeted, overt, and obstructionist activism engaged in by some bystanders, often framed as "getting in the way" and "obstructing my investigation." According to a few officers, a small number of well-known local "cop watchers" were particularly bothersome; one man who posted to YouTube was mentioned multiple times, due to his particularly confrontational tactics and publicly accessible YouTube channel. These concerns about obstruction (and distraction) were also frequently framed as problems of spatial proximity—that is, officers were concerned that bystanders "get too close," and officers also expressed concerns about bystanders baiting officers or communicating with suspects, witnesses, or victims. To address some of these issues, some officers would reorient their bodies so that their own body cameras would capture parts of an encounter they wished to have documented or, when on scene in a backup role, they would stand back at a distance and aim their cameras to capture a wide view of the scene.

Officers also frequently expressed concerns based on their perception that the bystanders who recorded them were motivated to do so for reasons the officers found offensive or unwarranted. For example, officers felt that bystanders were motivated by anti-police sentiment or the patent desire to document police misconduct, misrepresent police-public encounters in a way that makes officers look bad, or reveal police tactics, or simply by a desire for personal attention and recognition. These concerns, framed as they were to include elements of disclosure, also resonate with officers' concerns about the framing, disclosure, and interpretation of bystander video after it gets uploaded to sites like YouTube or Facebook.

The Dissemination of Bystander Video Online

Overall, officers' concerns about dissemination, visibility, context, and exposure can be boiled down into two categories. First, officers were concerned that bystander video would not adequately or accurately represent the context of the documented encounter—often manifested in the loss or manipulation of context. As I operationalize it here, this *loss of context* meant at least two different things to officers. First, it meant the recordings will not capture the full subjective experience of the officers, and thus the audience will view the video without understanding how the officers subjectively perceived the situation and why the officers chose to make the decisions they did—and relatedly, that the audience will view and interpret the video (evidence) in ways that did not match the officers' experience. Second, it means the recording (or the portion of the recording made public) is limited in its ability to capture or show the entire sequence of events that led to the incident (or interaction/use of force, etc.) of interest, because of limited visibility (on the recording), limited audio capture, distortion due to the camera's point of view, or limited coverage from the beginning of an incident until the conclusion for practical or intentional reasons (e.g., the bystander did not initiate the recording until after the incident had started, either intentionally or not).

Officers frequently expressed concerns about civilians' motivations for sharing video online, citing what they perceived as biased "personal agendas and narratives" (Jesse, detective, BPD, 2017) or the intention to "edit their videos so that pieces are taken out of context and better illustrate their viewpoint" (Emerson, senior patrol officer, SPD, 2016) or to "create a false narrative" (Oliver, detective, BPD, 2015) that "demonizes the profession" (Blake, neighborhood resource officer, SPD, 2016). Some officers felt that bystanders would "only show what they want people to see" rather than "the complete event" (Sidney, lieutenant, BPD, 2017). Some officers feared that bystanders would edit, manipulate, or frame their recordings in ways that would decontextualize the documented events. These perceptions led to frustration and concern about how bystanders (and the news media, in some instances) would disseminate, frame, and interpret the video, leading to an increase in "illegitimate complaints due to editing" (Wayne, patrol officer, BPD, 2016) and the "misrepresentation of what actually happened" (Kara, detective, BPD, 2016). These expressions of concern are indicative of the sense of fragility or vulnerability felt by officers in the face of potential visibility and of how these concerns fed into problematic "us versus them" mentalities.

Concern about "the ten-second clip taken out of context" (Christian, patrol officer, SPD, 2016) was one of the most frequently cited reasons officers didn't like bystander video, as such video only depicts "a very small piece of what happened" (Truman, sergeant, BPD, 2016). As one officer put it, "Most [bystander] video doesn't show what led up to the use of force[;] it only shows police 'beating down' a subject" (Taylor, patrol officer, BPD, 2015). Bystanders "only record and release the things that are provocative. People don't understand that the camera only tells a brief account as to what really happens" (Ross, undisclosed rank, SPD, 2016). Relatedly, officers were concerned that the "selective editing of video footage and then release on social media" (Ward, captain, SPD, 2016) would lead to unwanted and "selective scrutiny" (Stan, patrol sergeant, BPD, 2016), or that visibility and exposure in the public realm would depict officers "in a negative light" (Blanche, patrol officer, BPD, 2016). Some of these concerns over exposure and visibility were driven by questions of accountability. These accountability-related concerns fit into three general categories: (1) after-the-fact review ("armchair quarterbacking") by supervisors, the media, and the public; (2) an increase in formal complaints; and (3) punitive sanctions for otherwise "innocent mistakes." The feeling that their "every move is scrutinized" (Alex, sergeant, SPD, 2015) suggested to some officers that there was a "need to do everything perfectly, every time. If not, the evidence showing errors in officer decisions, actions etc., is front and center for everyone to dissect after the fact" (Cary, sergeant, BPD, 2015). Such constant surveillance would likely even capture officers' "occasional unprofessional comments or conduct while under stress" (Ralph, patrol sergeant, BPD, 2015).

Beyond accountability-related concerns, some officers reported that being recorded was "just unnerving. It's like being under constant observation and scrutiny" (Herb, undisclosed rank, SPD, 2016). Some reported that having video of them posted online, especially when they were identifiable, could create a safety risk for themselves or their families, even when they were off duty. Some also expressed other privacy-related concerns—for example, "I don't want to be shared around even when I do nothing wrong" (Alan, undisclosed rank, SPD, 2016)—or concerns about civilian privacy interests, for example, "People are just hoping to be the next one to uncover a corrupt police department when really they are just invading people's privacy who are trying to report a crime" (Sandra, patrol officer, BPD, 2016). Officers also reported that it was generally inappropriate for civilians to post recordings to the internet at much higher rates than they did when asked about civilians recording officers (in general or in arrest-related situations) (see figure 1 in appendix B).

VISION, CONTESTED; OR, THE LOSS OF INFORMATIONAL POWER AND "ACCOUNT ABILITY"

Within the two departments studied here, we see that officers' primary concerns regarding bystander video stem from fears about visibility and exposure, the misrepresentation or misinterpretation of their conduct, and physical interference with their daily work. In their daily work, the camera became a signifier for a difficult witness and evoked both temporal and visibility-related concerns. Additionally, recorded video often becomes "a politically charged theater for contested vision," as evidenced by the aftermath of the Rodney King beating as different sides sought to use the same visual evidence to support competing interpretations of the events.[65] Undoubtedly the world has changed since George Holliday's recording was first broadcast. However, while we should be careful about comparing that moment with the present for a variety of reasons, not the least of which is the important cultural shift instigated by the Black Lives Matter movement, we continue to see vision contested as alternate narratives are offered by parties competing to frame events in certain ways for political purposes.

The officers' responses summarized earlier evoke anxieties based in the perception that bystander video foregrounds decontextualized police-civilian interactions, often intended to make officers look bad or hold them accountable (wrongly or rightly) for misconduct. These concerns originate from the officers' condition as *affected bystanders*: although they are in a position of great power, they feel vulnerable; in their work, they are "surrounded by technology" and "often involuntarily, subjected to the effects that *others*' technology use entails."[66] But unlike the typical affected bystanders, who background much of the technological interference generated by those around them, police officers are frequently forced to foreground the technology use of civilians around them, based on their training and the need they feel to ensure their safety as they work. They notice. And they sometimes alter their performances when they are being recorded, not only because they know they are being watched, but also because they are concerned about the sort of exposure that the perpetual and persistent memory of the internet makes possible.

The connections between the civilizing- and accountability-related aims of police body-worn camera deployment and bystander video are also evocative of Foucault's notion of governmentality and government as the "conduct of conduct"; each is a "rational attempt to shape conduct" by varied entities for "definite but shifting ends and with a diverse set of relatively unpredictable consequences, effects and outcomes."[67] Indeed, the crossed lenses of police body cameras and bystander cameras likely incentivize both officers and bystanders to engage in forms of self-government, as cases "in which governor and governed are two aspects of the one actor."[68] These situations challenge the distinction between sousveillance and surveillance in practice.

Alongside their attempts to map the possible effects of being recorded, officers are also working within a context in which the "new transparency encourages beliefs in images speaking for themselves, in cameras as mechanically objective witnesses, and in information as self-evident."[69] Officers reported substantial concerns about popular acceptance of the "mechanical objectivity" of these video recordings of police-public encounters when the concern was their own visibility (but perhaps hypocritically, they extolled the benefits of body-worn camera footage as evidence useful to criminal prosecution).[70] Fears about perceived objectivity of video were only heightened by the fact that officers are working in an environment filled with increasing calls to "release the tapes," especially because these calls are often based on assumptions about the "objectivity" of these visual records of police-civilian interactions that run counter to many officers' opinions that the recording, selection, and presentation of these videos manipulate, distort, or remove vital contextual information.[71]

Interestingly, officers expressed concerns about the perceived objectivity of video in terms of physical presence (e.g., limitations on what bystanders choose to record and the field of view captured by individual recording devices) as well as physical absence (e.g., being disconnected from the online audience and their interpretation of events). Linking these two, however, was the overarching concern that video (as a technology, and as consumed online) was unable to put the viewer in the place of the officer and convey the perception and experience of the officer in the recorded moment, thus leading to distorted understandings and judgments about an officer's actions. To this point, various studies empirically support concerns that the interpretation of video footage is subject to differing perspectives and forms of perspective bias, suggesting that the mechanical objectivity of these videos is an impossibility.[72] Indeed, as Goodwin put it, "The ability to see a meaningful event is not a transparent psychological process but instead a socially situated activity accomplished through the deployment of a range of historically constituted discursive practices."[73]

In the context of their qualitative responses, the more negative views officers held about bystanders uploading video to YouTube and Facebook (etc.) versus merely recording officers also suggests that officers are more concerned about the risks brought about by visibility and the persistent and perpetual memory of the internet than they are with the perceived distraction- and safety-related effects of bystander video on their physical, day-to-day work. Essentially, concerns rooted in their loss of (informational) power and the resulting information politics were seen as more important than the more temporary, fleeting physical inconvenience caused by the presence of camera-wielding bystanders. Indeed, it was apparent that these concerns were often rooted in information politics, as the perceived loss of context and loss of control over how and when information about their work was disclosed suggests that officers are losing power in their struggle to frame and control the narrative and explain their interpretation of the events depicted on the video (their "account ability"). Indeed, when bystanders control the video, officers are limited in their ability to frame and anchor the narrative around their interactions with members of the public.

CHAPTER 4

Policing as (Monitored) Performance

Society trusts video footage, even private recordings that fail to show the entire incident, over the word of a sworn officer. Thank you, mass media and idiots.

—Henry, patrol officer, BPD, 2015

Our officers do things right 99 percent of the time, and it would be nice for those with an open mind to have objective evidence that this is in fact the case. Even when mistakes are made, it is seldom with the malice portrayed by some of the very vocal members of the public. Cameras have proven officers truthful more often than otherwise.

—Garrick, undisclosed rank, SPD, 2015

FROM THE TRAINING ROOM . . .

In September 2014, just prior to initial training meetings with the command staff and users (volunteering officers) at one of the departments, I met representatives from the body-camera manufacturer in the police station lobby. After we were led to the department's evidence room, it became evident that there was some confusion between the evidence room staff and the corporate representatives about who was responsible for setting up the docking stations for the cameras (which were opened but not yet installed in the room). The company representatives expected the police to have already installed them, but the evidence room supervisor was apparently not sure where or how they should be set up. He asked the reps to install the docking stations on the wall behind the door, but they responded by telling him they weren't comfortable doing that because there was no doorstop and the docks might get knocked off the wall inadvertently. As a compromise, they set up a folding table and placed the docking stations on top, ran cables to nearby outlets, and declared the installation complete—for now.

In the meantime, an officer who had participated in the department's earlier evaluation of the cameras stopped in the doorway and stuck his head into the room. He exclaimed that he couldn't wait to get his camera later that day. "I want it right now, give me my camera!" he called out, jokingly. During his evaluation of the cameras, this officer had recorded a man who began arguing with him, claiming his Terry-stop detention was racially motivated, prior to leading the officer on a foot chase. After the suspect originally pleaded not guilty to evading the police, the department provided his defense attorney with a copy of the footage, resulting in a speedy change of plea. Some of the officers, like the officer who had recorded the footage, saw these events as strong evidence that the cameras would capture important evidence and improve their work.

After the cameras were set up, we were ushered into a meeting with the department's command staff. As the meeting progressed, it became clear that department leadership had some concerns about how the law might regulate or impact some aspects of their camera program. They expressed concerns about whether officers were required by state law to announce to anyone they contacted that they were recording. (An existing state law exempted officers using car-mounted dashboard camera systems from the requirement to announce and notify members of the public, but it didn't explicitly extend to body-worn cameras like those purchased by the department.) Additionally, members of the command staff were concerned about some aspects of the state Public Records Act (PRA). Specifically, they noted concern that the system-generated email links to unredacted footage that could be sent to prosecutors, for example, might become subject to public disclosure, allowing requesters access to unredacted video files they were otherwise not permitted to view.

One SWAT commander asked why public disclosure issues were of such concern. In response, multiple administrators around the table agreed it was because Washington had one of the broadest FOI laws in the country. Indeed, the discussion around the table made it obvious that the breadth of the PRA was felt keenly by administrators, as something they knew they would have to deal with in the months and years ahead. Against this backdrop, the chief also noted his desire that their officers be reminded that, since they were relatively early adopters (in Washington and elsewhere in the country), the department might be scrutinized, and so officers needed to really pay attention to how they did their work on camera.

After the command staff meeting, we moved to a different room, where about thirty officers (mostly men) were seated at small desks. After my first survey questionnaire was distributed to the officers, the meeting was turned over to the corporate representatives, who introduced the cameras to the officers. As noted in the introduction to this book, the officers appeared to be excited to unbox their cameras. Most had volunteered, although one newer recruit told me that he had been told to attend under a policy that would require new recruits and officers transferring in from other departments to wear cameras as soon they started working (even during any probationary period).

The officers were shown videos recorded during the Rialto (California) Police Department's pilot program. In one clip, the video depicted officers moving through a private home and, eventually, onto a back patio, where the camera-wearing officer fired his TASER, causing the suspect to fall into a swimming pool. The video then depicted the officer entering the pool and retrieving the suspect. As they watched, I heard officers in the training room comment, "oh, that's amazing video" and "that was very well done." Others expressed concerns about knowing how to orient their own cameras to get such good results—one noting that the orientation of a head-mounted camera used by one of the department's officers who had evaluated the camera months earlier made it appear as if he were staring at the breasts of a woman he had pulled over for a traffic violation, rather than at her face or hands. This concern seemed to be shared, as I heard another officer ask his neighbor, "How is this orientation?" as he tried to attach and orient his new camera on his glasses for the first time, to which the second officer responded, "You might get a lot of cleavage with that."

As noted earlier, some officers also perceived body-worn camera adoption as a needed response to bystander video. They joked about having a "direct-to-YouTube" button installed on the cameras. After discussing how they could create a "training" category for clips that could be flagged for use in internal training programs, some officers joked about also creating a "YouTube" flag that they could attach to footage that was particularly worthy of being watched by others. Officers were upset at videos of police work that were edited or taken out of context and posted to the internet, and they saw a chance to gather their own evidence and provide more context to events. One sergeant, who was glad that cameras were being introduced, told me that a prior chief at the department had refused to install dashboard cameras in patrol vehicles because, in his words, he "didn't trust his officers enough to have them on video." In the sergeant's opinion, it was about time they moved past these reservations.

Of course, not all officers shared these feelings. From the beginning, some officers were concerned about the accountability that wearing a camera might generate, particularly when they didn't see the need for discipline. Others were simply apprehensive about adopting a new technology, adding something else to their already burdened uniforms, or understanding the department's new and evolving body-worn camera policy. One officer raised her hand during the meeting and asked whether they would need to record every traffic stop, or only those they thought had escalated or might be problematic. Should a simple warning with no terse language or interaction be recorded? "No," they were told, the department's policy allowed discretion.

. . . TO THE STREETS

The Bellingham and Spokane police departments both started their body-camera pilot programs in September 2014. In each agency, officers volunteered to wear cameras during the pilot phase (although some told me they felt that they had been "voluntold" to wear them). In Bellingham, broader adoption grew slowly over the first couple of years (as additional officers began to request cameras and new recruits or experienced officers who transferred into the department from elsewhere were required to wear them), until cameras were finally rolled out to all officers in the department in the summer of 2016.

In Spokane, officers also began wearing cameras in September 2014, but deployment across the agency was eventually dictated by the methods of a randomized control trial run by researchers at Arizona State University.[1] Thus, approximately half of the sworn patrol officers in the department were assigned cameras in May 2015, and the other half were assigned cameras in November 2015. Due to the methods chosen, this meant that some of the officers who wore cameras during the initial pilot phase of the body-camera program were asked to stop wearing them in May and were reassigned in November, if randomly selected to be part of the initial control group. (Some of these officers complained to me that they didn't want their cameras taken away from them, as they had begun to appreciate the cameras during the first nine months or so of deployment.) A small number of officers also asked to stop wearing a camera before the pilot phase had concluded. As also found by the Arizona State University researchers, the primary complaints these officers expressed were related to the broad public disclosure requirements in Washington State (discussed further in the conclusion).[2]

During my early rides with officers in these two departments, they expressed a variety of reasons for having elected to wear a camera. For some, body-worn cameras were seen as the future of law enforcement—a future they might as well get used to early. One corporal said that he volunteered to wear a camera because he liked the idea and wanted to generate good habits and be up to speed on best practices prior to when adoption would become mandatory. For a few officers, the fact that their department had promised to not hold officers accountable for policy infractions related to the cameras during the pilot period was also important. This allowed some of the officers, including those who generally didn't like the idea of wearing a camera, to get on board early.

Some officers saw the cameras as a response to bystander video or fraudulent claims of misconduct—essentially, a means of protecting themselves and having some control over how their work was documented. For example, one patrol sergeant told me that he had volunteered to wear a camera to generate better visual evidence, document his point of view, and fend off false claims of misconduct. For others, the positive experiences other officers had reported influenced their decisions. As a case in point, another officer who had volunteered, in part, to be better able to counter false claims of misconduct, had also heard (anecdotally, from other officers) that a camera might make people change their behavior. He repeated a story he had heard from other officers who had broken up a college frat party: the frat kids, who were usually disrespectful, had changed their behavior and were more respectful after they were told they were being recorded.

During one ride-along conducted a few weeks into the pilot program in 2014, one BPD patrol sergeant told me that he felt the administration had different motivations for adopting the cameras than the frontline officers did for volunteering to wear them. That is, in his opinion, the administration was really concerned about budgets, limiting exposure to legal liability, and image management. The sergeant also articulated why he thought some officers didn't want to wear a camera:

> I hate to say it, but I think it's really, mostly about ego. Most cops are type "A" personalities and we like to talk about what we did, but not the things

> we didn't do, well. Officers don't want to see or hear themselves on tape, or have their peers or others see and judge them when they don't perform their work without any mistakes.

Notably, some officers who were hesitant to volunteer at the outset also began asking to be assigned cameras shortly after the initial deployment as they received positive reports from their colleagues. BPD also reiterated their policy that new hires would have to wear the cameras, but not during their field training—where they are always watched, and pressure is intense—as the administration decided it would help make the initial training period less complicated.

Beyond the findings I report throughout this book, a growing number of studies of police officer attitudes toward body cameras have been published in the last few years, and many of these evoke similar findings. For example, in England, a study of police perceptions of body-worn cameras in 2015 found that very high percentages of officers expected cameras to have positive implications for their work.[3] The "most appreciated benefit" of body cameras reported by these English officers was the capacity of the cameras to capture evidence—evidence some saw as "indisputable."[4] Some saw body-camera footage as potentially exonerating in cases of alleged misconduct, holding the power to mitigate complaints and affirm the appropriateness of officer conduct.[5] And while most officers reported that the cameras would not cause them to change their own behavior, they cited the "prevention of antisocial behavior" and the improvement of police-public interactions as primary reasons for their positive perceptions of the cameras.[6] That is, they said that cameras would change civilians' behavior, but not their own. However, a minority of respondents in that study did acknowledge that body cameras would make them more aware of their own behavior. Officers also noted that body cameras would "let the public see exactly what we deal with day to day," echoing responses from several officers in my study.[7] Negative perceptions, on the other hand, included concerns about potential discipline, limited discretion, and the role of body-worn cameras in "policing the police," as well as increased administrative duties.[8]

Like officers from my study in Washington State, some English officers were also concerned that body-worn cameras are "not able to capture everything your eyes can see[;] [t]herefore, the full reasons of your actions will not be recorded," evidence that not all officers were convinced that video evidence was indisputable.[9] Similar findings have emerged in other studies as well, "refut[ing] the assumption that viewers of a video clip see and hear the same things."[10] Officers have linked body-worn cameras to a growing lack of trust in police and expressed fears that the public would not interpret or view footage of officers' conduct in ways that matched the officers' own expectations, or that the public would misjudge "appropriate" officer conduct based on bias or a lack of understanding.[11] Concerns about limited discretion, armchair quarterbacking, and increased visibility to internal affairs personnel also appear in research.[12]

In a randomized controlled trial in Tempe, Arizona, White et al. found that most officers viewed body-worn cameras positively prior to deployment within their agency, with over 90 percent reporting that body-worn camera footage "would produce more accurate accounts of incidents."[13] Roughly two-thirds of respondents reported that body cameras would civilize both officers' and citizens' behavior toward each other.[14] However, officers did express concerns about limited discretion, technological questions about how easy the cameras would be to use, and the feeling that their colleagues would not appreciate their use of a camera while in the field.[15] However, while the Tempe officers' perceptions became more positive over time across a variety of measures, the percentage of officers who felt that body cameras would improve citizen behavior decreased to below 50 percent by the end of the study. In another study in nearby Phoenix, Arizona, researchers found that officers who volunteered to wear cameras were more likely to report that body cameras improved civilian behavior than officers who resisted camera adoption.[16] These volunteers were also more likely to have college degrees, and those with prior body-camera experience were more likely to volunteer to wear one again—indicating that prior experience generally led to more positive perceptions of the cameras.[17] An experimental study in Amsterdam, Netherlands, also found generally high levels of officer satisfaction with the cameras and their ease of use, as well as enhanced feelings of officer safety.[18]

Some studies have found low rates of body-camera acceptance and approval by officers. In a study in Pittsburgh, Pennsylvania, for example, less than a third of officers reported that cameras should be adopted and less than half of all respondents reported that body-worn cameras would not erode trust with their supervisors.[19] In a study of police administrators, one-third of respondents reported that they did not support the use of body-worn cameras in their department, while only 50 percent did.[20] Another US-based study found that body cameras "increase burnout and decrease perceived organizational support."[21] That is, officers who wore body cameras were more likely to report burnout than those who did not, and they were also more likely to report the perception that their agency offered less organizational support.[22]

OFFICER PERCEPTIONS OF CAMERAS

On questionnaires distributed once each year from 2014 to 2017, I asked officers to respond to a series of five questions designed to gauge their general attitudes toward body cameras and body-camera adoption within their agencies. An index was calculated (averaged) from these five response items, referred to as the Approval Index, with a value from 1 (negative) to 5 (positive) (see table 1). The five questions, discussed in more depth below, asked officers (1) how positive or negative of a development the adoption of cameras within their department was, (2) how appropriate it was for officers to use body cameras, (3) how useful the body cameras were, (4) how comfortable the officers were with the idea of wearing a camera while they work, and, if applicable, (5) how they rated their prior experience with wearing a camera.

First, officers were asked *whether they saw the implementation of body-worn cameras within their department as a positive or negative development* (see table 2 in appendix A for numerical findings). On the first survey, nearly two-thirds (66%) of respondent officers (across both departments), indicated that the adoption of body cameras by their department was either a "very positive" or "somewhat positive" development (63% BPD, 67% SPD). From the first survey (2014) to the second (2015), the percentage of positive responses increased in each department, while negative responses also grew slightly at SPD. Positive responses from SPD respondents increased again to a high of approximately 83 percent on the third survey (2016), before dropping almost all the way back to what they had been in 2014 on the fourth survey (2017). Positive responses from BPD respondents dipped slightly in 2016 but rose again sharply to a high of over 91 percent in 2017. Notably, zero BPD respondents indicated that body-camera adoption was a negative development on the final survey in 2017. In general, BPD officers reported continuously more favorable attitudes toward camera adoption within their department over time than did SPD officers. This trend was also observed among those identifying as serving in supervisory roles at SPD and, for the first three surveys, frontline officers, although the responses from these officers dropped back to essentially the same level as on the first two surveys on the fourth survey.

TABLE 1 APPROVAL INDEX: 1 (NEGATIVE) TO 5 (POSITIVE)

Sample	Survey	Rank	n	Mean	Standard Deviation	Change
SPD	1	Supervisor	24	4.17	0.75	—
		Officer	62	3.75	0.96	—
		Unknown	12	3.54	0.96	—
		Total	98	3.83	0.93	—
	2	Supervisor	24	4.36	0.70	0.19
		Officer	40	3.59	0.94	(0.16)
		Unknown	20	3.83	0.68	0.30
		Total	84	3.87	0.88	0.04
	3	Supervisor	23	4.27	0.77	(0.09)
		Officer	30	4.08	0.84	0.49
		Unknown	17	4.06	0.73	0.22
		Total	70	4.14	0.79	0.27
	4	Supervisor	18	4.46	0.51	0.19
		Officer	31	3.73	1.05	(0.35)
		Unknown	19	3.55	1.22	(0.51)
		Total	68	3.87	1.04	(0.27)
BPD	1	Supervisor	11	4.41	0.37	—
		Officer	32	3.53	0.89	—
		Unknown	7	3.85	0.62	—
		Total	50	3.77	0.84	—
	2	Supervisor	12	4.42	0.44	0.01
		Officer	24	3.67	0.84	0.14
		Unknown	13	4.15	0.57	0.30
		Total	49	3.98	0.75	0.22
	3	Supervisor	14	4.54	0.46	0.12
		Officer	30	3.76	0.84	0.09
		Unknown	12	3.84	0.72	(0.31)
		Total	56	3.97	0.80	(0.01)
	4	Supervisor	13	4.37	0.62	(0.17)
		Officer	15	4.24	0.57	0.48
		Unknown	6	4.67	0.45	0.83
		Total	34	4.36	0.58	0.40

Numbers in parentheses indicate a negative change.

There were, however, some noticeable and consistent differences in responses based on rank and race. On individual surveys, there were differences observed based on sex, political preferences, and prior body-camera use, but none of these differences persisted across surveys. Nonwhite respondents consistently reported more favorable attitudes toward the adoption of cameras than white respondents—with between 75 and 90 percent of respondents ranking adoption as a positive development, while only 65 to 79 percent of white respondents reported similar positive attitudes, across surveys. (It should be noted, however, that the numbers of respondents reporting being nonmale and/or nonwhite on any given survey were very small, making any generalizations based on these findings difficult to make regarding those groups.) In all but one instance (SPD, Survey 3), those who identified as serving in a supervisory capacity responded more positively about cameras than those who identified as regular officers, although a majority of both sets of respondents reported that body cameras were a positive development in both agencies across all four surveys.

Second, when asked *how appropriate they thought it was for police officers to use body-worn cameras*, most officers reported that it was either "very appropriate" or "somewhat appropriate" (80%, 81%, 85%, 80%, by survey) (see table 3 in appendix A for more details). These percentages generally increased through the third survey and then decreased slightly on the final survey due to a smaller percentage of positive SPD responses (73% positive on the final survey versus 94% at BPD). Positive responses from BPD respondents varied from a low of 76 percent on the second survey to a high of 94 percent on the fourth, while negative responses ranged from 20 percent on the second survey to 0 percent on the fourth. Positive responses from SPD officers peaked on the second survey at 85 percent and dropped to a low of 73 percent on the fourth, while negative responses peaked at 20 percent on the first survey and dropped to 7 percent on the third. In both departments, supervisors reported noticeably higher percentages of positive responses than did regular officers, reaching 100 percent at BPD on the first (n = 11), third (n = 14), and fourth (n = 13) surveys, and at SPD on the fourth survey (n = 18) (even though regular officers reported their lowest percentage of positive responses on the same survey, at 68%). Regardless, most regular officers in each department also reported that body-camera use was appropriate (between 80% and 68% at SPD, and 88% and 71% at BPD).

Third, officers were asked *how useful body cameras were for achieving law enforcement objectives* (see table 4 in appendix A for more details). As with responses to the other questions, respondents indicated mostly positive responses, with supervisors reporting higher percentages of positive responses on almost every survey (the exception being SPD respondents on the third survey). Respondents, across departments, reported that body cameras were somewhat or very useful for achieving law enforcement objectives between 75 and 95 percent of the time, across all four surveys.

Fourth, officers were also asked to self-report *how comfortable they were with the idea of wearing a camera while they worked*, and (in line with the responses to the questions already discussed) most officers in both agencies reported being either "very comfortable" or "somewhat comfortable" with the idea (see table 5 in appendix A for more details). However, it was obvious that supervisors generally responded more positively than regular officers on this question as well; across both departments, the difference ranged from thirty points on the second survey to eleven points on the third, with 82 to 100 percent of supervisors at BPD responding positively and 75 to 94 percent of supervisors at SPD doing likewise, while 53 to 87 percent (BPD) and 55 to 83 percent (SPD) of respondents identifying as regular officers responded positively across all surveys. Within BPD, "very comfortable" responses increased from only 16 percent on the first survey to 53 percent on the fourth, with an additional 46 to 35 percent also reporting being "somewhat comfortable" across all four surveys. Within SPD, "very comfortable" responses increased from 25 percent on the first survey to a high of 49 percent on the third, dropping a little to 43 percent on the fourth, with an additional 45 to 25 percent reporting being "somewhat comfortable" from the first to the final survey. Negative responses dropped survey to survey from 38 to 6 percent within BPD and from 36 to 11 percent within SPD, rising to 22 percent again on the fourth survey.

On three of the surveys, officers with ten or more years of law enforcement experience responded more positively than those with less than ten years' experience. Perhaps most telling, though, was the difference between respondents who reported having used a body-worn camera and those who had not, which might also be one of the reasons that positive responses generally increased over time as more and more officers gained experience with the cameras. However, the percentage of positive responses among those who reported prior use declined across each survey, from 97 to 77 percent (although this was largely due to decreasing positive responses from SPD respondents, as 90 percent of respondents at BPD who had used a camera still reported being comfortable with the idea on the fourth survey), while the positive percentages of those who had not used cameras prior to responding to the surveys remained essentially stable, increasing from 59 to 65 percent across surveys. It is not entirely clear, from my data, why SPD officers' attitudes toward the cameras dropped so much on the fourth survey.

Fifth, officers who had previously used a body camera were also asked to *rate their experience with wearing a body camera*, from very negative to very positive (see table 6 in appendix A for more details). A majority in each department, from 62 to 90 percent across surveys, reported a positive experience, with roughly a third of these respondents on each survey (28% to 34%) reporting a "very positive" experience. Fewer than 25 percent of respondents reported having a negative experience with the cameras on each survey.

Despite the generally high percentages of positive responses to questions about body cameras, many officers did express concerns about the cameras (during the pilot phase as well as throughout the study), although some also cited positive outcomes as reasons to accept or prefer cameras. When asked, within the first few months of adoption, whether they would choose to wear a body camera at that moment (if the choice were completely theirs to make), roughly half of the officers responded affirmatively (53% SPD; 44% BPD; 50% overall), while about four out of ten indicated they would not (40% SPD; 36% BPD; 39% overall). However, when asked the same question over the following three years, officers' responses were generally increasingly positive. (Positive responses by BPD officers went from 44% on Survey 1 to 76% on Survey 4, while negative responses decreased over each survey to a low of 15% on Survey 4; although the percentage of positive responses from SPD officers increased from 53% on the first survey to 60% on the third, they decreased to 51% on the fourth, the lowest rate across all four surveys, with 31% of officers reporting that they would no longer choose to wear a camera.)

PERCEIVED BENEFITS

Officers who reported that they would choose to wear a camera cited a variety of perceived benefits, although a few types of responses were shared broadly and repeated by numerous officers in their qualitative responses. The two most-cited reasons for preferring a camera were (1) the perceived ability to counter false claims of misconduct and (2) the possibility of generating useful evidence that could be used in criminal prosecutions or to document bad civilian behavior. Both of these reasons are directly connected to the evidentiary benefits of body-worn camera footage. Officers also saw cameras as capable of serving as an independent witness to their work, documenting their actions and the actions of others in a way that could be employed to provide additional context or perspective when needed. Less frequently, but still repeatedly, officers also noted that cameras were "another tool" to be tried that could assist officers in carrying out their work, improve the perception of the police among the public, and be useful for report-writing purposes. A number of officers also noted the perception that body-camera footage would generally only depict law enforcement positively (interestingly, this sentiment arose much more frequently in later surveys than at the beginning of my research). The following was a common sentiment:

> I think there are positives and negatives to wearing it, but I don't have a problem with wearing it. I think it can help protect us from accusations and, sometimes, when people know they are being recorded, they are on their best behavior. (Blanche, patrol officer, BPD, 2016)

Others focused more on the negative. One officer, for instance, stated that he would choose to wear a camera "only because of Baltimore," referring to the (then recent) death of Freddie Gray while in the custody of the Baltimore Police Department, in which there was no visual evidence of what the officers had or had not done to cause or exacerbate Gray's injuries. Others found the whole idea of mandated body-camera adoption distasteful, despite being willing to wear one voluntarily as a form of protection. For example, one officer stated:

> I would wear one only because I think it would protect me from false claims against me. I have a disagreement in [principle] with making officers wear them because of people making claims against us that we are inherently dishonest and racist people. I have this job because I chose to live my life a certain way. I was subjected to more scrutiny to qualify for a job in law enforcement than any other job I can think of in civil service. The mandatory wearing of body cameras is a spit in the face to that hiring process. (Dennis, corporal, SPD, 2014)

Many of my respondents cited their belief that cameras could help protect officers from false complaints and allegations of misconduct. This was also commonly cited as the primary reason officers would choose to wear a camera if they had the choice themselves.

This idea—that the presence of body-worn cameras will quell complaints against officers—has been one of the most frequently touted claims in favor of mass body-camera deployment in the United States over the past decade. Initially, much of the fervor for this claim can be attributed to the Rialto Study, initially published online in 2013. In that study, year-to-year complaints against officers were shown to have dropped about 90 percent (compared to the previous three years) after the adoption of body-worn cameras within the relatively small Rialto (California) Police Department, along with a coinciding, and statistically significant, 50 percent reduction in use-of-force incidents.[23] In a study of body-camera adoption in Las Vegas, the presence of cameras resulted in decreased numbers of officers who generated at least one complaint during the study period.[24] However, in research with the Denver (Colorado) Police Department, researchers found that the presence of a body-worn camera *increased* "the odds of a misconduct complaint" while reducing the odds of use-of-force-related complaint, adding some nuance to the idea that cameras reduce complaints.[25] In Las Vegas, officers who wore a body camera were slightly less likely to have complaints against them sustained, and complaints against them were generally concluded more quickly.[26] A large experimental study in Washington, DC, found no significant effects of body-worn camera adoption on the number of complaints filed against officers.[27]

In my study, numerous officers noted the perception that cameras would help reduce their "exposure to lawsuits and unwarranted complaints" (Oliver, detective, BPD, 2015). The ability to "protect myself from liability," said one officer, "is by far the best use of this technology in our current societal circumstances" (Damon, detective, SPD, 2015). The refrain that "the camera protects me from complaints" (Gilbert, sergeant, BPD, 2014) or false allegations was echoed by officers of all ranks. For many officers, the body camera served as a form of protection or insurance in the face of what they saw as frequently misguided complaints from members of the public—"it shows how much people lie" (Mark, patrol officer, SPD, 2016)—as well to validate the appropriateness of how they conduct themselves during their work and what they write in their reports. Importantly, these responses echo concerns rooted in the changing information politics within these police agencies, as officers sought to manage and frame information about their activities in ways that would benefit them (or at least not hurt them).

A commonly stated perception was that "more often [than] not," body-camera footage will "backup an officer's statement" (Joseph, lieutenant, SPD, 2018) or "confirm or support an officer's account of what took place. In any event, it provides more information on contacts where facts are disputed" (Bert, sergeant, SPD, 2018). A lieutenant with experience in his department's internal affairs division noted his perception that body-camera video would generally "protect officers against false allegations, while protecting citizens from 'he said, she said' stalemates" (Craig, lieutenant, SPD, 2018). Officers noted that they had "nothing to hide" and that body cameras would "quickly shoot down false complaints" (Woody, patrol officer, SPD, 2014). In confirmation of this perception, some officers (often supervisors) noted that they "have seen how the camera has vindicated several officers from false allegations" (Lawrence, captain, SPD, 2018) by showing that "officers acted appropriately in several incidents where citizens were alleging inappropriate behavior" (Ward, captain, SPD, 2016). These perceptions, linked to the generally growing positive attitudes toward the cameras over time, signal an incentive to wear a camera and to use it regularly, despite obvious tensions between consistent recording and police discretion.

For some, it was also important to capture footage because it "shows that citizens lie about cops" (Philip, sergeant, SPD, 2018). This was especially important for some officers because they also felt that society was generally becoming more anti-police. As expressed by one officer, "In our current society, law enforcement is the only entity that is held accountable for our words and actions" (Bruno, undisclosed rank, SPD, 2018). Some officers also recognized that the release of body-camera video could harm individual officers, especially in the context of actual or alleged misconduct. However, officers often wrote these problems off as the "frustrating" result of the misconduct of "a few bad officers across the country," lamenting what "media sensationalism [has] done to . . . trust in law enforcement" (Buck, senior police officer, SPD, 2014).

Beyond simply protecting officers from "frivolous complaints," body cameras were also seen as helpful when officers "need to use force" (Ruby, corporal, SPD, 2018). This transparency and documentation of police work was needed, according to some, because of the increasing anti-police sentiment in society aggravated by "biased media coverage" that "has created too many false perceptions in the public's mind about how police use force" (Charlie, patrol officer, SPD, 2014). As put by one patrol officer, "Unfortunately, in the past two years it feels like our society expects officers to produce video in order to justify their use of force. . . . Video only tells part of the story, but it's the world we're living in" (Lovell, patrol officer, BPD, 2017). Another noted that he would choose to wear a camera only because of the "immediate attack on my integrity by the media after a high-profile incident" (Brad, patrol officer, BPD, 2016). Against this backdrop, officers liked "the security of it" and the ability to "capture the reasons I use force" (Eric, patrol officer, SPD, 2014).

THE CAMERA AS INDEPENDENT WITNESS

While many officers noted that body-camera footage doesn't capture everything (and particularly not the officer's own perspective of an incident), many also relied on the footage to be an objective, factual, and independent witness of events (indeed, this was critical to the cameras' perceived usefulness in producing exonerating evidence: information that gave them power). These claims often focused on the capability of video to hold both officers and civilians accountable for their actions, to support the credibility of the police, and to document police-public encounters more comprehensively. However, some officers focused more directly on the power of documenting the bad behavior of citizens. Additionally, a few officers noted appreciation for how the video could serve to aid their memory of events when writing reports or affirm their written narratives. Behind many of these reports was the perception that the body cameras allowed officers to capture evidence that could provide additional context and perspective to their actions, especially should controversy or claims of misconduct arise.

Interestingly, and flying in the face of rhetoric about the oversight potential of the cameras, some officers saw the cameras as a form of "extra 'insurance' for what [they] do out on patrol" (Cliff, patrol officer, BPD, 2015), while others noted that "in this climate of transparency and the questioning of police activities, the camera validates and confirms my actions" (Glen, sergeant, SPD, 2016). I often heard officers make comments such as, "I stand by what I do and feel that much effort is wasted in court as the defendants battle my character. Having that independent witness with me is empowering" (Cliff, patrol officer, BPD, 2015). Another officer referred to his camera as "my reliable witness" (Del, senior patrol officer, SPD, 2014). Relatedly, a handful of officers also expressed the belief that body-camera video would affirm their credibility. Another noted, "I feel that it is important to document how well our officers perform their duties and their high level of professionalism while at work" (Arnold, sergeant, SPD, 2014).

> I believe that a certain segment of society has lost trust in law enforcement and the body worn camera gives me the ability to prove my side of the story. There are drawbacks to wearing the camera, but, overall, I feel it gives me more confidence because I know that the truth will come out despite any media spins or false allegations that might result from a dangerous or violent encounter. (Vernon, patrol officer, BPD, 2016)

Numerous officers also said something comparable to the following: "It makes me more comfortable knowing it is no longer just our word against a citizen's. Now we have factual documentation that can be seen by all" (Jesse, detective, BPD, 2017). As cameras began to proliferate throughout the departments (in contrast to the earlier phases of adoption, when only a small number of officers were wearing them), large incidents could be captured from multiple points of view, providing a "great painting of the full picture" (Michael, senior patrol officer, SPD, 2016) of what had occurred. In the opinion of one sergeant, wearing a body camera was important "because it actually proves what we as officers have been saying for years—that we are not corrupt, we don't use excessive force, we are compassionate, [and we] use massive restraint when we would be justified in using force" (Homer, sergeant, SPD, 2016). These responses shed light on how officers saw the cameras, and the footage they captured, as changing the information politics of their work, allowing them to frame the visible evidence, and their own increasing visibility, within their own preferred narrative.

Providing Useful Evidence (in Criminal Prosecutions)

Numerous officers also reported that body cameras were useful because they allowed officers to document their interactions with members of the public, generating evidence that might be useful in subsequent criminal prosecutions. As one officer framed this, "It is a very useful tool [for gathering] evidence" (Michael, senior patrol officer, SPD, 2016). Several officers noted that one of the benefits of the cameras was that they would capture evidence, whether by recording statements by witnesses or victims (or even confessions or admissions of guilt by suspects), or simply by capturing the demeanor, threats, or intoxicated behavior of those with whom the officers interacted. "It keeps people accountable and is good evidence in trials," noted one officer (Virgil, senior police officer, SPD, 2014). According to another, "A body camera . . . very often captures behaviors of citizens that would be hard to articulate in a report or not [be] very believable if they were" (Morris, sergeant, BPD, 2016).

Multiple officers told me during ride-alongs that they appreciated how body cameras would capture evidence of a suspect's demeanor, especially in situations involving sobriety tests after suspects were contacted for allegedly driving while intoxicated. This sentiment was also noted in qualitative responses to survey questions as a reason for using a camera. Relatedly, other officers stated that video evidence "lets the public see and hear what we deal with at the time of a contact or arrest, rather than when the suspect is all cleaned up in court" (Callie, lieutenant, BPD, 2014), and that "it also shows how real and violent our job really is and the types of people and calls we deal with every single day" (Homer, sergeant, SPD, 2016). However, others held more qualified positions, agreeing that while cameras carry the potential to capture aspects of an incident not documented elsewhere, "they do more harm than good [because] they do not show everything, and citizens expect them to" (Darren, patrol officer, SPD, 2018).

Officers also appreciated the ability to capture victim and witness statements more accurately. One detective also noted that recording an initial victim statement in cases of domestic abuse allowed prosecutors to press charges even when the victim might have "become averse to proceeding with criminal charges after the initial arrest" (Amanda, detective, SPD, 2016). Relatedly, a lieutenant noted that "anything that can help me write better reports and provide better evidence is helpful. It will also remind me to always do what is right and document all contacts with citizens (good or bad)" (Jim, lieutenant, SPD, 2015).

Educating the Public

This new reality, for some officers, underscored the possibility that body-camera footage might be used to educate the public about what police work was really like, including showing "that the police are doing things right" and that "people complaining are not always telling the truth" (Roy, lieutenant, SPD, 2016). For some, this was a fruitful form of transparency that could promote a "better understanding of what we do" (Maynard, crime scene investigator, BPD, 2016), including showing "citizens how much restraint officers use" (Bennett, sergeant, SPD, 2014) when dealing with unruly members of the public. At least one officer was optimistic that "the people that are most vocal about officers needing cameras are going to be disappointed that the footage does not confirm their misguided views that the police are the bad guys" (Osmond, patrol officer, SPD, 2014). Again, these views represent an officer-centric focus on how the information generated through the use of their cameras could empower police in their attempts to frame officer conduct as understandable and appropriate, shifting blame for officer violence to unruly members of the public: the real "bad guys."

Interestingly, officers also occasionally expressed the perception that the potential for body-camera video to be made publicly accessible could help hold civilians more accountable for their behavior when interacting with the police. As noted in an earlier chapter, one officer stated that "the portion of the population we typically deal with often believe they will not be held to any standard of behavior. At the same time the public at large is unaware of the lowly behavior of these people and don't believe it unless they can see it for themselves" (Travis, sergeant, SPD, 2015). In a more qualified response, one senior patrol officer stated that he would choose to wear a camera if he had the choice,

> but not for the reasons politicians and media believe. This tool captures law enforcement doing the job correctly. The bad news it captures the unattractive side of law enforcement. Many people cannot stomach what is dealt with on a daily basis and they want someone to blame. They don't blame the lack of jails, funding for mental health facilities, they blame (inappropriately) law enforcement for the events that end up occurring. Cameras put this in their living rooms and may make the job even harder. (Conrad, senior patrol officer, SPD, 2016)

Self-Critique, Training, and Improvement

Some officers liked the ability to watch footage after incidents in order to critique their performances, so, for example, they "can operate more safely in the field" (Caldwell, patrol officer, BPD, 2016). One female officer told me during a ride-along that she would often narrate to the camera prior to arriving at a call, essentially to ensure that her state of mind was captured on the video. During my ride with her, I observed her activating her camera as soon as she received calls for service and then explaining to the camera (and me) what she expected to find when she arrived on scene. This process, she informed me, would help explain and contextualize her actions should she act aggressively on a call she expected to be difficult or with an individual known to the police to be violent or agitated. Indeed, the fact that this narrative might influence the interpretation of the video by a subsequent viewer was precisely the point of the officer's actions.

PERCEIVED RISKS; OR, REASONS TO NOT WEAR A BODY CAMERA

Officers noted a number of concerns about wearing cameras, regardless of whether they had volunteered to participate in their department's pilot program or not. A corporal at SPD told me that he first heard about the possible adoption of body cameras within the department when it arose in union negotiations as part of the contract put forward by the city government. The "usual crowd" voiced objections and didn't like the idea, he said, or were trying to use it as a bargaining chip to get a salary increase. (He wasn't convinced that was the right battle to fight.) A common concern was that recordings could capture innocent or unintended mistakes, leading one officer to exclaim, "If you make one error, the attorneys will crucify you for it" (Ross, undisclosed rank, SPD, 2016).

> Look at the NFL and how many camera angles it takes sometimes to get a split-second call right for something as trivial as a football game. Now apply that to a real-life scenario with a life or death situation and a subject who is drunk, drugged, or deranged and wants to hurt you. (Buck, senior police officer, SPD, 2014)

Sitting through a small shift briefing at the Bellingham Police Department in the fall of 2014, I listened to a handful of officers expressing frustration at recent news reports by a Seattle-based news outlet that stated, "In an effort to reduce use-of-force complaints, Bellingham Police officers are now wearing cameras to record audio and video of their interactions with the public."[28] A sergeant in the room stated firmly to others there (including myself), "We do not have a use of force problem, and the Chief is very proud of our record on that front." Apparently the public information officer for the department, who had given a statement to the news outlet, had not mentioned that reducing use of force was a motivating reason behind the department's adoption of cameras, and thus he was seeking a retraction in light of the report. Additionally, officers expressed concern about other news reports that mischaracterized the terms of camera adoption within the agency by stating the department was requiring officers to wear the cameras when, in fact, most had volunteered to do so. One of the patrol officers in the room voiced a concern: "What will the public now perceive about those of us who have volunteered to wear the cameras—that we have a use of force problem?"

Although officers' self-reported perceptions of body cameras generally became more positive over time, largely because officers found them to be very useful tools with the power to exonerate them from false claims of misconduct, most officers still had questions or points of concern. Some of these concerns are addressed in later chapters.

For example, various concerns related to the law, departmental policy, report writing, and the perceived need to change behavior while performing on camera are addressed in chapter 5. Likewise, many of the officers' concerns about privacy (for themselves as well as the citizens with whom they interact) and public access to their camera footage are examined in chapter 6.

Officers' other primary concerns revolved around accountability, increased visibility (with attendant questions about how others would interpret their conduct as mediated and presented in video form), privacy, safety and distraction, and the feeling that body cameras were being relied on too much at the direct expense of trust in individual officers and their written reports. Officers also expressed frustration at the amount of time that using body cameras added to their back-end administrative tasks, like report writing and logging video. These heightened administrative duties were perceived as taking officers off the street and keeping them from doing more important work in the field. For some, especially those who saw limited benefits to wearing a camera in general, the "time spent labeling and categorizing video" outweighed any perceived benefits (Chris, patrol officer, SPD, 2018). While officers saw body-camera adoption as a response to the perceived threat that citizen video posed to their work, many were also concerned that body cameras would not provide a neutral and objective witness of events, and that body-camera footage might also be interpreted in ways that did not match officers' experience and point of view. All these fears were underscored by officers' perception that the sociopolitical environment in which they worked had generally become anti-police in recent years, with significant focus on making misconduct more visible and reforming and overseeing policework (with both the public and the media seen as culpable actors).

Accountability

Popular rhetoric suggests that body cameras improve evidence and accountability precisely because they capture a reasonable approximation of an officer's point of view during an incident. However, from the beginning of my research, officers expressed worry that the cameras did not actually depict their field of view or even capture sensory evidence that might inform an officer's behavior, especially in high-stress or rapidly evolving situations. Officers worried that video would capture details that the officer missed, and that officers' decisions would be held to higher than reasonable standards when critiqued by "Monday-morning quarterbacks" or when presented in court. These concerns are important, and not only for officers who might have their reputations challenged. However, these worries evoke much broader concerns about the nonobjectivity of the video and the subjective, often bias-filled processes by which individuals view and interpret visual evidence—a reality that potentially hurts or helps either side in contests to anchor subjectively preferred interpretations of the footage into broader narratives about the events and conduct that the cameras "witness."

My data are replete with officers expressing concern about links between body-camera use and being held to account for their actions, including concerns related to both internal and external visibility and accountability. Some of these concerns are directly tied to formal discipline, but many are more focused on officers' perception that using a camera would make them more likely to be judged, second-guessed, or held to a higher standard, even if formal discipline did not result. The imposition of this heightened, but impossible, "perfect standard" was, according to some, inconsistent with the notion that officers "are simply fallible human beings" (Andy, undisclosed rank, SPD, 2014). Officers also expressed concerns that heightened surveillance of their work was essentially "undue scrutiny" (Byron, patrol officer, SPD, 2014) and the result of a "micro-managing administration" (Stephan, patrol officer, BPD, 2014).

For others, "due to the narrow incomplete perspective they provide, [body cameras] massively increase the ability of future supervisors to abuse the officers through use of the video" (Jerry, corporal, SPD, 2016). Still others expressed concern that the cameras might capture video that was simply "embarrassing to me or the department" (Clay, lieutenant, SPD, 2014), especially as cameras allow "no mistake to be undetected" (Ken, patrol officer, SPD, 2014). For some, wearing a camera was only important, as a practical matter and despite these concerns, because it allowed the officers to prove their "statements and actions" in an environment where law enforcement "is the only entity that is held accountable" for what they say and do (Bruno, undisclosed rank, SPD, 2018). Of course, in the past few years numerous officers have been held to account for misconduct based on footage captured by body-worn cameras, so these subjective concerns are largely predictable. However, these themes also link up to questions about whether police work—and the array of functions it is typically tasked with carrying out—simply needs to change because it has evolved into a broken, discriminatory, and unnecessarily violent series of confrontations between police and the communities in which they work. Of course, body-worn cameras also link to critical concerns surveillance scholars have with intrusive, employer-mandated workplace surveillance. Surveillance can both improve and destroy the employment experience and employee-employer relations. But police, as employees themselves, are rarely viewed in this light, perhaps as a result of the coercive powers they wield in society.

Armchair (or Monday-Morning) Quarterbacks

Many officers expressed concern that the split-second decisions they had to make during their daily work would now be subject to increased scrutiny, with multiple other people second-guessing their decisions, from police administrators to members of the press and public. Cameras were seen as technologies that "encourage second guessing [and] armchair quarterbacking" (Theo, patrol officer, BPD, 2015), leading to "post-event scrutiny from the public, elected officials, and department administrators who just see video, not the entire context of the call" (Stanley, captain, SPD, 2018). For many officers, being made more visible—"being placed under a microscope" (Marvin, undisclosed rank, BPD, 2015)—was just generally uncomfortable. As noted by an experienced patrol officer, "Nobody wants to be constantly recorded for 10–11 hours a day for somebody else to second guess the decisions they make" (Buck, senior police officer, SPD, 2014). One officer even called out a specific administrator, claiming that "officers are reluctant to take appropriate action because Lieutenant [redacted] is using body camera footage against officers" (Georgie, patrol officer, SPD, 2016). Another stated that although officers might perform their job correctly, people will "second-guess[] it when watching it on TV" (John, detective, SPD, 2014), especially when viewers have "the ability to slow an incident down frame-by-frame to evaluate an officer's decision that was made at real time" (Ward, captain, SPD, 2016).

Fishing Expeditions

Some officers also felt that supervisors and administrators would comb through footage on "fishing expeditions" (Elliot, senior patrol officer, SPD, 2014) "purely to find policy violations" (Darren, patrol officer, SPD, 2018), even in the absence of formal complaints or other evidence of wrongdoing. As stated by one officer, "Recordings will be used against officers when they are routinely viewed by administration even if there is no complaint. Our Lieutenant in charge of cameras is reviewing recordings at this very moment with no justification or complaint from the public" (Noah, patrol officer, BPD, 2014). For some, this was tied to the perception that administrators were "overly consumed with whether or not our cameras are on as if we are not trusted" (Chad, senior patrol officer, SPD, 2018).

Perspective, Misinterpretation, and the (Non-)objective Observer

Much like their reaction to bystander video, officers frequently noted concerns about the potential for manipulation or misinterpretation of body-camera video. "It's difficult for people to place themselves in another person's shoes. They will never really get it. Videos can be edited and taken out of context as well" (Truman, sergeant, BPD, 2016). The statements, "Everything is taken out of context like we're robots and devoid of feelings. Sometimes we make off-color comments to each other that when taken out of context makes us look bad. People don't understand the job and how ugly the world is through our eyes" (Bond, senior patrol officer, SPD, 2018) make clear how body cameras have thrust previously offstage officer conduct into the limelight. These concerns were often grounded in the idea that the video divorced the officers' actual subjective experience in the moment from the interpretation of those events, as depicted on video, by outsiders who may or may not have police training or understand how the police were trained to operate. According to one experienced officer, "The negative side of body cameras is that it doesn't show everything an officer senses in a rapidly evolving situation and most people don't have the training that officers have to be able to second guess split second decisions" (Buck, senior police officer, SPD, 2014).

More broadly, the claim that "the camera does not capture the whole event" (Roy, lieutenant, SPD, 2016) was made by officers at all ranks. Officers noted that a single camera's perspective of a situation was limited: "one camera may not present [the] entire picture causing false perspectives" (Theo, patrol officer, BPD, 2015), or "a camera is unable to capture the full scope of what is going on. It's easy for an outsider to look at and decide over the course of weeks if action was appropriate but a camera will not give that same person a true sense or feeling of what was going on" (Noah, patrol officer, BPD, 2014). "Sometimes what is seen on film and what is seen by the eye is different, so in a case where the film does not match what the officer sees, the officer may be hung out to dry" (Jenson, patrol officer, BPD, 2016).

Officers also expressed concern that video would lead to the "misinterpretation of an incident" (Kara, detective, BPD, 2016) by those who might watch the video. The same officer noted that "what the camera shows isn't always accurate and may be misinterpreted." Officers also expressed concern that the "misinterpretation" of officers' "language and actions" (Eden, patrol officer, SPD, 2015) might also have disciplinary outcomes. As claimed by one patrol officer, "We all know one camera angle does not show what happened. I have seen officers prosecuted because [of] what was captured on camera" (Harold, patrol officer, SPD, 2014). Some officers also connected their fears about misinterpretation and misrepresentation of their conduct to broader sociopolitical concerns. One officer noted, "Unfortunately, in the last two years it 'feels' like our society expects officers to produce video in order to justify their use of force. I feel that's unfortunate, since even the video only tells part of the story, but it's the world we're living in" (Lovell, patrol officer, BPD, 2017). As noted by another,

> How would the general public like to have EVERY minute of their day filmed? Still, I'm conflicted on the issue. I want to believe it's only there to help me but fear it might be used against me. The camera may see everything, but it does not know or show what the individual might or might not see/focus on when under extreme stress. (Miles, crime scene investigator, BPD, 2014)

Officers sometimes worried that "minor reporting errors between what the camera can see and what an officer [saw] could hold officers to an impossible standard of personal perception, especially with the newer cameras coming out with enhanced night vision" (Herb, undisclosed rank, SPD, 2016). "My biggest concern still is that the camera is pointing one direction, and my eyes are pointing another, and I will be judged when I use force, but the camera does not see why. Makes me look like a liar when I did nothing wrong" (Edric, senior patrol officer, SPD, 2015).

What Happens When the Camera Is Not Recording?

Officers were also concerned about what they perceived as an overreliance on the cameras and the associated assumption that whenever a camera was not activated, an officer must have acted with ill intent.

One officer explained, "I hate wearing it for the fact that as soon as I forget to turn it on, I will be accused of hiding something by the media, public, or even my own admin. This may in fact be the sharpest double-edged sword ever!" (Aiken, senior patrol officer, SPD, 2015). As noted by another, "What the camera DOESN'T show or when it WASN'T on will become the focus" (Russell, sergeant, BPD, 2014). Officers also expressed concern that if they reacted in response to something they saw, but that wasn't captured by their cameras, "the assumption will be made that it didn't occur and the officer's integrity will be called into question" (Louie, patrol officer, SPD, 2018).

Others noted that problems with the technology—for example, batteries that "can't last a shift without going dead" (Vivian, patrol officer, SPD, 2016)—were not considered by those reviewing officer conduct ex post, and that officers were being held accountable as if the technology never failed (or as if officers never simply made mistakes). As expressed by one officer,

> The equipment is not that well-built. The switch is sticky, and the cord breaks easily. Occasionally it does not work, and my fear is that I will try to record an incident and through my inability to turn it on under stress or the fault of the equipment, it won't record. If it is a high-profile incident, the media will be relentless in their blame that I did this on purpose when I would never do that. It worries me very much that the equipment will not function when I need it do so. (Maynard, crime scene investigator, BPD, 2016)

Alternatively, officers were also concerned that they might forget to activate their camera during, for example, a rapidly evolving call for service, and, in those cases, "I believe the media and public would not accept I 'simply forgot'" (Fletcher, crime scene investigator, BPD, 2016) as an excuse.

Overreliance on Body-Worn Cameras

Officers had a sense that the public expected them to have video evidence of all their contacts with civilians, and that there were incentives for recording everything because "in America's current climate our judgement is not trusted" (Hale, patrol officer, SPD, 2018). These concerns about the overreliance on video were generally focused on officers' perception that the video would detract from or replace the officer's word (or written reports) and, in more extreme instances, that when footage wasn't available (for whatever reason), officers' own recollections of events and written reports would not be trusted. To return to one of the quotes that began this chapter, some officers felt that "society trusts video footage, even private recordings that fail to show the entire incident, over the word of a sworn officer" (Henry, patrol officer, BPD, 2015). One officer explained this concern as follows:

> An unreasonable weight or significance placed on the video evidence in a case . . . may not fully capture the essence of what occurred, or the viewpoint of the officer involved. During controversial incidents videos are sometimes used similarly to an instant replay in the NFL. The official on the field reacts to what he sees in real time during the play. Later, others can view the incident from a number of camera angles (potentially), slow the video down, etc. In police work, an officer will react to his/her environment in real time and potentially later be judged based upon a two-dimensional video taken from a different vantagepoint. (Les, undisclosed rank, SPD, 2015)

I discuss this issue further in the following chapter, as many of these perceptions arose in the context of officers discussing the impacts of body-worn cameras on their report-writing practices.

Privacy

Some officers noted concerns based on privacy, most notably due to the cameras' ability to inadvertently record private conversations or, at the extreme, trips to the bathroom when the officer forgets to turn off the camera. Due to becoming habituated to wearing a camera, officers expressed worry about "forgetting that it is on and speaking to coworkers or civilians and saying something that could be construed in a negative way, even if it is not meant to be" (Rita, patrol officer, BPD, 2017) or, further along the spectrum, "saying something inadvertently that could be misconstrued or used against me during a trial or court proceedings" (Darlene, patrol officer, BPD, 2016). One officer I interviewed showed me how his camera, mounted on his chest, had a perfect view of the screen of his smartphone whenever he was using it. He expressed concern that the camera would reveal, through inadvertent public disclosure or improper redaction, his passwords and the contents of his private text and voice conversations with his wife and friends. Some officers also expressed concerns about invading the privacy of the civilians with whom they interacted—for example, by recording inside a person's home or when taking a sensitive statement from a victim or witness of a crime. However, most of these concerns about privacy were not about the fact of recording, but rather about the potential for broad visibility should the recordings be requested and released under the state PRA.

Significant privacy concerns do emerge when police create audiovisual records of their encounters with civilians, especially, for example, when they record the interior of people's homes or sensitive or vulnerable moments in people's lives. Courts have not always granted heightened Fourth Amendment protections to police video recordings, largely because in early cases, they "analogiz[ed] video to still photographs rather than to audio recordings."[29] However, perhaps neither analogy is quite right. Indeed, body cameras are perhaps better viewed as "bulk and indiscriminate sensor-based data collection devices" that may soon carry a number of additional environmental sensors (beyond audio and video) that could acquire or process a broad range of information that could potentially be privacy relevant in some cases (consider the application of facial recognition, gait recognition, and other biometric identification techniques that could be become basic, expected functions that body-worn cameras provide).[30]

Safety and Distraction

Officers frequently complained that cameras were a distraction, forcing them to think about activating their cameras (and about what discretion they might have in certain circumstances, due to departmental policy) or to second-guess their words or actions prior to engaging with the public as they ought to. Cameras were seen as just "another piece of equipment to worry about operating instead of concerning ourselves with the incident or call" (Sterling, patrol officer, BPD, 2014). Many of these statements echoed concerns about officer safety, as officers distracted by turning on their cameras or "ensuring contacts are captured on camera" (Shaun, patrol officer, BPD, 2014) would not adequately pay attention to "more pressing . . . issues and their own safety" (Lance, patrol officer, BPD, 2015). The scenario of concern, as sketched out by one patrol officer, included officers being forced to "think about activating the camera" while also "advising [civilians] of the recording, constantly evaluating if they can legally or within policy continue the recording, and thinking about if the camera is providing footage that would assist in the investigation" (Robert, patrol officer, BPD, 2014).

Some officers also expressed concerns about requirements to notify civilians that they were recording audio and video, generally noting that notification (or "warning" citizens) made contacts less natural. In this vein, officers stated that "warnings . . . are an unnecessary burden" and "unjustly favor and bias different police contacts" (Ralph, patrol sergeant, BPD, 2015) or "disrupt the flow of conversation" (Hale, patrol officer, SPD, 2018). For others, the notification requirement was "just one more thing to think about or get in trouble for not doing" (Ford, sergeant, BPD, 2017). Thus, the hesitation to act that officers thought might increase risk and allow contacts to escalate more quickly was not just due to concerns about officers not engaging for fear of being second-guessed; it was also about concerns over an increased cognitive burden placed on officers when they had to determine when to activate their cameras or not, taking departmental policy and, sometimes, public disclosure law into account. (Notably, the movement in the industry to automate camera activation could ameliorate some of these concerns, while admittedly generating others.)

CONCLUSION

Drawing from the findings outlined throughout this chapter, I argue that most of the concerns that officers expressed about wearing body-worn cameras can be explained, at least in part, by two things. First, just like bystander video, body-worn cameras affect police officer's "account ability," that is, their "ability to control the accounts of what happened on the street" and "to provide a record of activities that explains them in a credible manner so that they appear to satisfy the rights and obligations of *accountability*."[31] As noted earlier, this is essentially a matter of "negotiating control," and the visibility brought about by body-worn cameras either reduces or increases the informational power available to any given officer, depending on the circumstances and nature of the recording.[32] As such, the adoption of body-worn cameras is clearly an act of information politics, and it changes the way individual officers engage with and exert power in the course of conducting and explaining their work. As discussed earlier, the recording of nonarrest, "peacekeeping" activities may subject officers to oversight from a variety of sources that may diminish their ability to "act alternatively" in situations in which they might otherwise have chosen not to, for example, make an arrest. For example, report writing becomes a task of aligning narrative and documentary evidence. Consequently, officers must now "perform" satisfactorily (in the streets and on paper) for a vast audience or risk losing their jobs and being put at substantial risk of reputational harm.

Second, the mandated adoption of body-worn cameras also runs counter to, and strongly challenges, officers' perception of themselves as "skilled practitioners" who ought to be sheltered from meddling by citizens (and other outsiders) who don't understand the nuances of the profession.[33] As such, body-camera adoption, in conjunction with citizen video, is intruding into (and problematizing) the historical separation of police work into law enforcement and peacekeeping functions. Herbert argues that the police's desire for separation is implicated by both the legal order (their ability to engage in coercive action is in some conflict with a purely subservient role, albeit regulated by formal law) and their desire for professional status (the "skilled practitioner" discussed by Bittner).[34] That is, as professionals, the police have special knowledge and training, can make appropriate decisions that could not be made by ordinary civilians, are distinct from the citizenry, and should be sheltered from citizen meddling.[35] Separation is also sought as officers feel the need to "possess unquestioned authority, particularly in situations where danger may be present," often as a consequence of their desires to remain safe in dangerous circumstances and to receive deference because of their professional skills and training, and because they are putting themselves in harm's way for a higher purpose.[36] The recording of these potentially dangerous encounters also threatens to expose the use of force, even when arguably appropriate or necessary under the circumstances, to heightened levels of scrutiny. This may be one cause for the significant drop-off in the use of force by the Rialto police officers, and it is possible it signals an unwillingness by officers to engage physically on camera, even when to do so might be appropriate, not only when force is unwarranted.[37]

Police practices and policies also have the potential to shape social life, and the use of officer-mounted cameras poses an obvious challenge to the status quo of officer-citizen interactions and, likely, the perception citizens form of officers in general. In any case, there is a certain disconnect between public sentiment and officers' self-recognition as "deeply virtuous . . . risk-taking protectors of society" that is likely to play out in interactions after adoption of these surveillance systems.[38] When officers begin to use body-worn cameras, attempts to prohibit the public from also recording their encounters with police—or accessing the officers' footage—become even less legitimate (if a case for their illegitimacy can even be made in the first place), despite the fact that officers continue to have concerns about bystander video even after donning their own cameras.

In line with Herbert's arguments about police practices shaping social life, we can expect body-worn camera adoption to shape and modify the nature of routine police work as well as public perceptions of police.[39] Observational and interview data, discussed in more depth in chapter 5, reveal that some officers consciously or unconsciously change their behavior—for example, their use of harsh language, orienting their bodies to direct the camera lens toward a subject—and review their own footage to self-critique and improve their public-facing behavior. Others assert confidently that they don't need to attend to such things, as they "don't act inappropriately" or, in any case, altering their performance would sacrifice their effectiveness or safety. Body-camera footage also affects how some officers perceive report writing and approach documenting their civilian encounters after the fact.

CHAPTER 5

The (Techno-)Regulation of Police Work

> The current camera program does more to sacrifice officer safety than to ensure it. We have officers double pressing buttons on a camera when they should be focused on their surrounding[s] or possible threats. These officers also spend precious attention thinking about the camera, its position relative to the contact, adjusting their position, not for safety, but for the camera angle. The camera also makes the officer second-guess their actions and language, which again takes even more attention away from where the officer should be directed.
>
> —Ambrose, patrol officer, BPD, 2015

REGULATING THE POLICE

As a response to the deepening community mistrust of police and the image management problems spurred, in part, by the rise of citizen video, body-worn cameras are changing the very nature of what it means for officers to "perform" while on duty (and how officers report their encounters in post-incident reports or audibly narrate for their body cameras while in the field). Officers are changing the way they perform their work as a consequence of wearing body cameras. Officers are under the impression that they must perform in particular ways on camera or risk censure—evoking McKenzie's claim that a failure to perform (the requirement to "perform *or else*") can lead to significant negative repercussions.[1] Similarly, when law enforcement operates on "a political stage for the performance of control," utilizing "a showy set of symbolic gestures" that conjure up "the sheen of securability and controllability," the introduction of new technologies and increased visibility have the potential to alter these officers' front-stage (and even some backstage) performances.[2]

Body-camera adoption, at least in much of the United States, has been driven by public desire for accountability (a call to perform at the risk of negative consequences). Within that context, both internal review and external disclosure of body-camera footage threatens officers' privacy by forcing higher levels of visibility onto backstage performances.

A rapidly growing body of scholarship has, again and again, found that body-worn camera adoption either regulates officer and/or civilian behavior or, at least, leads officers and others to believe such behavioral regulation is occurring. As we saw in the previous chapter, studies have shown that high percentages of officers in some contexts believe that body cameras will lessen or prevent "antisocial behavior," improve police-public interactions, and make officers more aware of their own behavior, even though some of these perceptions may wane over time or vary by demographic characteristics of individual officers.[3]

Some studies have found that body-worn cameras *decrease* the likelihood that officers will make an arrest, others have found that body-worn cameras *increase* the likelihood that officers will issue citations and make arrests, and others find that cameras make officers more likely to initiate encounters and issue citations (but not more or less likely to make arrests).[4] Multiple studies have shown that body-camera adoption has the potential to decrease the number of incidents in which officers use force.[5] However, in other studies, body cameras were found to have no significant impact on overall use of force—although in at least one of these studies the number of formal use-of-force reports filed by officers did increase significantly.[6] Based on the findings of a large, experimental study of the Metropolitan Police Department (Washington, DC), researchers concluded that "we should recalibrate our expectations of BWCs. Law enforcement agencies (particularly in contexts similar to Washington, DC) that are considering adopting BWCs should not expect dramatic reductions in use of force or complaints, or other large-scale shifts in police behavior, solely from the deployment of this technology."[7] Importantly, the form and amount of self-regulation that occur in a given context are a consequence of a variety of contextual factors. However, the possibility that recordings might become visible—and how visible the recording might become—appear to be shared across a number of agencies, as officers often express concerns about the Big Brother implications of body cameras and the role they play in narratives about "policing the police."[8]

Beyond broader concerns noted in the previous chapter about limited discretion, officers have expressed their desire to retain discretion in choosing when or whether to record an encounter, as well as whether to delete recorded video after the fact.[9] Although these sentiments may be expressed as abstract concerns and not as descriptive evidence of actual behavioral change, they do indicate areas in which granting officers discretion may lead to predictable outcomes or forms of possible officer resistance to being under (near-) constant surveillance.

Regulation itself can be defined as "the sustained and focused attempt to alter the behaviour of others according to standards or goals with the intention of producing a broadly identified outcome or outcomes, which may involve mechanisms of standard-setting, information-gathering and behaviour-modification."[10] Thus, regulation is intentional, normative, and directed at modifying human behavior to achieve specific goals. On the one hand, *law* (and various levels of policy—e.g., internal police department policies) regulates much of police work, from the constitutional regulation of search and seizure to, in the context of my fieldwork, the constitutional and statutory privacy provisions within Washington State law. On the other hand, *techno-regulation* is a specific form of regulation involving the "deliberate or intentional use of technology to regulate human behavior."[11] Understanding how each of these forms of regulation impacts frontline police work helps us unpack a richer picture of what body-camera adoption really means in practice—for the police, but also for the communities being policed by officers wearing cameras.

LEGAL REGULATION

There is much that can be said about how law regulates police work. However, this section focuses on ways in which officers evoked the law, or concerns about law, as an item of concern or as justification for how they changed their behavior in line with their use of body-worn cameras. Thus, what follows is not a full examination of how law applies to the conduct of the police in a broader sense. I leave that discussion to the law reviews that are filled with such doctrinal analyses. Here I provide a relatively brief examination of the law-related issues and concerns that arose—or were raised by officers—during my study, and how the officers understood these laws and policies as impacting their work. Officers' concerns generally focused on questions such as: Does the law require officers to notify civilians that they are recording? Which recordings are subject to public disclosure under the state's Public Records Act? In this context, I observed that officers sought answers to questions about the law for two reasons: first, so that they could conform their actions to legal expectations; and second, so that they could exercise greater discretion in deciding how to carry out their work (e.g., by resisting notification in situations in which they deemed it inappropriate). These findings align with Manning's conclusions: "The police in general tend to 'push the envelope' and let the courts decide the limits of their actions. The effects of the law are ex post facto because the rules, regulations and practices are focused on 'stay out of trouble' and 'keep your head down.' As a result, violations of the law are seen as mistakes at work rather than guidance in future enforcement."[12]

I noted that officers (especially more experienced officers) generally had very high levels of awareness and understanding of laws that regulate their ability to stop, detain, or arrest a person or to conduct a search or enter a private residence. Because they frequently found themselves the subjects of citizens' smartphone cameras, officers also clearly understood that citizens had a legal right to film them while they worked. However, the advent of body-worn camera programs in these two departments forced officers into the middle of a situation filled with legal ambiguity and uncertainty, and it was not clear to officers where, how often, and when they needed to record, as well as when they should not record, how state eavesdropping and privacy laws might regulate recording inside homes and without the consent of civilians at a scene, whether officers were required to notify civilians that they were being recorded, how courts and juries might deal with and interpret video, and when footage might be subject to public disclosure under the state Public Records Act. Officers initially relied on informal networks and limited administrative direction (e.g., in the form of draft body-worn camera policies) to understand how the cameras impacted what they could or could not do, but officers remained concerned about the legal ambiguity that existed in the guidance they received.

Camera Activation

In the past few years, questions about when police officers should activate their body-worn cameras during police-public encounters have come into the foreground of public and scholarly debate. Instances in which camera-wearing officers have failed to activate their cameras have received significant media scrutiny. Concerns about activation policies and practices are often tied to normative arguments about proper levels of police accountability and transparency, the appropriateness of (and limits on) officer discretion and, potentially, the adverse impact that increased recording may have on privacy interests. Understanding how officers perceive body-worn cameras and policies surrounding activation (and how they view these as impacting their ability to make discretionary choices while on the job) can provide greater insight into why, when, and how officers may attempt to exercise their discretion in the form of resistance to or avoidance of body cameras, seen as "technologies of accountability."

The choice to record—that is, when, where, and in what circumstances officers should or should not activate their cameras—was a point of consternation for many officers over the course of the study. They were frequently concerned about this issue due to perceived ambiguities in legal and policy requirements involving camera activation. This concern is summed up nicely by the following statement from a patrol supervisor: "The technology exists but the law is unclear as to what is appropriate to record. I'm afraid we are wasting time and money figuring out how to deploy the cameras, when the legislature has not stepped up to lay out guidelines" (Travis, sergeant, SPD, 2015) (interestingly, an example of an officer arguing for the ex-ante legal regulation of police work). A few officers said that, if they had the choice, they would choose not to wear a camera precisely "because it does not yet appear to be clear when and when not the camera should be recording," especially when this potentially complex question was just one more thing "that officers have to think about, when they may already be concerned with more pressing, and lifesaving issues and their own safety" (Lance, patrol officer, BPD, 2015).

Notification

During early ride-alongs in the fall of 2014, several officers expressed frustration and concern that they had not gotten clear guidance about whether they were legally required to notify civilians that they were recording with a camera under the state's restrictive eavesdropping law. Under Washington law at the time, recording a private conversation without the consent of all parties would violate the state Privacy Act. Officers could obtain consent, and thus not violate the law, by notifying those they contacted that audio was being recorded (as long as officers also recorded their verbal announcements). The law did include an exception for audio recorded by the use of on-officer microphones connected to "video cameras mounted in law enforcement vehicles," essentially immunizing the use of dashboard camera systems from the notification requirement, but there was no similar exception for the use of body-worn cameras. However, in practice, the prohibition on audio recording private conversations was probably only applicable to police use of body cameras in very limited circumstances. Under state law, conversations between a police officer and a civilian in a public place (or within the hearing of passersby) would not constitute a "private conversation" for purposes of the Privacy Act, since whatever a person had "voluntarily exposed to the general public and [that is] observable without the use of enhancement devices from an unprotected area is not considered part of a person's private affairs" under Washington State case law.[13]

However, because the law wasn't completely clear on this point in some circumstances, officers were initially told to always announce that they were recording when contacting civilians. Some officers noted benefits (e.g., that citizens occasionally changed their behavior in positive ways after being told they were being recorded), but others disliked the requirement outright or argued that in some circumstances notification might do more harm than good—for example, "announcements disrupt the flow of communication" (Hale, patrol officer, SPD, 2018) between officers and those they contact or are simply "just one more thing to think about or get in trouble for not doing" (Ford, sergeant, BPD, 2017).

In the words of another officer, "It's not important, yet it is required. People that make things mandatory either never did the job or are too far removed from it!" (Paul, senior patrol officer, SPD, 2018). Another noted concern that investigations involving rape, deceased persons, "and other private investigations should not be recorded," and that the state's "two-party consent laws are prohibitive to this mission and should be reviewed" (Brigham, senior patrol Officer, SPD, 2014). Other officers expressed the feeling that required notification made their conversations with civilians unnatural and more imposing—for example, "officers will have to start every encounter with citizens with 'you are being recorded'" (Harold, patrol officer, SPD, 2014). One officer stated that if he were required to record all encounters, "I would avoid contact with people. It is awkward telling everyone 'just to let you know, you are being audio and visually recorded,' especially during casual encounters with the public. Not everyone is comfortable with being recorded and I respect that" (Ned, senior patrol officer, BPD, 2014).

Another officer, reflecting on why he would prefer not to wear a camera, included mandatory notification issue as one of his concerns:

> I had to advise people I was recording them. This may sound simple until you place yourself on the street talking to multiple people who come and go into the situation you are investigating. I was spending a good deal of time and distraction telling people, "just to let you know, you are being video and audio recorded." Then I would spend another minute explaining the camera when someone would ask "why?" Or, "you're doing what?" This became a bigger issue when I recorded after I showed up onto a scene where officers were already present and were talking with witnesses, victims, suspects, etc. (Robert, patrol officer, BPD, 2014)

Within a few months of initial camera adoption, the state attorney general released a long-awaited opinion announcing that police officers were under no legal obligation to announce their recordings (on the theory that any conversation with a uniformed, on-duty police officer was, de facto, not a "private conversation" under state law).[14] City lawyers quickly began to issue legal guidance to their police departments to that effect. Over the subsequent months, some officers placed significant reliance on the attorney general's conclusion, changing behavior to fit their interpretation of the opinion. Under the attorney general's interpretation, even body-camera recordings made by uniformed officers inside private residences would not be subject to the Privacy Act, as the conversations would not be considered private conversations. This legal interpretation is clearly in line with Fourth Amendment decisions around the country that diminished the perceived intrusion of video cameras, based on judges "analogizing video to still photographs" rather than to more intrusive data collection devices.[15] However, if we view body cameras as "bulk and indiscriminate sensor-based data collection devices," it is clear that the cameras bear the potential to be much more intrusive than our current Fourth Amendment jurisprudence alleges.[16]

Over time, body-camera policies changed, and some officers occasionally complained that the legal and policy positions taken by their departments and city legal counsel were not always clear to them. In 2015, one officer noted:

> Current policies require that warnings be given that recordings are occurring, and recording is allowed in some places and not in others. There is no expectation of privacy when dealing with on-duty uniformed officers while performing their required duties. Warnings and restrictions are an unnecessary burden and unjustly favor and bias different police contacts. (Ralph, patrol sergeant, BPD, 2015)

Others felt that the choice of when, and whether, to announce that they were recording should be a matter of discretion, based on their interpretation of what was needed in any given set of circumstances. As noted by one officer,

> The choice should be dependent on the circumstances. I've been in situations where announcing that my body camera is activated makes the contact disingenuous. For example, we often respond to suicide threatened calls and when we encounter people in a crisis, it's extremely awkward to contact them, attempt to show compassion and gain understanding, and find any appropriate time to announce [to] them they're being recorded during an absolute low point in their life. This is just one example but the one that I encounter the most. (Vernon, patrol officer, BPD, 2016)

Body-Camera Video in Court

A handful of officers expressed concerns about how their video footage would (or would not) be used in court. Some of these concerns were rooted in a desire for clearer legal or policy guidelines and more clarity about how the footage could be used. For example, one officer stated, "I think it's ignorant and somewhat dangerous for the department to put cameras on officers when we don't know exactly what the courts are going to set as guidelines for use" (Cyril, patrol officer, BPD, 2014). Others expressed concerns that their footage was "often not admissible into court even though they provide excellent evidence" and, even when footage was admitted into court, it was "often redacted" (Chad, senior patrol officer, SPD, 2018). Officers blamed this on defense attorneys, whom they saw as "successfully keeping a majority of the video out of the courtroom so even though the video is fantastic evidence, many jurors aren't able to see it which seems like a waste of resources" (Lovell, patrol officer, BPD, 2017). Even when footage was admitted into court, officers sometimes felt it wasn't helpful or that the video might not be interpreted fairly. For example, officers noted that videos admitted into court may "do more harm than good in that they do not show everything, and citizens expect them to" (Darren, patrol officer, SPD, 2018). However, it should be noted that there was no clear evidence that what these officers were concerned about was actually happening in practice. In a conversation with a local prosecutor during my early fieldwork, it was apparent that prosecutors may have not been actively asking for body-camera footage, at least during the early stages of camera adoption, as they were also busy, and these sorts of requests had not yet become part of their standard procedures.

Some of the officers' concerns also had to do with officers' belief that courts, juries, and the public *might* place too much weight on their own interpretation of what a single video depicts, rather than also considering an officer's written report and testimony. Thus, it appears that many of these concerns were focused on possible future problems and may not have been based on actual past experience. Officers stated that differences between their written reports and video might be due to the fact that "different angles lead to completely different interpretations of the incident" and that "one view does not give an accurate account of what occurred, and I doubt that the general public will understand that" (Osmond, patrol officer, SPD, 2014). They suggested that the answer was "educating the courts and the public on perceptions and possible differences in reports versus what is on video" (Percy, sergeant, BPD, 2015).

At the beginning of 2018, one officer expressed concern that "right now, we're having issues getting our footage into court and then having it used against us," for example, "officers discussing [probable cause] and defense saying we didn't know what we were doing. It's a double edge sword in court right now" (Ruby, corporal, SPD, 2018).

Public Disclosure of Body-Camera Video Footage

The possibility that their video might be subject to public records requests quickly became a pressing concern for more than a few officers. Some of these concerns were based on the belief that public disclosure could place the officers in a bad light or subject them to investigation or prosecution, while others were focused on privacy-related aspects of broad disclosure and dissemination of the video: "I am hesitant about the public dissemination of the private information of citizens . . . that may be encountered on a daily basis" (Orson, undisclosed rank, SPD, 2014). As framed by another:

> We record civilians at their worst. These recordings can then end up on YouTube and severely damage that individual's reputation in the community. Public disclosure needs more legislation in posting these documents/videos for all the world to see with no end date. A "right to be forgotten" law needs to be enacted where the videos can only be posted on the internet for "x" amount of time. (Tom, patrol officer, BPD, 2016)

Due to the prevalence of concerns about public disclosure among officers in both departments, I address these issues in greater depth in Chapter 6.

TECHNO-REGULATION

The practice of designing and deploying ICTs with particularly normative qualities, such as body-worn cameras, fits easily within Lessigs's concept of "code as law."[17] Relatedly, behavioral change due to technological change has been termed *technicways*, in contradistinction to folkways, or "the traditional behaviors . . . of life of a particular community or group of people."[18] In any case, the idea is that people's behavior changes in response to, or as a consequence of, technological innovation and the deployment or use of that technology in ways that touch their lives. Much scholarly ink has been spent in examining how behavioral change might be spurred by technological innovation. However, Manning urges caution, arguing that "the belief that technology drives change and is the source of organizational 'efficiency,' or 'effectiveness' hyper-elevates technology, ascribing it both excessive power and granting it far too much positive potential."[19] Instead, technology "takes its meaning from social context, how it is used and defined."[20]

In some countries, body cameras are worn alongside brightly colored text or symbols that help inform civilians that the officer may be recording. In the agencies I studied, the cameras were small black boxes worn on the chest or small cameras attached to an officer's eyeglasses or lapel, sometimes obscured against dark uniforms, radios, and other tools. During one of my interviews with tech developers working for Axon, I asked about whether privacy or other human values played a role in how the cameras were designed. A developer told me that, yes, they did take privacy into account. In fact, they had modified a camera design that initially included a forward-facing light to inform civilians that the camera was activated by moving the light to the rear of the camera, so it was only visible to the officer wearing the camera. This was done, after feedback from users, to better protect the privacy of the *officer* in low-light situations where a forward-facing light might give away an officer's tactical position.

Much of the rhetoric surrounding body-worn camera adoption, as well as the existing academic research, focuses on the techno-regulatory effects of body-worn cameras on police-civilian interactions (e.g., the rates at which officers use force, decreasing numbers of complaints against officers as a proxy for officers improving their previous bad behavior, etc.). However, beyond these more public or front-stage police interactions, body-worn cameras may also regulate the information-related behavior of government employees in ways that are not quite so visible from the outside. As discussed earlier, the possibility that police officers' (mis)conduct might become more visible as a result of increased recording creates problems for law enforcement image management, as well as for individual officers, and the recording of nonarrest, "peacekeeping" activities may also subject officers to oversight from a variety of sources that may diminish their ability to "act alternatively" in situations where they might otherwise have chosen not to make an arrest; for example, to merely give a warning in a situation where an offense was not patently illegal.

Attempts to regulate human behavior using technology often drive, or leverage existing, technological design choices. The particular properties and characteristics of any given environment (including the technologies in use, governing policies or laws, and social norms within that environment) are sometimes referred to as *affordances* because, as boyd notes, "they make possible—and, in some cases, are used to encourage—certain types of practices, even if they do not determine what practices will unfold."[21] Normatively, boyd argues that, "Understanding the affordances of a particular technology or space is important because it sheds light on what people can leverage or resist in achieving their goals."[22] Thus, in the context of police adoption and use of body-worn cameras, understanding the environment and the affordances made possible by the particular technologies employed is an important first step in understanding the techno-regulatory implications of body-camera adoption within that particular site (department). This is especially so because, if police officers change their behavior because of the deployment of body-worn cameras within their working environment, these behavioral changes may be closely linked to the attendant laws and policies governing the appropriate or intended use of the cameras, the affordances available to them, and the level of enforcement realized in the officers' everyday practice and experience.

Drawing from Black's definition of regulation (noted earlier), we can see how the deployment of body-worn cameras evinces all three regulatory mechanisms: standard setting, information gathering, and behavior modification. First, at the hierarchical level, *standards* are set by laws and policies (including police department body-camera policies and applicable local laws), although standard setting also occurs as the (intended) by-product of technological design choices. For example, designing body cameras that activate at their user's command (e.g., by double-tapping a button) establishes certain standards and reinforces particular user behavior in ways that differ from designs that, for example, automatically activate upon sensing certain environmental conditions or that allow remote activation by supervisors located elsewhere. Second, *information gathering* involves monitoring and data collection, either by supervisors or automatically as the device interacts with the environment and records data while in use. Notably, this mechanism often encompasses surveillance directed at the user of the device. Third, *behavior modification* is often the product of enforcement—that is, behavior is more likely to change in the desired ways when users are held accountable for adherence to, or divergence from, the standards established, often judged by qualitative or quantitative analysis of the information gathered during the monitoring process.

Obviously, then, information politics also intersect with the new forms of police visibility generated by the advent of body-worn cameras in a variety of ways, from the "antisurveillance affordances" of officer resistance to workplace surveillance to the capacity of individual officers to negotiate the emerging visibilities that the cameras foist upon them.[23] When body-camera footage is shared publicly or posted online, this police visibility is mediated and enhanced by the affordances of online social media identified by boyd, namely,

- persistence: the durability of online expressions and content;
- visibility: the potential audience who can bear witness;
- spreadability: the ease with which content can be shared; and
- searchability: the ability to find content.[24]

This, in turn, may drive even more behavioral change.

In practice, these behavioral changes might be as minor as the introduction of hand signals that some officers developed to signify to other officers that their body camera was recording (as noted in chapter 3) or the practice of simply announcing their cameras to other officers when they arrive on scene (both indicating the potential that officers would be "hesitant to speak freely when there is a body camera being worn" [Baldwin, patrol officer, SPD, 2014]). However, the changes most hyped and promoted by the media and police department administrators as a possible (or likely, certain) outcome of camera adoption included decreased use of force by officers, decreased complaints from civilians, and overall greater civility in police-public interactions.

Indeed, when I first attempted to gain access to both departments for this study in 2014, the Rialto Study (which claimed dramatic decreases in both uses of force and citizen complaints after body-camera adoption in Rialto, California) was really the only existing US-based study of how body cameras would impact policing. The findings in that study seemed to be instrumental to my acceptance by departmental leadership. One senior administrator, who was responsible for administering the body-camera program within his agency, essentially quoted the Rialto Study's findings to me when he invited me to conduct my research with the department. My sense of things was that the agencies couldn't imagine that studying camera adoption could do anything but validate these widely circulated claims about positive outcomes and behavioral modification.

On the other hand, it is entirely possible that body cameras do not impact officer behavior at all, or, if they do, they impact certain types of behavior but not others.[25] Additionally, as has been shown by research into the effectiveness of CCTV cameras in deterring crime, the deterrent (regulatory) effects of cameras fade with time unless publicity, accountability, and enforcement are consistent.[26] In one interesting recent case, a Seattle police sergeant drove to the workplace of a civilian who had gotten angry with the officer for towing his car and, in retaliation, the officer pulled up a chair and sat outside the store for an hour "telling passers-by he was waiting for an apology."[27] The officer was quickly demoted from his supervisory rank, largely based on review of his own body-camera footage (he had recorded the entire incident). Tellingly, the officer acted in this way despite wearing (and activating) his camera.

In my research, I found that some officers report becoming more conscious about their use of harsh language when interacting with civilians, some report that they actively review their footage to self-critique their performance and correct for deficiencies in future encounters, and some report that the presence of a camera makes civilians less (or more) aggressive toward the police. However, some officers remain suspicious about the cameras and try to avoid being captured on another officer's footage as much as possible. As noted by one patrol officer early in the study, "The public appear to be unwilling to accept that though such devices may have positive aspects, they also have a negative impact on the way officers will interact with the realities of street policing" (Terence, patrol officer, BPD, 2014).

Civilizing the Police; or, "Sometimes You Need to Talk Street When Working the Street"

Civility is described by the *Oxford English Dictionary* as denoting "good citizenship and orderly behavior" and defined as "formal politeness and courtesy in behaviour or speech."[28] Much rhetoric has assumed these to be desirable virtues in both police and members of the public. However, quite a few officers from my study sought to challenge this assumption insofar as it relates to them and how they do their work—for example, "officers may be too friendly or polite due to the camera and not handle business appropriately" (Walter, patrol sergeant, BPD). Others react seemingly with offense at the notion that their behavior needs to become more civil or, indeed, that cameras will change their behavior at all. As one officer bluntly put it, "The idea that a camera makes us more professional is bunk. I work with very squared away officers" (Jamie, detective, SPD).

However, one of the more common refrains from officers (both in ride-alongs and on survey responses) was that cameras pressured them to modify the way they spoke to some members of the public, especially when the use of harsh language might violate departmental policy. Officers told me that they had stopped swearing so much in their conversations with civilians (one candidly reporting that she hadn't realized how much harsh language she used until she watched her own body-camera video), but most who broached the subject expressed the belief that harsh language was necessary in a range of situations. "Sometimes you need to talk street when working the street," stated one officer, "'please do this for me' just won't cut it with a very high percentage of our client base" (Terence, patrol officer, BPD, 2014). Or, put differently, "Sometimes our job is ugly, and we have to say bad words to people to get their attention" (John, detective, SPD, 2014). According to another, "Sometimes you have to use the language these people understand, and it doesn't always look nice and pretty on the TV or internet" (Douglas, undisclosed rank, SPD, 2015).

Others felt that cameras would diminish officers' "humanity," removing their ability to be "candid" with people they interacted with on a daily basis (Frank, senior patrol officer, SPD, 2014). This might be expressed by a feeling that they should become more formal, which "takes some of the humanity out of interviews" (Tad, corporal, SPD, 2016) or other personal contacts:

> Anyone who has tried talking with a known street criminal with a "Hello Sir, the reason I'm contacting you today . . ." will instantly lose credibility with this contact, thus compromising officer safety. But if you approach this same street criminal with a "Bro, what's the word on the street?" you'll be called a racist, insensitive or otherwise unprofessional. (Ambrose, patrol officer, BPD, 2015)

Relatedly, some felt that body cameras, coupled with the requirement to activate the cameras frequently, would also limit their ability to joke around with other officers in ways that might seem (or actually be) offensive, racist, or sexist. Some officers saw these behaviors as a way of "coping" with the "evil nature" of what they experienced while doing their work: "Our P.C. [politically correct] culture doesn't understand what it's like being an officer and to view carnage day in and day out" (Ross, undisclosed rank, SPD, 2016). Others were simply concerned their words might be misinterpreted by those who viewed the videos divorced from context, or, more generally, that they might simply be disciplined for the way they spoke to people. "When dealing with unreasonable individuals, my words and actions may seem unprofessional to those who have never been hurt or in danger of getting hurt by a violent and unreasonable individual" (Jasper, patrol officer, BPD, 2015). On a more general note, one officer stated that body cameras have generally "taken the fun out of our job. Before we could joke around with each other on calls or after calls but now everyone is worried about being recorded and saying something that could be taken the wrong way" (Ross, undisclosed rank, SPD, 2016).

These comments are not reproduced here in an attempt to provoke sympathy for the police—especially within those communities that have often suffered as the butt of these jokes. They are offered to demonstrate how individual police officers experience vulnerability and a loss of power, which might motivate particular types of behavior in response, inform our understanding of how the police "create the social reality that they police," and define "the environment in which officers act."[29] Many of these responses also demonstrate a lack of trust or respect directed at those individuals whom the police contact frequently.

Some officers also felt that the use of body cameras would "deter officers from engaging in normal and acceptable law enforcement engagement, like uses of force or verbally dealing with very difficult individuals" (Rex, undisclosed rank, SPD, 2018). For these officers, body cameras presented "a tremendous officer risk, and risk to the public, as we will be constantly second guessing our actions, which will lead to slow or non-reactions to threats" (Austin, patrol officer, SPD, 2015). For some, these concerns were triggered by what they saw as a codification of the requirement to act according to the moral compass of others, removing their own judgment and discretion. This outcome might mean that officers might feel prevented from acting in the way their training and experience suggested was the most appropriate "because of the fact it may not be, in someone else's opinion, the 'right' way to handle it[;] staying professional, safe, and courteous is always at the forefront," suggested one officer, "however, some situations may call for unorthodox methods" (Jack, undisclosed rank, SPD, 2018).

Generally, the sentiment was that "officers might worry more about the camera during interactions than on threats and handling the situation" (Jane, master patrol officer, BPD, 2016) or that "officers might sacrifice their safety due to not wanting to appear too aggressive or heavy-handed when dealing with violent offenders" (Jesse, detective, BPD, 2017). For some, this deterrent effect, causing officers to pause or refrain from acting (to "de-police" or become less proactive), was making officers less effective and, in the view of others, amounted to an officer safety issue. One officer mentioned research by Ariel et al. that found body cameras increased the rate of assaults against officers and offered his own explanation of those findings: "This may be a result of officers being slower to issue commands or use force than they would have if they were not wearing a camera" (Billy, sergeant, BPD, 2016).[30] As another respondent explained,

> I am concerned that officers in general may second-guess their authority to keep themselves safe during contacts with aggressive individuals because they are worried about how it could look on camera. This is where the increase in assaults against officers is a plausible outcome. (Cole, detective/sergeant, BPD, 2017)

In all four surveys, I asked officers whether they agreed that wearing a body camera would put an officer at greater risk of being subject to violence. Only a very small percentage of officers strongly agreed that body cameras would increase the risk of violence (5%, 6%, 7%, and 9%, respectively, by survey), with a similarly small percentage reporting that they "somewhat agree" that such risk was realistic (16%, 11%, 17%, and 6%, respectively, by survey). Much higher percentages of officers reported some level of disagreement (70%, 78%, 44%, and 58%, respectively, by survey). Additionally, on the final two surveys, I also asked officers whether they thought it was likely that body-camera use would result in increased numbers of assaults against officers (16% and 33% of officers reported that increased numbers of assaults were at least "somewhat likely," respectively by survey, which is consistent with responses to the question about risk of violence, as expected).

One outcome of camera adoption, in the eyes of some of my respondents, was that officers would not use force when force was needed, even "when that use of force is justified and appropriate, for fear of getting in trouble" (James, senior patrol officer, SPD, 2015). Framed slightly differently, "officers will delay using appropriate force when justified and create increased risk of being assaulted. This will happen out of concern for being 'Monday-morning quarterbacked' by administration and the public" (Jason, patrol officer, BPD, 2017). When confronted with a situation in which force might be appropriate, police officers are not only forced to determine, prior to acting, whether force is necessary and justifiable, but they must also "decide how others will view that force" (Conrad, senior patrol officer, SPD, 2016).

On the other hand, some (senior, administrative) officers did note that they appreciated the behavioral cues offered by the cameras. For one, "the awareness that a camera is in use can result in positive results" (Simon, lieutenant, BPD, 2016). Additionally, another senior officer saw wearing a camera as positive by because "it will . . . remind me to always do what is right and document all contacts with citizens" (Jim, lieutenant, SPD, 2015). However, as these specific comments were made by high-ranking officers with supervisory responsibilities (and who reported *not* having used a body camera), it is likely that their positive remarks only reflect generalized opinions about body-camera use (and appropriate officer behavior) more broadly within their departments.

On the survey questionnaires, I asked officers two different questions about how they thought body-camera adoption would impact officers' use of force behaviors. I also asked two additional questions that sought to probe how likely officers thought it was that body-camera use would lead to "better officer behavior" (the term "better" was not defined, as I wanted to let officers attach their own meanings) or make officers more cautious when dealing with civilians. Across departments, nearly half of respondents indicated that body camera use was "very likely" or "somewhat likely" to lead to improved officer behavior (48%, 52%, 42%, 45%, by survey). Only a handful of respondents reported that better behavior was a "very likely" result of camera adoption (4% to 12% of BPD respondents, 6% to 10% of SPD respondents). However, more than a third of respondents from each department reported that better behavior was "somewhat likely" (ranging from 35% to 57% at BPD, 34% to 39% at SPD). Interestingly, as time went by, the percentages of respondents who indicated that better behavior was somewhat or very *unlikely* dropped consistently within each department (from 38% to 15% at BPD, and from 46% to 24% at SPD) (for more details, see figure 2 in appendix B). Relatedly, most officers generally indicated at least some agreement with the proposition that wearing a body camera was very or somewhat likely to make officers more cautious while interacting with civilians (the only exception was SPD respondents on the third survey, with 46% agreement) (see table 7 in appendix A).

Officers generally reported fairly substantial agreement with the proposition that wearing a body camera would decrease officers' willingness to use force even when such force would be justified, although rates of agreement did decline over time (see figure 3 in appendix B). A majority of BPD respondents on each of the first two surveys reported at least some agreement (58 and 55%, respectively, reporting either "strongly agree" or "somewhat agree"), rising to 66 percent on the third survey before dropping to 47 percent on the fourth survey. Rates of disagreement (respondents choosing either "strongly disagree" or "somewhat disagree") ranged from 32 to 47 percent across surveys. Rates of agreement were generally higher at SPD, with rates of agreement at 71, 73, 61, and 59 percent, respectively by survey (with rates of disagreement ranging between 24% and 32%).

When asked how likely officers thought it was that body-camera use would actually lead to less use of force by officers, nearly (or more than) half of the respondents across surveys agreed that decreased use of force was at least somewhat likely (50% to 61% of all officers across both departments, by survey, reported that such an outcome was either "very likely" or "somewhat likely"). While SPD respondents reported agreement at slightly higher rates than BPD officers on the first two surveys (at 55% and 62% agreement, respectively), this agreement dropped considerably on the latter two surveys (to 41% and 46%, respectively) while BPD agreement rates remained roughly stable across surveys (ranging from a low of 54% on the first survey to a high of 61% on the third).

The "New Cat Videos"

Police officers like to watch police videos. Most of the officers I interviewed had watched many of the highly publicized bystander videos of police-involved killings that occurred during my fieldwork (those of Eric Garner, Walter Scott, and others). Most of the time, when I asked, they expressed concern that the officer's side of the story had gotten lost or subdued, and that it was hard to make judgment calls about whether individual killings were a "good shoot" (justified) based solely on the video evidence. In almost every conversation, the officers took the side of the officer involved: supporting one of their own, finding some way of explaining why the officer's conduct might have been justified. However, in one surprising conversation, I asked an officer what he thought about the shooting of Walter Scott by Officer Michael Slager in South Carolina in 2015. The officer paused for a moment and then said, emphatically, "That was a bad shoot." He said that he had watched the bystander's cell-phone video of the shooting multiple times because he was so surprised by what he saw. There was no way he could justify what he was watching, he said. The video evidence seemed clear. And on YouTube, it was there for all the world to see.

After some of my ride-alongs, officers would welcome me into a small room where they would watch the videos they had recorded during their shifts and complete their reports. Most of the time, this was rather uneventful. However, occasionally, usually after a high-stress day, officers would banter about their various calls and the "crazy" people they had been forced to deal with during their shifts. Frequently these conversations were continuations of earlier discussions begun when officers had crossed paths during the day (or had been at the same calls for service). After one particular shift, in the very early hours of the morning, a couple of officers were in good spirits as they sat down to complete their reports. As they excitedly discussed a call that one of the officers had taken and joked about the belligerent actions of an intoxicated civilian, one of the officers turned to his computer and told the other they should just watch it. Moments later, a handful of officers and I were huddled together behind the officer watching footage from the incident that had been recorded by the officer's body camera.

On Writing Reports; or, Should the Video Speak for Itself?

Having the ability to watch these sorts of encounters after the fact no doubt allows officers some time to decompress, vent, and bond with their colleagues. Other studies have also highlighted officers' desire to be able to watch their recordings.[31] Of course, the ability to watch also increases the visibility of the actions of the individuals depicted in the video and raises questions about when, where, and in what circumstances officers should be allowed to watch their own body-camera footage or the footage of others (e.g., before or after writing a report?) and for what purposes. As my fieldwork progressed, it became clear that officers were watching their own video (though not all of it) and the video of other officers, especially when the videos depicted high-stress incidents or civilians behaving badly. Indeed, a majority of the officers in each agency who had experience using a body camera consistently reported that they had watched body-camera footage at least "sometimes" for purposes of informing their written reports (officers from SPD reported watching their footage at slightly higher rates than those from BPD), with roughly a quarter to a third of respondents in each agency watching footage "very often" to "always." For those officers who reported having watched body camera footage, 94 to 100 percent (across surveys, by department) reported watching the footage prior to writing their reports. Only between 3 and 7 percent of responding officers reported never watching footage for report-writing purposes.

Despite civil rights groups calling for limits on the ability of officers to preview body-camera footage prior to writing incident reports, agencies have generally not imposed these sorts of limits on officers.[32] Upturn and the Leadership Conference on Civil & Human Rights issued a report and "Policy Scorecard" in 2017, alleging particular concern that widespread, "unrestricted footage review" by officers prior to writing incident reports constituted an institutional failure of police organizations at safeguarding constitutional rights, "plac[ing] civil rights at risk and undermin[ing] the goals of transparency and accountability."[33] Indeed, their analysis found that "most major police departments [in the United States] that use body-worn cameras allow officers unrestricted footage review . . . including after a controversial use-of-force incident."[34] Some major police agencies, like the Los Angeles Police Department, even *required* officers to review footage in the process of writing reports.[35] Research by the Brennan Center at New York University Law School supports these findings.[36]

Initially, in 2015, 90 percent (BPD) to 100 percent (SPD) of respondents from both agencies reported agreement that officers should be allowed to review their body-camera footage *prior* to writing a report, with 73 percent (BPD) to 94 percent (SPD) reporting that they "strongly agree" with that statement. In 2016, these numbers remained roughly the same (with 80% to 94% of respondents reporting strong agreement, respectively by agency). In 2017, BPD respondents reported 100 percent agreement (79% strongly agree, 21% somewhat agree). However, in 2017, support for prior review of footage dropped considerably among SPD respondents, with only 12 percent reporting strong agreement and an additional 13 percent reporting some agreement, with more than a third of respondents (35%) reporting that they "strongly disagreed" that officers should be able to watch their footage prior to writing their reports. From my data, it is not clear why this shift occurred at

SPD, although (as noted later), SPD respondents on the 2017 survey did report concerns about the time it took to review footage as well as heightened concerns that body-camera footage was detracting from the value of an officer's written report or testimony about what had occurred during a police-public encounter.

As an alternative to policies that allow unrestricted review, the Leadership Conference and Upturn recommend what they call "clean reporting," defined as "a simple two-step process where an initial report is recorded based only on an officer's independent recollection of an event and then a second, supplemental report can be added to a case file to address any clarifications after footage is reviewed."[37] This process (i.e., write the report first, then watch the video and add an addendum later) was noted by multiple officers at BPD, as one of the department's supervisors had initiated a dialogue with officers and had promoted this as the ideal process. The idea, as explained to me by another officer in the summer of 2015, was that it was okay to recognize the fallibility of your memory and to not remember everything perfectly ("you don't have to be Superman") but you should make the full report as accurate as possible. Although he liked the idea of "clean reporting," he was still critical of the public's ability to understand and recognize fallibility as an aspect of human memory rather than presuming the officer was simply trying to align a written narrative with the video recording to avoid accountability. In the end, he told me, he didn't think this process was a viable solution because the public, defense attorneys, and the press would have a field day with all the misremembered details in police reports prior to the post-viewing addendums, and defense attorneys would "eat officers alive" on the witness stand in court because of their supposedly false statements made in police reports, based on misremembering something.

Additionally, this officer stated that he would be very concerned about a policy that wouldn't allow officers to view their footage prior to writing a report or at least an addendum. To illustrate his point, he told me about how he had recently apprehended a suspect as the suspect tried to escape through the back door of a home, but he couldn't remember which arm he had initially grabbed as he put the suspect into a detention hold in the backyard. What if he wrote down the wrong arm in his report or misremembered other details about this use of force? As it was, he had video and was able to check. "If we weren't allowed to view our videos, my reports would look something like, 'I saw a guy in a house, he tried to run, and I apprehended him.'" Such a policy, in this officer's opinion, would absolutely decrease the specificity of language and description that officers would include in their reports, simply because officers don't want to be caught "lying." However, another officer told me during a ride-along that he was concerned that watching video before writing his reports would taint his narrative and remove its authenticity. Regardless, though, he would watch video after writing his reports and sometimes write an addendum to "fill in gaps" because he was worried about signing the perjury statement at the bottom of the form without having previewed the video first.

During one of my ride-alongs, the officer I was riding with stated that he really liked to be able to rely on the videos his camera recorded, as it allowed him to take fewer notes while he was interacting with people. To him, the camera allowed him to just "be in the moment" and talk to people, which made his conversations with other people feel more natural. Additionally, having the footage allowed him to review witness or victim statements, to refresh his memory about what people told him as he wrote his reports. For another officer, reviewing video allowed him to tag or mark segments of video that might be useful for prosecutors or supervisors, a process he found useful. During another ride-along, an officer expressed the sentiment that she also appreciated the ability to watch footage when writing reports, but that she was concerned that perhaps officers should note in their reports if they had or had not referred to their footage, just in case discrepancies arose. There just wasn't time to watch all the video for every report, she said, and she saw the benefit of just writing reports as she had always done, but she was concerned that what she might write down would not match what the video showed due to misremembering something.

For those who appreciated the ability to watch footage, body-camera footage "affirms what I do and write in my report" (Tommy, patrol officer, BPD, 2015), "aids in [the] recollection" of high-stress or quickly evolving events (Jake, corporal, SPD, 2014), and frequently "captures behaviors of citizens that would be hard to articulate in a report or not very believable if they were" (Morris, sergeant, BPD, 2016). As one sergeant put it, "A picture has always been worth a thousand words. It can help fill in parts of a police report that would take several hours to articulate on paper" (Leon, sergeant, BPD, 2014). It was apparent from many of these responses that officers appreciated the perceived ability to generate more accurate reports by referring to video, especially due to the affordance of capturing victim or witness testimony verbatim rather than relying on quickly written notes (although one officer strongly voiced his opinion that audio recording would be sufficient for what he wanted to capture, and that video provided a bit too much information in most circumstances).

Officers contrasted the accuracy of their written reports with the objectivity of footage and with the fallibility of their own memories, seeing body camera footage as having the ability to act "as an impartial witness to events that may be hampered by lack of detail or quality in memory" (Timothy, patrol officer, SPD, 2018). One supervisor noted that having a body camera was "very helpful for writing Use of Force review reports as a supervisor" because it enabled him to "record the statement of the arrested [person] after force has been applied to him, and most of the time get them to admit it was justified" (Winston, sergeant, SPD, 2015), limiting the ability of the contacted person to complain at a later date. A very small minority of officers also felt that video should substitute for their written reports, which would allow them to spend more time in the field unless they wanted to write addendums to the video reports (to include, for example, "officer feelings" [Penelope, senior patrol officer, SPD, 2018]). Put simply by one officer, "If I'm capturing video, why do I need to write detailed reports? It should direct readers to the video" (Jed, investigator, BPD, 2016).

Most of the concerns that officers expressed about the impact of body cameras on report writing had to do with the possible inconsistencies between officers' written reports and the viewers' interpretation of the video recording of the events or, relatedly, the perceived role of footage as discounting or detracting from officers' own words and written statements. Some also reported that referring to video would make report writing "a more time-consuming process" (Gresham, patrol officer, BPD, 2014) that would pull them away from doing "real police work" in the field. Others expressed concern that supervisors might criticize them for "taking longer to write reports" (Grayson, sergeant, BPD, 2014), or that they might feel pressure from their administrators to "change written reports to reflect what [administrators] see in the video" (Shaun, patrol officer, BPD, 2014). In the SPD, where body cameras had been incorporated into officer-use-of-force training, officers had also noticed how multiple camera angles offered multiple perspectives on an incident. One officer told me about a training exercise in which he wore a body camera, and a neutral second camera was placed in the corner of the room. After the mock use-of-force exercise, he remembered using his baton twice. His body camera footage seemed to confirm his initial report. However, the camera in the corner clearly depicted him using the baton three times as he subdued the other officer.

Officers' anxieties about inconsistency were generally connected to larger underlying concerns about accountability or the ability of defense attorneys to negate the usefulness of officers' statements in subsequent prosecutions. For some, "there can be many explanations for why" these inconsistencies could occur, "but people will not listen or try to understand how that could happen. They will rush to judgment against the officer and disregard any explanation" (Reese, sergeant, BPD, 2017). Officers saw "accusations of dishonesty" (Abram, sergeant, SPD, 2015) or "being accused of lying or covering [something] up" (Nick, sergeant, SPD, 2014) as likely outcomes. As a result, one officer suggested that "we should just say 'see video' for any report writing" (Ross, undisclosed rank, SPD, 2016). Others also felt that having camera footage "could hold officers to an impossible standard of personal perception" (Herb, undisclosed rank, SPD, 2016), especially when newer cameras (e.g., those with enhanced low-light capabilities) had the capacity to see better than the officers could themselves.

The "Video or It Didn't Happen" Effect

One officer told me during a ride-along that the adoption of body cameras signaled "the end of an era" when people would trust an officer's word for what it was. Although he stated this rather matter-of-factly, I sensed a bit of sadness in his demeanor as he described how he saw body-camera footage taking the place of an officer's word and written report, and the beginning of a new era in which something had to be on video or else no one would believe it had happened. Other officers reported the perception that "society is becoming programmed to seeing body camera footage" (Hansen, sergeant, SPD, 2018) and that "if the officer says something happened and the video doesn't capture it," public perception will be that "it didn't happen" (Guy, senior patrol officer, SPD, 2016)—essentially, "if it isn't on camera, it didn't happen" (Rowan, patrol officer, BPD, 2016). One officer called this "the 'video or it didn't happen' effect" (Leo, undisclosed rank, BPD, 2017). Officers also expressed concerns that "what should be an additional tool and a piece of the puzzle becomes *the only piece* of the puzzle that matters to the public, prosecutors, or judges" (Bert, sergeant, SPD, 2018), or that "the courts and public opinion will rely *only* on the footage and not the entire scope of the incident, such as what occurred prior to the incident and what actions simply were not captured on the video because of camera angle" (Lionel, senior patrol officer, SPD, 2018). One officer explained that a body camera

> can be a good tool or addition to our police reports, but what they record is not the whole truth or story. In the courts and media, if there are any inconsistencies based on perception . . . the officer is always "the liar." The biggest problem is the Monday-morning quarterbacking . . . which causes officers to be slow to react when they see danger or a problem. If the camera didn't see what the officer saw, the camera is held as gospel. (Matt, patrol officer, SPD, 2014)

For another officer, report writing was all about justifying what he did, including "providing a rationale for why I did things, so I can show why I was within the law, within my legal rights as an officer." "I have to justify what I do," he said, "the camera can't do that for me. The camera can't justify what I do. The camera is not going to explain why I did what I did, or what I saw or thought I saw, or what I smelled, or what the experience was." Other officers stated that cameras should "never replace a thorough investigation, which may become biased by an overreliance on video" (Theo, patrol officer, BPD, 2015).

On one occasion, while I was sitting in the Bellingham police station's report-writing room with an officer who had recently transferred into the department from another agency in a different part of the country, these ideas came up in our conversation. He emphasized that despite the benefits of the cameras, the focus should be on the narrative. He didn't want the video to replace the narrative from the officer's report. "You know, you still have the narrative," he said, "and if you have footage, that's just icing on the cake. That's great, you have an extra bit of evidence." However, at the opposite extreme, some officers seemed resigned to the idea that "without supporting camera footage, an officer's testimony is useless" (Heath, sergeant, SPD, 2018), and an officer's "written word no longer matter[s]" (Sam, patrol officer, BPD, 2016).

Civilizing the Public

Besides civilizing the police, body cameras have also been touted to diffuse potentially violent encounters with members of the public. Researchers have tried to capture this in a variety of ways, including a quantitative focus on the number of complaints filed by citizens after the introduction of body cameras into these police-public interactions. In one experimental study of body-camera adoption in Amsterdam, the Netherlands, where cameras were adopted for the express purpose of civilizing members of the public and better ensuring police officer safety, researchers found some evidence that officers who had worn a body camera also reported a significantly improved sense of security and safety when compared to their colleagues who did not wear a camera, and that they also reported fewer instances of civilian violence.[38] However, as discussed earlier, most of these quantitative, often experimental studies find varying results. The qualitative data from my study do not answer all of these questions; however, they do help present a picture about how frontline officers perceive the presence of cameras affecting their interactions with civilians.

In my study, officers noted varying agreement with the notion that their use of body cameras affected the behavior of civilians. A couple of officers stated that the cameras did not change or only rarely changed behavior. Others stated that they "have had a lot of positive outcomes when people know they are being recorded" (Digby, corporal, SPD, 2016), or offered qualified responses, such as the following: "I think it depends on the circumstance and type of encounter. Sometimes announcing you are wearing the camera shuts people down or alters the genuineness of their statement. Other times it assists, and subjects are on their 'best behavior' if they know the camera is on" (Darlene, patrol officer, BPD, 2016). A few officers reported that cameras had a "calming" or "positive" effect on civilian behavior, resulting, for example, in situations where it seemed that they were "more compliant and less likely to be hostile" (Tina, patrol officer, BPD, 2015). However, others, as noted in the previous section, felt that de-policing due to the cameras might also lead civilians to act more aggressively toward the police.

However, some officers felt that the presence of cameras (and the associated video) would make it less likely that civilians would file complaints against officers for misconduct or inappropriate demeanor. One supervisor noted his belief that "the cameras will help almost completely stop some of the frivolous complaints we have" (Laurence, undisclosed rank, SPD, 2015), while another stated, "I believe it reduces the ability of a citizen to make a false claim regarding use of force, how they were treated, or any other items in which a complaint or a lawsuit could be initiated" (Billy, Sergeant, BPD, 2016).

A few officers also reported that body-camera use might create tensions between the police and the public. These responses generally involved two types of concerns.

First, some officers felt that civilians would not want to be recorded or would be "less inclined to speak to an officer if they were being recorded" (Mike, patrol officer, BPD, 2014), a concern that could be exacerbated by policies that gave officers little discretion to turn off the cameras during encounters. Relatedly, issues about whether officers should notify civilians that they were recording are relevant here, as they highlight the camera when it might otherwise not be noticed. "A lot of times when you tell someone they're being audio and visually recorded, they tend to stop talking" (Aubrey, undisclosed rank, BPD, 2016). One officer stated that in certain circumstances he would consciously make the choice to *not inform* civilians that he was recording:

> Most of the time, it seems appropriate to announce that I'm recording audio/video at the beginning of a contact. However, we respond to a large number of mental crisis-type calls and it feels extremely insensitive to tell a suicidal subject that you're recording everything. Often times, I do not make the announcement in those circumstances because it sets the person off and hurts our rapport. (Matthew, investigator, BPD, 2015)

Second, officers expressed concern that the possibility for public disclosure of the video under the state Public Records Act would make people afraid to talk to the police when the cameras were on. Underlying this concern was the perception that distribution or "misuse of video obtained under Freedom of Information" would have "a chilling effect on day to day interactions once people realize they are being recorded," and that this held "the potential to become another barrier between citizen and police" (Samuel, patrol officer, SPD, 2014). Officers shared the general concern that "many citizens would be reluctant to provide information to officers about suspects if they know they're being recorded and that recording is subject to freedom of information laws" (Noah, patrol officer, BPD, 2014), especially if they feared "being labeled as a 'snitch'" (Markus, patrol officer, SPD, 2014). From the perspective of an investigator, this concern was especially relevant when dealing with "individuals . . . who might want to become an informant" (Stephen, detective, BPD, 2016). Others stated that they would prefer not to wear a body camera, precisely because "I work with informants" (Jackson, patrol officer, SPD, 2015) or because "it has a chilling effect on my ability to conduct interviews" (Phil, patrol officer, SPD, 2015). One officer noted:

> I believe that once more routine interactions with police are placed on social media, YouTube, and similar sites there will be a chilling effect between citizens and officers (citizens with little contact with officers will be less likely to engage in non-call related conversation). I have already had people ask if the camera was on before starting a conversation. Other EMS personnel are already limiting contact with the cameras on. (Eden, undisclosed rank, SPD, 2015)

These concerns became quite clear to me one day during a ride-along in 2015. The officer I was riding with was called to the location of a man with an outstanding warrant (he was being detained by a corrections officer). On the way, the officer explained that this particular individual was a violent gang member, and that he had arrested him before. After making the arrest, the officer led the handcuffed arrestee to his patrol car and had him sit down inside. Next, the officer turned off his body camera and sat down in the back seat beside the man. A few minutes later, after exiting the vehicle and closing the rear door, the officer told me that the man he had arrested was also one of his confidential informants, and that they had discussed information that might be valuable to the police. He then turned his camera back on and recorded our drive to the county jail. On the one hand, a broad always-on activation policy would require officers to record such conversations. In a legal context in which public disclosure laws might cover such video (as was the case at the time in Washington State), access to this video might put the arrestee in danger, as it would reveal his cooperation with the authorities. On the other hand, allowing officers the discretion to turn their cameras off in these situations could lead to accusations that the officers were hiding misconduct. Additionally, public disclosure of the videos before and after the break might also suggest the confidential informant relationship. In either case, broad public disclosure aggravates the risk to the informant in potentially significant ways—as a form of collateral visibility—and regulates the officer's use of the camera, even in ways that may not align with agency policy.

CONCLUSION

Officers recognized various ways in which their adoption of body-worn cameras is regulated by law as well as by the technology itself. On the one hand we see, again, how officers' conceptions of themselves and their profession as skilled professionals or practitioners are challenged by camera adoption, especially as rhetoric surrounding the cameras has focused on making police work more transparent and officers more accountable (for purposes that resonate with Herbert's notion of subservience).[39] Body cameras, in some ways, push back on the police desire for separation and special treatment, while also empowering the police in other ways (e.g., using footage to convict offenders or exonerate officers). Officers report vulnerabilities, and that they change their behavior in various ways due to the presence of the cameras. As such, we see how visibility and accessibility of information about how they do their work causes behavioral change. However, officers also find ways to use the cameras and resulting footage in their favor, capitalizing on the affordances the technology provides to capture evidence and retain some control over the narrative. Relatedly, officers' comments about changes in civilian behavior were predominantly linked to concerns about reducing safety risks and civilians providing less information to police—again, an issue of how information plays an important role in defining power in these interactions.

On the one hand, the presence of cameras may civilize officer behavior by encouraging tempered tongues, but on the other, many officers also clearly report a perceived need to use "unorthodox methods" in some cases or to use harsh language and tactics to subdue and overpower those they distrust, disrespect, or perceive as threatening and not amenable to more humane treatment. These are entrenched perspectives within police culture, uttered frequently by officers who seem to believe deeply in their own professional ability to utilize discretion absent oversight. In the end, attempts to regulate the police, whether through law or technology, should not serve to entrench or exacerbate existing problems of trust between the public and the police. Reinforcing "us versus them" and "warrior" mentalities will get us nowhere. Unfortunately, it seems that body-worn cameras may do just that.

CHAPTER 6

Public Disclosure as "Direct to YouTube" Alternative

I personally would NEVER provide my personal information to an officer with a camera. It all ends up on the internet. That is wrong, and unsafe.

—Tyler, patrol officer, SPD, 2015

Not everything should be filmed (for example, rape victim or child abuse interviews) and our public disclosure laws are too liberal to keep those out of the hands of people who would exploit or abuse such video.

—Larry, captain, SPD, 2015

"SMILE AND SAY HI TO THE CAMERA, HONEY!"

One winter afternoon in 2015, I attended multiple domestic violence calls with a Spokane police officer. We were first called to a home where a couple, roughly in their late forties, had been fighting. We were the second car on scene, and another officer had already separated the two in their driveway along the side of their house. After parking by the curb, we walked up the driveway to where the man was standing. The officer I was shadowing turned on his body camera and called out, "Just so you know I'm wearing a camera." He then turned to the woman, who was about twenty feet further up the driveway, and said, "Did you hear that? I'm filming. I have this camera on, this body-worn camera." At this point, the man we had approached yelled down the driveway to his wife, "Smile and say hi to the camera, Honey!"

As the officer began to question the man, seeking to determine what had occurred, the other officer began to question the woman. As it turned out, during the fight the woman had taken a metal baseball bat, swung it, and smashed in the man's face across his eye. When we approached him, he had blood leaking from his eye and eyebrow and rolling down his nose and cheek. His eyebrow looked caved in; the bone was obviously fractured. After a few minutes of questioning, the medics arrived in an ambulance. Upon seeing that the man's eye was filled with blood, they rushed him quickly to the ambulance and prepared to leave for the hospital. At the same time, the officer and I followed them to the ambulance, where the officer continued to question the injured man, seeking to get a statement or confession out of him on camera. When the ambulance left, we entered the couple's home, where the woman had been taken to be questioned. The officer continued to record in case the woman might offer a confession as well. In the end, the woman was arrested, cuffed, and taken to the local jail, where she was booked on a charge of assault.

A few months later, while sitting around a table eating lunch with a group of five officers at a coffee shop in Bellingham, an officer loaded one of his body-camera videos, recorded a few weeks earlier, onto his laptop. He stood and placed the laptop on the table in front of me and said, emphatically, "Here, tell me this should be on YouTube." On the screen, I watched a video, apparently with a view from the officer's body camera as he quickly exited his vehicle and ran across a lawn and through the open front door of a private home. I heard multiple people screaming and a woman wailing loudly in the background as he entered the house. Quite a few people appeared to be crowded into a small living room. I saw the officer suddenly turn and take a small infant (who I later learned was two months old) from the wailing woman. The infant's head and arms hung limply as the officer carefully transferred the baby's body to the floor and attempted to resuscitate it, unsuccessfully. In the background, I saw a couple more small children, held back by another adult, before I turned away from the screen in shock at what I had just seen. *There is no legitimate reason for the public to access this video*, the officer claimed. The others around the table nodded and quietly voiced their agreement.

The problem was, and is, however, that many of these videos are potentially disclosable under state FOI laws. Such provisions threaten to make even the most sensitive moments of private individuals' private lives visible on a massive scale, especially if and when they are posted online, even when they bear little connection to alleged officer misconduct.

PUBLIC DISCLOSURE AND ONLINE DISSEMINATION OF VIDEO

Public disclosure and the online dissemination of video have the potential to cause significant issues for the police and members of the public.[1] Indeed, if law allows, or even requires, disclosure of footage like that recorded in the preceding examples, the personal details and private lives of individuals may be projected for all the world to see, especially when posted to online social media platforms like Facebook, Twitter, Instagram, or YouTube. Making the police more visible through the use of body-worn cameras and public disclosure laws will also expose those with whom the police interact to new, radical levels of visibility. As a form of "refractive surveillance," the body-camera-to-public-disclosure pipeline promises to reveal vast amounts of sensitive personal information about victims, witnesses, suspects, and bystanders.[2] Under such access-to-information frameworks, the visibility of individual citizens (innocent, presumed innocent, or guilty) is inextricably tied to the visibility of the state. This suggests the urgent need to imagine comprehensive and coherent new approaches to public records regimes.

Within the two departments I studied, as well as other agencies within the state (e.g., the Seattle Police Department), public disclosure quickly became a serious issue after the first blanket request was filed by Tim Clemans in September 2014.[3] One police employee charged with responding to records requests confirmed that the process of previewing and redacting footage took up to three times longer than the length of the footage itself, and that current staffing levels could not support a high volume of requests or, indeed, even a single broad request like that filed by Clemans. In one of the two departments in this study, the threat of the broad request caused administration to briefly consider halting or canceling the program, due to the potential administrative and fiscal burden of responding to such requests over time.

Some patrol officers indicated concerns about the cost and personnel required to adequately handle public disclosure requests. Several officers also indicated that providing entertainment to the public was not an appropriate reason to release footage, and some expressed concern that disclosed video would be edited and taken out of context before being placed online. Other officers cited safety concerns, attorneys trolling through footage looking for potential lawsuits, and increased scrutiny from departmental administrations as issues of concern. One officer stated, "Many times, officers seek privately given intelligence from informants and other persons that is essential to the mission and should not be subject to public records request" (Brigham, senior patrol officer, SPD, 2014).

To some extent, officers' concerns about public disclosure of their footage (or just body-camera footage in general) mirrored the concerns they had about the online dissemination of bystander recordings. Frequently, officers expressed concerns about the accessibility of the footage as well as the heightened visibility that occurred when the video was posted to the internet (something that they saw happen quite quickly in their own departments, as the "PoliceVideoRequests" YouTube channel became host to body-camera videos sourced through public records requests to each of these departments). Additionally, the fact that members of the public had broad access to most of the officers' videos—including, prior to 2016, those filmed inside homes and with citizens in very sensitive personal situations—made many officers uncomfortable.

Few officers expressed concerns about citizens editing or altering the disclosed body-camera footage, in contrast to more frequently stated concerns about the manipulation of bystander videos, but some did echo concerns that the requesters or media outlets would acquire footage and only use portions of it, amplifying certain aspects of the events while concealing others. For example, some expressed the concern that "only a 10 second video [would make] the news and not the complete story" (Lincoln, crime scene investigator, BPD, 2015). And as discussed later, officers generally appear much more accepting of limited-access public disclosure policies than they are of the broad and all-encompassing public records law that existed in Washington State at the time this study began. On the one hand, it is not at all surprising that officers would generally dislike public disclosure of their video, especially when much of the information politics related to body-camera adoption in these agencies was driven by the accessibility or nonaccessibility of this footage. On the other hand, the broad accessibility of some of this footage under state FOI laws raises significant privacy concerns.

As described earlier, requests for body-camera footage under state FOI law began almost immediately after agencies began deploying cameras in September 2014. Within months, sensitive video footage (e.g., of interviews with alleged prostitutes in hotel rooms and other officer-citizen interactions and arrests) began to be posted to YouTube after the agencies were required to disclose almost every recording made by the cameras under broad state FOI law. After these initial disclosures began to hit YouTube, officers began to talk openly about the problems they perceived with broad public disclosure. Many of the conversations I had during subsequent ride-alongs changed dramatically, and officers frequently shifted the conversation to the issue of the state Public Records Act without any prompting. Officers frequently expressed dismay that all their footage was likely to be visible to anyone on the internet. In the domestic violence context, specifically, one officer reported, "I believe it is likely that after a [domestic violence] victim sees herself on the internet she will be less likely to call police in the future" (Samuel, patrol officer, SPD, 2014).

Officers frequently made statements to the effect that "recordings should only be for people legally attached to a case, not for YouTube videos. If an officer decides to turn a camera off because they are taking a sexual assault case, there is going to be serious argument by the defense once it goes to trial" (Wade, patrol officer, SPD). Importantly, officers were concerned about the privacy of (some of) the citizens they contacted during their shifts, not *only* about violations of their own privacy. As one sergeant explained, "My only reservation about the [body camera] program is that all the footage is subject to a public records request and could possibly put a victim into further harm or ridicule if the footage is viewed by a person [who] does not have any legitimate interest in the incident" (Arnold, sergeant, SPD, 2014).

In this context, *collateral visibility*, or the unintended increase in the visibility of ordinary citizens due to a combination of body-camera usage and liberal public disclosure laws—ostensibly adopted to make the *police* more visible—becomes an important variable to consider when developing law or public policy in this area. Body-worn cameras are often adopted for the stated purpose of making police officers more accountable and amenable to oversight, but we need to remember that these cameras point away from the officers' bodies, and their lenses are primarily focused on those with whom the officers interact. These are often not regular middle- or upper-class members of the community, but people who are experiencing difficult and painful circumstances and/or who suffer from mental illness or homelessness, or those who are members of other communities who receive heightened police attention, for whatever reason (including race, religion, etc.). To some extent, the ability of an officer to exercise discretion by choosing *not to record* a citizen contact may have significant (positive) implications for a citizen's privacy interests. However, officers expressed the concern that, if they choose not to record an interaction, the media and the public will distrust their decision and assume the officer was acting badly.

Additionally, by not recording, the officers will not capture potentially exculpatory evidence to ward off unfounded complaints of misconduct.

In the end, the officers I interviewed and surveyed were primarily concerned about either the public disclosure of their footage itself or the subsequent dissemination of that footage online, especially in online social networks, where highly increased visibility was almost assured. Within this context, popular cries from communities, protestors, and activists for release of the video—for example, "Release the tapes!"—were not always about providing full (or at least more) information or context about an incident. These calls for greater transparency can be seen to have at least three primary purposes: first, they seek to gather evidence in order to "prove" the claimants' preferred interpretation of events, vindicate their preexisting concerns and interests, and/or prosecute the police officers involved; second, they aim to provide a more complete and accurate picture of the events and conduct at issue, also as a form of evidence, in order for the truth to come out and for justice to be done (no matter which side has its story bolstered); and third, they reflect a general call for less government secrecy and more popular and democratic oversight of government action and are not always about procuring evidence. In sum, advocacy for access to police video is about power and framing information and (a particular) interpretation of information for political ends.

OFFICER ATTITUDES ABOUT PUBLIC ACCESS TO BODY-CAMERA FOOTAGE

Many officers held strong views about public access to their body-worn camera footage. When asked whether they would choose to wear a body-worn camera if they had to make the choice again, several officers stated that existing public disclosure rules were a primary reason they would choose not to wear or continue to wear a body camera. Some also expressed anxiety about "recording stuff that should NOT be allowed to be released to the public under public disclosure laws" (Sandra, patrol officer, BPD, 2016). Officers frequently noted their feeling that there should be "better laws addressing disclosure of the videos" (Erin, detective, BPD, 2014). One officer stated, "I would not wear a camera today despite the benefits it offers. Right now, there are too many unresolved issues dealing with who, when, and where to record as well as the public disclosure fiasco" (Fred, patrol officer, BPD, 2014).

Some officers questioned whether public access should be allowed at all or, even if it was, whether video recorded in certain contexts—for example, in private homes, during interviews with sexual assault victims, or when officers were engaged in post-incident conversations with other officers—should be redacted prior to disclosure. Officers also expressed concerns about *who* ought to have access to particular video—that is, should all members of the public have a right to obtain footage or, for example, should access be limited to only those with some connection to the incident depicted in the video? Moving beyond those broader questions, officers voiced concerns that public access to footage would invade the privacy of those they interacted with (including possibly leading to other forms of embarrassment or revictimization), make officers' mistakes more visible, and cause officers to alter their behavior in unwanted ways.

Interestingly, the police often seem to be unaware of or insensitive to the fact that they themselves invade the privacy of citizens on a daily basis, in routine and scripted ways. Implicit in these comments about public access being intrusive on privacy is the view that it is okay for officers to violate the privacy of people—presumably for public safety or law enforcement ends—but that creating a visual record of that invasion that might be disclosed to the public is problematic.

Should the Public Have Access to Body Camera Footage?

Across surveys, I asked officers how appropriate they felt it was for citizens to gain access to body-worn camera recordings. In the 2014 survey, 39 percent of officers indicated that broad public access to body-camera footage was either "somewhat appropriate" or "very appropriate," with 58.9 percent reporting that access was not appropriate. The percentage of positive responses fell to 28.8 percent in 2015 and 12.9 percent in 2016, rising somewhat in 2017 to 24.5 percent, while negative responses increased to 66.7 percent (2015) before falling slightly to 62.1 percent (2016) and 51 percent (2017) on the final two surveys.[4] Notably, very few officers felt it was "very appropriate" for citizens to access police body-worn camera video footage (fewer than 6% across the first three surveys, rising to 9% in 2017), while between 23 and 33 percent reported that it was "not at all appropriate" for civilians to access footage. The percentages of positive and negative responses to this question were similar in both departments on each survey (for more details, see figure 4 in appendix B). Supervisors were slightly more likely to report that access was appropriate than those identifying as regular officers (see figure 5 in appendix B), but there were no consistent differences across surveys in terms of sex or race.

Some officers specifically expressed concerns about permitting access to certain types of content captured on video, rather than to all video in and of itself, including segments of video documenting officers' conversations that were unrelated to their enforcement activity, officers' bathroom breaks (if accidentally recorded), police tactics, footage recorded inside homes, sensitive information provided to officers by civilians (especially by victims of crime), or personal information about civilians accessible to officers through their computer systems. Some of these worries were expressed due to safety and privacy concerns, but some officers also felt that some footage should not be released (or recorded in the first place) because of its perceived entertainment value (at the expense of those depicted). Others noted that video, if publicly accessible, might be used for other unintended purposes, including employers screening potential employees or as evidence in divorce proceedings. "Should that video be available to future employers [or] to the divorce attorney? How will that change police-citizen interactions once those stories start to get out?" (Landon, undisclosed rank, SPD, 2016). Some officers postulated that his sort of public disclosure of video might "have a chilling effect on day-to-day interactions" with members of the public "once people realize they are being recorded," creating "another barrier between citizens and the police" (Samuel, patrol officer, SPD, 2014).

The refrain that there was "too much video being released to the public and media," thus putting the "citizen's worst moments out there for everyone to see" (Joseph, lieutenant, SPD, 2018), seemed to pervade many officers' sense that public disclosure law allowed too much access (in terms of content) and also made access too easy (both in the breadth of requests and allowing requests from any member of the public who wanted access). As expressed by another officer, "We record civilians at their worst. These recordings can then end up on YouTube and severely damage that individual's reputation in the community" (Tom, patrol officer, BPD, 2016).

Who Should Have Access?

Assuming some level of public access to footage, the question then becomes, *who* do officers believe ought to have access? During rides with officers, I was repeatedly told that officers didn't mind persons involved in contacts getting access to footage, but in many cases, officers were generally adamant about not wanting "any anonymous person" to be able to access their footage, especially as officers felt much of the footage they recorded contained sensitive information about the people they contacted, the officers themselves, or even police tactics (e.g., on SWAT calls). These feelings were also expressed by several respondents on open-ended questions across the four surveys and informal interviews and were supported by responses to closed (Likert-scale) survey questions.

In qualitative responses, officers also made normative statements about who they thought ought to have access to body-camera footage (and, conversely, who should not). "Everyone and their mother will be requesting copies," argued one officer. "There has to be limits on who can obtain the recordings, not just some Joe Schmoe putting in a blanket request for everything. That is insane" (Clayton, undisclosed rank, SPD, 2015). Commonly, officers argued that people should not be able to access the videos "unless they are directly involved in the incident or are a member of the criminal justice system with a need to use that video [as] part of a criminal case, as a training tool, etc." (Liam, internal affairs sergeant, SPD, 2015). Requests from those not directly connected to an incident were sometimes seen as "unnecessary" or not worth the internal administrative cost to process (redact) and produce them, again highlighting distrust of the public and the motives of those who might make these requests.

Likewise, across the first three surveys, respondents overwhelmingly disagreed that body-worn camera footage should be accessible *to all members of the public* under state FOI law (with 78%, 92%, and 90%, respectively, indicating disagreement; see figure 6 in appendix B). While BPD responses remained roughly similar on the 2017 survey (77% disagreement), SPD responses shifted dramatically—with only 13 percent reporting disagreement and 69 percent indicating agreement. The percentage of positive responses ("strongly agree" or "somewhat agree") also decreased over time over the first three surveys, from 20 percent (2014) to 6 percent (2016), rising to 21 percent (BPD, 2017) and 69 percent (SPD, 2017) in each department on the fourth. It is not clear why SPD respondents reported such dramatically different levels of agreement in 2017. Qualitative responses from SPD officers in 2017 generally reveal continuing concerns about the privacy risks of public disclosure. However, a small number of responses also suggest that officers had seen body-camera footage also frame police officers in a positive light and serve as evidence that they had acted appropriately in use-of-force situations. As framed by one officer, "Body cameras are great for proving that we are not malicious people. It shows that we were within the law for using force, making arrests and searching etc." (Dalton, patrol officer, SPD, 2018).

However, when presented with a slightly altered version of the previous question (framed as access *only to those individuals who were captured on the body-worn camera footage itself* rather than any member of the public), officers were much more supportive of disclosure across all four surveys (see figure 7 in appendix B). Most respondents on each survey reported agreement (either "strongly agree" or "somewhat agree") that disclosure to these individuals *was* appropriate. Positive responses increased from 70 percent (2014) to 77 percent (2015) before falling somewhat to 59 percent (2016) and 65 percent (2017).[5] Correspondingly, officers who expressed disagreement (either "strongly disagree" or "somewhat disagree") dropped from a high of 28 percent (2014) to a low of about 20 percent in both 2016 and 2017. These findings suggest that officers may have become less averse to *limited* public disclosure over time, even while generally becoming more critical of broad, indiscriminate public disclosure policies.

Civilian Privacy

Over half of the respondents on each of the first three surveys indicated that they agreed that police use of body-worn cameras would intrude on the privacy interests of citizens (59%, 60%, and 51% choosing "strongly agree" or "somewhat agree," respectively by survey), while disagreement was reported by 38, 37, and 31 percent of respondents, respectively. Interestingly, however, this level of agreement was not shared across both police agencies. When analyzed by department, SPD respondents reported substantially higher rates of agreement that the cameras would likely invade civilian privacy on the first three surveys (64%, 75%, and 56%, respectively by survey), but the rate dropped surprisingly to only 26 percent on the fourth survey. On the other hand, fewer than half of BPD respondents agreed with this proposition on all four surveys, although the rates of agreement were more consistent (48%, 35%, 45%, and 47%, respectively by survey).

Officers frequently expressed concern that footage subject to public disclosure could cause harm. Even officers who expressed otherwise positive attitudes toward the body-camera program offered up concerns about the possible harm stemming from public disclosure. Officers suggested that the video might violate expectations of privacy by revealing "personal information that citizens share about themselves believing that the information they reveal was confidential" (Dalton, patrol officer, SPD, 2018). There was a general sense among many that "people do not need to see the inside . . . of someone's house" (Adrienne, patrol officer, SPD, 2015). Multiple officers also made statements to the effect that a "rape victim's statements should not be accessible [through] a simple public disclosure request," because release "could victimize them further" (Cory, senior police officer, SPD, 2014).

Quite a few officers seemed to feel that "the chance of [sensitive personal] information not being censored" (Dalton, patrol officer, SPD, 2018) or properly redacted prior to public disclosure was high, or that public disclosure requirements would result in the inadvertent disclosure of "private information, computer passwords, dates of birth, social security numbers, etc." (Steve, patrol officer, SPD, 2015). As a consequence of these concerns, one officer suggested the need for a "right to be forgotten" law, "where the videos can only be posted on the internet for 'x' amount of time" (Tom, patrol officer, BPD, 2016). For another, "I worry about public disclosure laws and victims' personal horrors being released for the public to watch like it is a TV show, or now perpetrators being able to see the inside of victims' homes, etc. The public should not be able to get online and watch what happened to their neighbor during the police contact just because they are nosey" (Madison, patrol officer, BPD, 2015).

Officer Privacy

On the other hand, many officers continued to feel opposed to the cameras for a variety of reasons more directly tied to their own interests. At the beginning of the department's pilot program, one officer stated that "a witch-hunt is about to begin and the cameras will be used to show us doing something—anything—wrong" (Miles, crime scene investigator, BPD, 2014). Over time, others had experiences that either improved or eroded their confidence in the cameras. Across surveys, officers were asked whether they thought that body-worn camera use would intrude on the privacy of individual police officers. Often, officers' concerns about their own privacy was related to supervisory review directed at finding small policy infractions (such as using profanity), the need for privacy in regard to things officers might say while venting after stressful incidents or in regard to critical comments an officer might make about a supervisor in the presence of a trusted colleague, or the perceived risk of "Monday-morning quarterbacking" and critique of officers' actions (by the media and the public) made possible by broad public disclosure rules.

Across surveys, the general distribution of responses to this question was similar to the distribution of responses about civilian privacy, with roughly half of respondents indicating agreement that body-worn camera use would result in intrusions on officer privacy. Responses by the departments were generally more alike than regarding the previous question (about civilian privacy intrusions), with the exception of the responses to Survey 2, in which BPD respondents indicated only 36.8 percent agreement (compared to 56% at SPD) and just over 50 percent disagreement.

Some officers expressed concern that public disclosure could negatively impact them or portray them or their departments in a negative light. Some concerns revolved around the fact that "anything you say can be recorded and is open to the public per public disclosure" (Maxwell, sergeant, SPD, 2018). Another officer stated that "this video WILL be abused by news media, lawyers, and all the troll citizens that spend their days trying to defame police" (Brigham, senior patrol officer, SPD, 2014), while others also echoed the concern that "citizens and/or anti-police groups" would acquire and review footage with the intent to "get officers in trouble for unintended mistakes" (Seth, patrol officer, BPD, 2015). Similarly, another noted the concern that "officers have minimal protection from admin, and zero from the public release of every word spoken on every day in every scenario by people who condemn a single misspoken sentence as though we are murderers" (Hugh, detective, SPD, 2018).

Discretion to (Not) Record

Several officers stated that liberal public disclosure of body-camera footage was a primary reason to afford officers broad discretion in when to activate their cameras, rather than to require recording in all or most situations. Alternatively, an administrator stated that "victims should have the option of not being recorded," because "a public records request could devastate" them and open their homes to the view of anyone who watches the video (Dave, patrol lieutenant, SPD, 2014). Similarly, another argued, "Yes, officers should have discretion especially with the public disclosure laws. If those were changed to not allow access to unrelated conversations by officers and only to those citizens involved in the incident, then I might have a different opinion" (Bert, sergeant, SPD, 2018).

Officers also repeatedly made connections between policy discussions about when and where officers should or should not record and the risk of public disclosure. Most of these responses (as well as other discussions I had with officers during the study) indicated that officers generally felt they should record (or were recording) less often in certain situations because of concerns about privacy and public disclosure. Relatedly, these officers felt that they "should have a fair amount of discretion" about when to activate their cameras and record, but that "interviews of victims, children, social contacts, etc., should not usually be recorded due to public disclosure laws" (Cynthia, undisclosed rank, BPD, 2015). On the other hand, one respondent stated, "If you are going to record, why not record everything? I am not necessarily for the cameras but if we are going to wear them, record it all! Then maybe public disclosure laws will change so victims don't become victims again with their calls being posted for all to see" (June, patrol officer, BPD, 2015). A lieutenant stated:

> Any officer-initiated contact should be videotaped. . . . [T]his is really what the public is looking for and provides true transparency into [an] officer's own enforcement actions. [However,] officers should have discretion when responding to private calls. Should my neighbors be able to view my personal family issues just because a police officer shows up to my house? What if my autistic son is having a breakdown? How about a juvenile who is suicidal or arguing with parents over doing the dishes . . . should this video forever be [accessible] by prospective employers for all time? (Ryan, lieutenant, SPD, 2015)

Behavior Modification

Some officers also reported modifying their behavior and choosing not to record certain situations (or inside homes) when they felt doing so could jeopardize a victim's or witness's privacy—although I only saw a little evidence of this in my ride-alongs, as the officers I accompanied generally recorded most of these sorts of contacts. One officer, explaining why he often chose not to activate his camera when inside private homes, stated (while pointing at his camera), "because I know where this goes" (referring to the video created by his camera).[6] Another noted that "knowing every word is available to be taken out of context [due to public disclosure law] prevents me from helping people in many ways I used to" (Hugh, detective, SPD, 2018). Elaborating further, this officer said that although a "body camera protects me," it also "stops me from using common sense solutions in favor of strict application of the law, rather than in the spirit of the law, even when it may not benefit the citizen." (The officer described letting someone go with a warning rather than citing her for driving with a suspended license, because the car was only a few houses away from the person's home and she had an infant in the car). The concern here was, in the end, that "if the wrong reporter or supervisor finds out," the officer "could receive discipline" for exercising such discretion.

THE DISSEMINATION OF BODY-WORN CAMERA FOOTAGE ONLINE

Along with concerns related to public disclosure, officers also expressed specific concerns about the dissemination of body-camera video on the internet. For example, some officers felt that the public accessibility of footage might be abused in various ways, such as by those who might wish to shame or humiliate someone, post "embarrassing footage [of ex-partners] on Facebook" (Patrick, patrol lieutenant, SPD, 2015), access footage to help facilitate stalking or harassment (e.g., to see "inside of a victim's house" or view their victim's statement to the police [Sandra, patrol officer, BPD, 2016]), or use information on the footage to commit or "plan future crimes" (Christopher, undisclosed rank, SPD, 2016). One officer noted that "a reoffender can ask for the video through a public records request and watch police tactics in catching and arresting him. He can use this knowledge to avoid capture or avoid being caught for committing dangerous/violent felonies in the future" (Dalton, patrol officer, SPD, 2018). Another claimed that officers should have discretion about when to record because "people may be less likely to report a crime if they know they are being recorded. And, now that it is under public disclosure, the suspect knows who reported it. This could lead to retaliation" (Sandra, patrol officer, BPD, 2016). In survey responses and during ride-alongs, officers stated that video recorded inside people's homes could be used by intended burglars, for example, by "shopping the insides of private residences from video requests" (Patrick, patrol lieutenant, SPD, 2015).

Frequently, officers targeted their frustration at what they perceived to be a significant violation of privacy; however, as noted earlier, they were not *only* concerned about violations of their own privacy (and the attendant accountability), but also about the privacy of the civilians they would contact during their shifts. To a survey question about what concerns body-worn cameras raise in the minds of officers, one lieutenant responded, "I have very significant concerns about WA State's [public disclosure] laws. I do not believe that the inherent privacy issues of citizens are being addressed. It is unfair for a family's personal laundry to be immediately accessible on YouTube" (Ryan, lieutenant, SPD, 2015).

One officer noted that officers needed "to be mindful of the fact that sexual assault interviews, inside of people's homes, medical issues, and mental issues have potential to be entertainment for others" (Christopher, undisclosed rank, SPD, 2016). As put bluntly by another, "people want body cam footage for entertainment, e.g., YouTube and LiveLeak.com, purposes" (Bond, senior patrol officer, SPD, 2018). For those who expressed these concerns, the online publication of body-camera footage was "a complete and total invasion of privacy for citizens who are going through a crisis" (Jake, corporal, SPD, 2014). Relatedly, one Spokane officer stated, "I don't think victims to sexual assault should have their reports put on the internet. I also don't think the entire dying moments of an officer need to be put on the internet. People [are] waiting to see and hear that last dying breath" (Adam, lieutenant, SPD, 2015). However, as noted in chapter 5, the police themselves frequently watch these videos, sometimes to write reports, but also sometimes for their own entertainment. This suggests one way in which the police understand their own actions (e.g., watching video as not invading privacy) as different than those of the public, removing themselves from the moral judgments they make about the conduct of others.

One officer who had recorded a lengthy interview with a young woman detained during a prostitution sting explained to me how he spent time after the video was posted to YouTube trying to figure out how, and whether, he could request the video be taken down for privacy reasons. He couldn't believe that such a sensitive interview could be disclosed and published without being redacted to protect the young woman's privacy. The interview, which remained on the internet for almost two years (and was eventually taken down voluntarily by the person who had uploaded it), included the woman stating her name and talking about her boyfriend and family, as well as the events and activities that had led to her arrest for prostitution. Other officers also reacted quite strongly to these instances of public disclosure.

Conclusion

Policing . . . has always been as much a matter of image as substance.

—Robert Reiner, "The Dialectics of Dixon," 11

Body cameras represent a liberal, legalistic approach to police reform. They are a techno-regulatory mechanism designed to acquire evidence for use in legal proceedings. And as a state-supported response to bystander video and other forms of increasing police visibilities, they predominantly legitimize official, state narratives and the use of state police power, often at the expense of individual privacy interests. Rather than representing the same form of "regulation by recording" that we see with bystander video (focused most directly on democratic police oversight), police body cameras predominantly serve state surveillance and investigatory purposes. Understanding how the police view body-worn cameras and the range of their subjective concerns provides a lens for unpacking the epistemologies and information politics that the body cameras generate within the police and how these might then be projected onto the communities they serve. Indeed, as noted earlier, if "the environment in which officers act is one they largely project, act in accord with, and reify," then understanding police officers' perceptions of body-worn camera technology and its emerging role in their work can reveal quite a lot about police power in society.[1]

At this point, we should return to where we began. My purposes throughout this book have been to examine how the crossed lenses of police body cameras and bystander video cameras make police and civilians more visible, to question how these forms of surveillance are changing the information politics at play within the police, to interrogate how the adoption of body-worn cameras is changing police work on the ground, and to develop an argument for how we ought to balance privacy and transparency interests within this rapidly evolving context. In reality, despite claims that body-worn cameras are different and more desirable than traditional surveillance technologies, my findings demonstrate that they are not. They are not simply a transparency mechanism for overseeing the police and ensuring "good" police behavior. Indeed, police body-worn cameras have become tools of information politics and police image work that legitimize official police narratives and do little to encourage greater trust between police and those who live in their communities. Indeed, the sense of police fragility or vulnerability exposed in my findings, as a consequence of increased police visibility at a time when police-community relationships are faltering, works to solidify destructive us/them mentalities. Body-worn cameras exacerbate preexisting police-society tensions related to subservience and separation, possibly forcing the police and society further apart rather than healing wounds and bridging rifts. They also make individuals, especially the most policed and marginalized members of society, more visible to the state as well as to the rest of society.

Even if police body cameras were primarily effective as sousveillance tools for watching the police, the collateral consequences for individual privacy are a substantial side effect that cannot be ignored. This refractive surveillance has already led to widespread visibility of various individuals' sensitive personal encounters with police. But what is the solution? As it is unlikely that police body cameras, and whatever new surveillance technologies they lead to in the future, are going away anytime soon, lawmakers must enact appropriate legislation to establish rules to govern and regulate these tools. Rules are needed to regulate the adoption and use of surveillance technologies by law enforcement agencies, both retroactively and in ways that future-proof such regulation rather than merely tying it to specific forms of technology. In the pages that follow, I argue that we should regulate the police in ways that forestall their ability to establish de facto information and surveillance policies through the unregulated procurement and deployment of surveillance technologies prior to public deliberation, debate, and consent. This argument is largely about limiting the potential for body-worn cameras to increase police power while also enhancing the ability of communities to understand and control the power their local police agencies wield. It is about moving away from a society characterized by surveillance and domination to one of sousveillance and antipower.

The world has shifted from a situation, which had existed for most of human existence, where citizens had virtually no power to demand access to government records, to a contemporary recognition of access to information as an important human and political right. The public sphere, which combines public access to the flow of information as well as public forums in which citizens may express themselves, is vitally important to the ability of citizens to critique government action and "its monopoly on interpretation of political and social issues" and is essential to protect basic civil liberties.[2] However, the proliferation of increasingly sophisticated surveillance and data-intensive technologies in concert with the consequences of some outdated information access laws has placed the legitimacy of current legal frameworks into question, as similarly important human or civil rights, such as the right to privacy, become the unintended victims of our legacy information policies.

Law defines the boundaries between police surveillance and information gathering, on the one hand, and public rights to access information or record police conduct, on the other. Restricting public access to information limits the ability of the public to oversee government activity, but it also protects the privacy and dignity of individual citizens whose information may be contained in government records, including surveillance footage. The First Amendment protects the "right to record," yet state and federal law places few limits on technology adoption by police departments, regulating such technology use only when it facilitates unwarranted searches in specific cases.

Freedom of information laws are vital to many aspects of democratic governance; they allow for transparency and heightened accountability within publicly funded agencies and government and provide the citizenry with information that can be used for a wide variety of social goods, including supporting free speech principles. (Of course they are only one of many checks on government power and should be viewed within the broader context of police transparency practices and accountability measures.) However, as governments collect increasing amounts of information about their citizens and others living within (or even outside) their borders, some of this personal information may be subject to public disclosure. Absent exceptions to disclosure, this information ceases to be private, no matter how sensitive, merely because a government agency holds it within its possession—and regardless of whether the information was obtained voluntarily and knowingly, surreptitiously, or by compulsion. We then have, as Solove has argued, a situation where governments "compel individuals to reveal a vast amount of personal information about themselves" and then "routinely [pour] this information into the public domain—by posting it on the Internet where it could be accessed from all over the world, by giving it away to any individual or company that asked for it, or even by providing entire databases of personal information upon request."[3] Such is the case with police body-worn camera adoption, as demonstrated in the preceding chapters in this book. As such, we have a situation where governments can compel a lack of personal information privacy, not just vis-à-vis the government itself, which arguably has a strong claim to need some personal information from its citizens. But there is no reason why these claims should then extend to unlimited—and *legally mandated*—disclosure of this information to any member of the requesting public, which can lead to significant privacy intrusions.

Much current liberal privacy theory fails to adequately protect privacy in an age of ubiquitous vertical and horizontal surveillance. Modern surveillance capabilities, including increasingly sophisticated forms of *vision*, the aggregation of personal information across time and disparate systems—related to various concepts (e.g., what Solove calls the "database problem," what Haggerty and Ericson call the "surveillant assemblage," and what legal commentators have called the "mosaic")—and the permanence of digital memory all point to a need to rethink how we structure privacy rights, from both a moral and a legal perspective.[4] Additionally, liberal conceptions of liberty and privacy based on restricting actual negative interference fail to coherently explain how covert surveillance that never results in actual interference with a person's life can constitute a privacy violation. However, viewing privacy and freedom through the lens of republican theory, we can explain the harm caused by these forms of surveillance by reference to the concept of *domination*. A republican conceptualization of privacy "grounded on the idea of freedom as non-domination can explain a loss of privacy where there is no subsequent interference in terms of negative freedom."[5] As Roberts has clearly stated, "At the root of our anxieties about loss of privacy, is concern about what republicans will recognize as domination. While liberals can explain how a loss of privacy that does not lead to any interference might affect the individual's autonomy, where she is unaware of the loss, they will have difficulty in explaining the value of privacy."[6]

Viewing freedom as antipower—as the absence of domination by another—allows us to respect the importance of noninterference, but also to recognize that some forms of interference (those that are not arbitrary or without recourse) do not necessarily restrict our freedom but may only condition it. In this view, we can see that proper application of the nonvoluntaristic rule of law (with opportunities for effective appeal and democratic participation) actually protects and preserves our freedoms, rather than restricting them as a means to some other end. A person living under a friendly despot is not in the same position—in terms of freedom—as the person living in a properly constituted constitutional democracy with limits on domination. Fully realizing a situation of more equalized reciprocal surveillance and rights to access information about government activities (with exceptions as may be needed to protect certain state or private interests) would give citizens greater ability to ensure their government was not overreaching and abusing its authority, to hold the state and state actors accountable for rights violations, and to maintain government as an entity that protects it citizens' freedoms without coming to subjugate them under the arbitrary exercise of power.

However, the public disclosure of personal information held in state surveillance databases should be weighed against its implications for personal privacy and its relevance to democratic self-governance, and redaction may be an important tool to help balance the tensions at play between privacy and access. Consequently, the version of neorepublican theory developed here as an instrumental means to construct an original information policy provides valuable insights into how one-sided surveillance powers and control of information vested in states can limit individual freedom. Applying neorepublican political theory to information policy concerns in this context represents an important and novel application of these valuable ideas with the capacity to inform future information policy research and the development of better laws and policies related to surveillance, secrecy, and access to information.

When an individual's personal information is captured—in identifiable form and without their knowledge—by a passing police officer's body camera, and this information is subsequently stored in a police database but not actually accessed or used in any way, no actual (negative) interference has occurred. Negative liberal theories of privacy have difficulty explaining how privacy is violated, in this case, prior to any subsequent access to or use of this information by the state. A control-based definition of privacy—which I have incorporated into my broader theory here—does provide an argument that such information collection would violate a person's right to control access to that information—especially when our presence in public spaces cannot necessarily be considered entirely consensual. However, this limit on access to publicly visible information—without deeper justification—seems overly broad precisely because it would effectively limit all surveillance in public spaces absent particularized justifications from the police. In effect, it would prohibit all forms of persistent surveillance, including the use of, among others, CCTV cameras, ALPR cameras, and body cameras, except in cases where police had acquired, for example, a warrant or some other form of particularized justification. The republican account, however, opens the way for such collection to occur, in the first instance, but only when citizens are sufficiently empowered to conduct oversight (i.e., when sufficient antipower exists) and when other limitations have been put into place to prevent the arbitrary use of the information against individuals.

The potential violation of privacy in these scenarios cannot be explained by simply resorting to a focus on subjective (extending to *actual subjective perceptions* of surveillance) or objective (requiring some actual "use of information about a person against that person") theories of privacy harm.[7] However, republican theory can explain the violation in these cases by reference to domination: the existence of a state of affairs in which one entity *could interfere*, should it choose to, with another person's agency. This sort of covert collection generates the potential for arbitrary interference by the state in the lives of innocent citizens and ought to be limited by requiring the institutionalization—into legal doctrine, the design of the technology itself, and institutional practice—of elements of semantic discontinuity as a means to increase obscurity and empower democratic deliberation and a state of "play in everyday practice."[8] Only then can a theory satisfactorily account for conflicts between personal information privacy rights, government surveillance, and government disclosure of personally identifiable information contained in public records under access to information laws. In the context of police body-worn camera adoption, this argues against always-on recording practices and the broad public disclosure of footage containing information about private members of the community.

In modern society, states are conducting enormous amounts of surveillance—both online and offline—and are amassing huge databases of information about citizens (and others) within the scope of their searches. In many cases, the state clearly has the actual capacity (rather than merely "virtual" or unrealized capacity) to exercise arbitrary power over dominated persons based on its power to collect and control information about those persons. The state may choose to enact its power through a variety of means, including by coercion, arrest (or threat of arrest or punishment), or limiting or refusing to release information. It is also clear that restricting (chilling) a person's free expression, First Amendment right to gather information, or right to acquire information about government activity causes harm and affects a person's choices. This is especially apparent when, under Pettit's account of freedom, a subjugating interference with a person's choices may be limited to certain choices of varying centrality or importance and need not totally remove all choices available to that person. Such interference by police officers or law enforcement (and the policy- or lawmaking processes behind the enforcement) also clearly equates to "an intentional attempt to worsen an agent's situation of choice" because it represents an intentional act that eliminates certain information that might be relevant to the decision-making process of the agent in that situation.[9]

Since the Fourth Amendment generally does not protect against the government's collection of information through surveillance in public spaces, many forms of surveillance (e.g., use of body cameras, drones, cameras, license plate readers, and mining personal information on the internet) may not be subject to much real scrutiny through democratic processes or legal proceedings in courts of law. The legal and practical restrictions on citizens wanting to document or access information about government conduct, combined with the power of government to watch its citizens, represents an imbalanced situation where citizens lack the antipower they might otherwise command. As a result, we should question whether this is a situation in which "the powerless are not going to be able to look the powerful in the eye, conscious as each will be—and conscious as each will be of the other's consciousness—of this asymmetry. Both will share an awareness that the powerless can do nothing except by the leave of the powerful: that the powerless are at the mercy of the powerful and not on equal terms. The master–slave scenario will materialize, and the asymmetry between the two sides will be a communicative as well as an objective reality."[10]

Perhaps this overstates the case somewhat. However, when the people do not have access to all the information that supposedly supports the government's need to conduct various types of electronic surveillance, they do not have full access to information about what the government has done with the powers it has been given. This is inherently problematic, especially under the neorepublican position that governments should protect their people's freedoms and ensure that the state does not come to dominate its people in any arbitrary fashion. Without some form of effective democratic check in place—some way for the public to make informed, deliberative choices based on real information—abuse (and domination) is always a real possibility. Perhaps it is best—even essential—that citizens grant their governments some power to restrict public access to information for various purposes like criminal investigation, but this does not mean that citizens should not have the right to insist on safeguards and the right to ensure that government complies with constitutional requirements in the exercise of its power. If that were so, the exercise of power would cease to be arbitrary, and the action would not be subjugating. The people would retain antipower.

OUTLINING A THEORY OF INFORMATION POLICY: ACCESS AND PRIVACY

There are compelling reasons to define freedom in republican terms as the absence of domination (itself defined as the potential for arbitrary interference). It is also clear that surveillance generates information, the control of which creates and facilitates power, potentially implicating domination. Because the people are sovereign and should retain antipower vis-à-vis their government, there should be a presumption that the people retain the right to access government information and to document information about how the government discharges its duties. Forms of reciprocal surveillance (e.g., filing public records requests or recording police officers with their smartphones) support this type of antipower—that is, the power of some over others that reduces domination.

However, a presumption, by definition, may be overcome in appropriate circumstances, and a more robust description and explication of the appropriate threshold is in order. In some instances, it might be appropriate for a state to withhold information from its people (potentially an act of domination if the people have not granted such power), acting unilaterally or on its own, for the protection of the people, as long as certain safeguards are put in place to properly respect the sovereignty of the people. Thus, building on this argument, we can see that the state, absent powers granted by its citizens, may not generally withhold information about its activities from its people or deny them the right to access information about government activity, because such actions are acts of domination. However, as stated earlier, this theory does have room to entertain the idea that certain state interests may sometimes justify the state in withholding information from its citizens, despite the possibility that such withholding may infringe upon the people's antipower, thus overcoming the initial presumption. Privacy should be seen as an adequate justification for overcoming this initial presumption in favor of access.

Of course the public disclosure of information collected through state surveillance may include personal information about civilians, implicating their right to privacy. When personal information that could create dominating power when controlled by the state is released to the public under the guise of state transparency, we have a situation where individual visibility becomes the collateral damage of our transparency regime—what I have referred to herein as *collateral visibility*. Absent clear and informed consent to access or use personal information, the state should be empowered (and required to) to protect citizens against violations of their privacy that would result in domination by the state, corporate interests, or other private individuals. Importantly, in this respect there is a significant difference (in terms of the threat to antipower) between government decisions regarding secrecy (and the related risks to law enforcement) of

1. the substantive information collected by the government (i.e., the actual information or metadata collected through mechanisms of surveillance), and
2. the procedural information about how the government conducts its activities (surveillance activities or otherwise) or the legal bases and processes that authorize such conduct.

This division rests on the idea that the Constitution protects the people from certain inappropriate actions of government (e.g., the Fourth Amendment prohibition on unreasonable and unjustified searches or seizures). Domination is also more clearly implicated in terms of government conduct (or the potentiality of arbitrary conduct) that interferes with a person's situation of choice than it is with the nature of the underlying information. Thus, the following distinctions need to be made.

First, there is a greater abrogation of the people's antipower when the state withholds information about the *methods and procedures* used by the state to collect the information and to approve information-gathering activities of the state than when the state withholds *substantive information* collected by the state about its citizens or other targets.

Second, if the state collects information about its citizens but denies them the right to know what information has been collected about them, the state has acted in a dominating manner, unless the people themselves have authorized the government to withhold such information and sufficient constitutional safeguards have been put in place to ensure civil liberties are not violated. Therefore, the state has an obligation to not disclose substantive personal information in some cases (those implicating domination), and this information should be redacted prior to disclosure, except when individuals are seeking access to information about themselves held by the government. If the state exercises its surveillance powers but denies its citizens the right to know or document how this information was collected and what procedural requirements were met to authorize such information gathering, then the state has acted in a dominating way by eliminating the citizens' antipower and has come to impermissibly dominate its citizens because it has eliminated the sovereign right of its people to ensure that their government protects their freedom and constitutional rights. Likewise, a government acts in a dominating fashion when it engages in the initial collection of its citizens' personal information without their knowledge and informed consent.

The preceding argument leads to the conclusion that because the people are sovereign, they should presumptively retain the right to access and document information about how their government conducts the activities and duties entrusted to it by them. This presumptive right of access encompasses information about how government agents conduct surveillance and what information is gathered through such surveillance activities, subject only to determinations by the people themselves that certain information be kept secret. In any case, the state may not withhold information about the methods and procedures used to gather the information or the procedural requirements used to authorize such information gathering.

However, at least one additional problem needs to be addressed at this point. The allowance just made for government secrecy must be tempered. If it is not, the people's antipower has been severely limited, and the state retains much of the power that the argument presented in this book has sought to limit. The allowance was predicated on the assumption that sometimes certain information ought to be secret to protect the people's interests in security and protection by the state from outside evils. But such secrecy does not necessarily need to persist for lengthy periods of time, and certainly not in perpetuity. Sunlight provisions, or enforceable and mandatory declassification provisions, would provide a balance between law enforcement interests (when those interests are present and legitimate) and the people's right to sovereignty and liberty by providing a form of retroactive accountability. This idea, despite its simplicity, is an incredibly important core issue and is vital to a proper balancing of the security and liberty interests at stake.

Thus, we may concede that substantive information collected by governments may sometimes be withheld from the people, because release would compromise legitimate privacy or security interests, without eliminating the usefulness or force of our neorepublican conception of freedom. But, as just stated, withholding this information in perpetuity always impermissibly infringes the people's antipower, unless the people effectively retain the right to override the state's ability to classify the information in perpetuity. Thus, when government surveillance information is withheld from the people, it should only be temporarily withheld, mandatory sunlight provisions should be specified clearly in the law, and the people should retain the power to ensure information is released consistent with the relevant sunlight provision(s). Importantly, such provisions might also contain clauses that allow the people to hold state actors accountable for violations of their rights after the information is lawfully declassified, should violations of constitutional or legal rights be identified.

This argument provides justification—based on republican concerns for liberty and a robust opportunity for citizen oversight of state action—for broad laws on access to information (as well as a robust right to record). Within this context, privacy and free speech should both be protected for two reasons: they limit the possibility of arbitrary interference by another with an individual's choices, and they promote the ability of the people to engage in open (or closed) democratic deliberation and active civic participation. When privacy and free speech are not in conflict, they both promote these ends and are not in significant tension. In some cases, government records might contain both information relevant to self-governance and purely personal information about individuals. When these pieces of information can be teased apart, we ought to require disclosure *after* redaction to protect the substantive personal information from disclosure. However, when these values conflict (i.e., when the personal information is inextricably tied to, or is itself related to, issues of state accountability or other aspects of self-governance), the presumption for access ought to prevail.

Each of these rights should be protected vigorously as far as they don't interfere with the rights of another person or group. The right to free speech—or to access government information—should trump the right to privacy when the speech at issue concerns information relevant to self-governance (a difficult question, admittedly), but when speech is not related to self-governance and another's privacy interests are implicated, privacy should prevail. When government records contain both sensitive personal information and information about government surveillance, for instance, partial disclosure and redaction is entirely appropriate as a means to separate the two types of information as much as possible. Speech in the public interest (defined narrowly to include speech relevant to governance and deliberation about social issues), then, may prevail over privacy rights in some cases, but ought to do so only when public access to the personal information is *necessary for informed choices about proper governance* (e.g., the public should be able to talk candidly about a public official involved in a scandal or the illegal activities or misconduct of a police officer). However, body-camera footage filmed inside a person's home during a domestic violence response should not become part of the public record unless, and until, an officer is charged with an allegation of misconduct. Even in this scenario, redaction of personal information not relevant to the misconduct allegation should be required under thoughtfully crafted public records legislation.

INFORMATION POLICY IN CONTEXT

The deployment of body-worn cameras may only support citizen oversight and law enforcement accountability efforts when either the cameras are always on (i.e., officers have no discretion as to when/whether the cameras are recording) or officers adhere to strict guidelines requiring activation during every citizen encounter (unlikely without strict policies, active oversight and enforcement, and engaged supervision). Additionally, when balancing privacy and oversight interests, it is important that citizens have ex post access to recorded footage to dispute charges or challenge officer conduct, that access to recorded footage is strictly regulated to information relevant to active (or potential) official investigations or prosecutions (of police OR civilian misconduct) and to proper personnel, and that footage is consistently and routinely destroyed in a manner that respects the requirements just described. Additionally, because "freedom from surveillance . . . is foundational to the practice of informed and reflective citizenship," laws and regulations that encode "gaps and imperfections in systems of control and surveillance" should be encouraged.[11]

Fundamentally, I agree with Westin that "the achievement of privacy for individuals, families, and groups in modern society has become a matter of freedom rather than the product of necessity."[12] Like Cohen, I also argue that "privacy . . . is an indispensable structural feature of liberal democratic political systems."[13] Viewed through the lens of republican political theory, privacy is also broadly valuable because it allows us to conceptualize how individual privacy can be violated in situations involving direct interference by another entity (the typical case addressed in many liberal theories), as well as when an individual is "aware that he has suffered a loss of privacy, but suffers no subsequent interference" and when the person "is unaware that he has suffered any loss of privacy, and suffers no subsequent interference."[14] This conceptualization of privacy would support the aims of antipower and provide robust privacy rights in an age of ubiquitous vertical (panoptic) and horizontal (omnioptic) surveillance, even when such surveillance is conducted covertly and results in harms not always detectable by reference to identifiable interference.

Obviously, then, the contours of public disclosure regulations play an important role at the nexus of privacy and oversight interests. In seeking to preserve the ability for oversight while also preventing state domination through the realities of secondary (collateral) visibility, a few principles are in order:

1. **Independent oversight.** We ought to challenge the common assumption that the agencies themselves should act as gatekeepers to the records they create. Independent oversight boards, who might be responsible for overseeing police agency and officer conduct more broadly, could also play a heightened role as informational gatekeepers to public records. This should remove some of the adversarial information politics from the request process, decrease the ability of police institutions to dictate how they become visible to their communities, and open up opportunities for less costly appeals and dispute resolution procedures (not requiring requesters to file suit in court as the first avenue for seeking redress).
2. **Access.** It seems reasonable to assert that the individuals depicted in body-camera footage should always have access to those recordings, especially when they are the subjects of the police-citizen interactions depicted. Without this rule, body cameras would play the part of state surveillance with no corresponding

oversight function, eviscerating the very possibility of oversight by those directly harmed by the police. This rule would allow those charged with crimes or claiming police misconduct to bring evidence to light that may (or may not) help prove their case, and it also respects the rights of individuals to be informed about what information the state's surveillance has captured about them so that they can exercise their right to control subsequent use of such information.

3. **Redaction.** Because the personal information of bystanders, victims, witnesses, and even suspects is not likely to be needed to demonstrate police misconduct, blurring or otherwise obscuring or redacting identifiable information about these individuals prior to disclosure should be built into public disclosure laws and agency policies. Excluding wider public access to the recorded footage may sometimes restrict the ability of the public and news media to serve important functions as watchdog. This limit to citizen oversight, on a basic level, reduces the effective antipower available to society and risks reifying dominating structures within government and law enforcement agencies. When the footage is recorded in public spaces, because of the claim that presence in public may involve a waiver of the right to access such information, the public's interest in access to footage may outweigh the full denial of requests for that footage, but this concern can be accommodated by requiring the redaction of the faces or other identifiable features of those individuals whose identities are not key to the oversight purposes of such access (e.g., innocent bystanders).

4. **Private space.** Footage captured within a person's home or other private area, or that depict particularly sensitive personal information or situations, should by default be protected more stringently than footage captured in public or outside locations or that does not implicate heightened privacy interests. Property rights, like speech and privacy, also serve important liberty interests. Property rights also encapsulate privacy interests, and in this case, spatial property rights should protect informational privacy interests in footage filmed in nonpublic spaces, particularly inside private homes. These limits protect individuals from interference and domination by states or private agents, as well as from the prying eyes of neighbors and the voyeuristic

> tendencies of strangers. Likewise, because of the enhanced claim to privacy in a person's home as opposed to in a public space (e.g., a park or public sidewalk), public access to such footage under FOI laws should only be allowed when the person whose property and privacy interests are at issue consents to such disclosure.

In addition, although much of the discussion here in the conclusion has shifted to issues of privacy and access to information, we should not lose sight of the empirical realities about how body-worn camera adoption is shifting power relationships and the informational practices of the police—those ideas explored in the central chapters of this book. Understanding and critically examining police perspectives can allow us to create better-informed law and policy in our attempts to regulate police behavior and police power in society. At a time when police reform and Black Lives Matter protests have been more sustained than at any point in recent decades, we have an opportunity to rethink the use and regulation of surveillance technologies by the police in our communities. Fixing the situation is clearly not as simple as merely placing cameras on cops, and we must do more, and more thoughtful, work on regulating the police in the months and years to come.

CONCLUSION

The findings presented throughout this book provide a clear link between existing studies of policing on camera; policing and new media; and the important, and evolving, state of information politics within contemporary police organizations. In the end, the negotiations of power in this context, from the choice to record—or resist—to navigating the presentation, disclosure and dissemination, framing, and interpretation of bystander and body-camera video, are all forms of information politics. Bystander recording confronts officers with two distinct challenges: dealing with video and the visibility it can bring and dealing with bystanders who may or may not be conventional witnesses, victims, or suspects. Officers are also beginning to use their own visual technologies (e.g., body cameras) to counter claims of misconduct or evidence they feel misrepresents their actions, including making conscious choices about how and what to record that impact their behavior on the job. Rather than being emancipatory systems of police oversight, body-worn cameras are an evolution in police image work and state surveillance power.

The concerns officers have about their own visibility—including about objectivity, documentation, transparency, and accountability—and their responses all manifest as parts of a broader intersecting of the politics of information, surveillance, and the police. Each side struggles to manipulate information access and information control for political gain and to use cameras and online hosting platforms as "decisive tool[s] of power-making."[15] This is an information politics fed by the coercive powers of surveillance and the ambiguity of vision. In an era referred to as the "The End of Forgetting," where "social power is not only premised on what is concealed" but rather "is increasingly constituted in the act of revelation," understanding the effects of this new visibility on policing and the role played by public disclosure law and the affordances of new media in this process has become vitally important to our tasks of organizing, understanding, and overseeing both the police and the new media platforms that afford such increased visibility.[16]

Likewise, understanding the subjective social reality of the police, as projected by the police themselves, along with observation of their information practices, we gain an understanding of how body-worn camera adoption is generative of information politics within the police and how this may impact the way they work in their communities. Indeed, understanding police officers' perceptions of the technology and its role in their work can reveal quite a lot about police power in society, because "officers create the social reality that they police" by "filtering information . . . sifted through officers' screening mechanisms," including information from the citizenry in their local communities, and "the environment in which officers act is one they largely project, act in accord with, and reify."[17] Indeed, my findings suggest that this projection flows from a sense of fragility or vulnerability and that this sense works to solidify destructive us/them mentalities. Body-worn cameras exacerbate preexisting police-society tensions related to subservience and separation, possibly forcing the police and society further apart rather than healing wounds and bridging rifts.

Methodological Note

In this note, I provide an overview of the methodological choices made throughout the planning and execution of my underlying empirical research.

I am greatly indebted to the many officers who took the time to allow me to ride along with them or ask them questions. There were, of course, barriers, and I had to gain the trust of those I was speaking with. However, in many respects, my experience with officers can be characterized by something one patrol officer from Bellingham wrote in (an anonymous) response to a qualitative survey question: "Buy me a beer sometime and I'll tell you more" (Terence, patrol officer, BPD, 2014).

METHODS

The findings discussed throughout this book emerged from a primarily qualitative analysis of data collected through fieldwork (interviews, observation, ride-alongs) and surveys of police officers in two municipal police agencies in the Pacific Northwest. At the midpoint of the study, the Bellingham Police Department (BPD) employed approximately 110 sworn personnel, with over 60 personnel assigned to patrol (including K–9) and over 50 non-sworn civilian personnel. The department had jurisdiction over 31.7 square miles and served a population of more than 83,000 citizens. The Spokane Police Department (SPD) employed approximately 310 sworn personnel, with over 140 personnel assigned to Patrol, and just over 100 non-sworn civilian personnel. The department had a jurisdiction of roughly 76 square miles and served a population of more than 210,000 citizens.

Washington State provided a particularly useful jurisdictional boundary for this research because of a confluence of factors, including the breadth of the state's public records law and its recently confirmed precedence over state privacy law; provisions in the state's Privacy Act that restrict audio recording in some circumstances without the consent of all parties to a conversation; and the fact that the recent release of largely unredacted body-worn camera footage to members of the public within the state has forced questions about privacy versus disclosure into the public spotlight—and, in 2016, resulted in a number of additional body camera–related exemptions being added to the state's public disclosure law. To be sure, Washington is not alone in experiencing the ramifications of the adoption of body-worn cameras, but the conflicts between privacy and public disclosure have come to a head in Washington as in no other state to date, and the lessons learned in Washington have the potential to inform the regulation of body-camera use in other jurisdictions. My access to the agencies that took part in this research was also a consequence of my physical presence in Washington—when the study began, I was a doctoral student at the University of Washington in Seattle—and is also partly due to connections made during some preliminary research with technology developers working for TASER (now Axon) on that company's backend software solution for agencies deploying its brand of body-worn cameras.

No experimental (i.e., treatment/control) conditions were implemented during the initial rollout of either department's body-worn camera program, although the SPD implemented an experimental deployment starting in May 2015, partway through the current study. Instead, each department allowed most officers to volunteer (opt-in) to wear a camera (BPD only mandated camera use by new recruits and lateral transfers to the department). Both departments used TASER AXON Flex and/or TASER AXON Body cameras, and the departments also both utilized TASER's Evidence.com digital evidence management platform for storage of, access to, and analysis of the captured footage.

The research was approved by the University of Washington's Human Subjects Division (IRB), and the electronic versions of the survey questionnaires were administered using the University of Washington's proprietary Catalyst survey system under the "anonymous/IRB" setting, which does not track IP addresses or time-stamp information related to responses. Participation in all research procedures was voluntary, and respondents were asked to agree only after being presented with an information statement outlining the nature of the research as well as the possible risks and benefits of participation.

The data collection encompassed forty ride-alongs with twenty-nine officers, ranging in duration from a few hours to entire ten-hour-and-forty-minute shifts, as well as numerous informal discussions with other officers and department administrators and a series of four surveys (in 2014, 2015, 2016, and 2017–18, respectively). Interviews were informal, and detailed written and audio fieldnotes were made during breaks and shortly after each ride-along. The survey questionnaires, which were designed primarily to inform the qualitative investigation and, as appropriate, validate whether certain themes drawn from the qualitative work were shared across the two departments, resulted in 148, 133, 126, and 102 valid responses, respectively, across both departments.

The first questionnaire (Survey 1) was administered in the fall of 2014, just at—or shortly after—the point when each department began issuing body-worn cameras to officers.[1] The first questionnaires were distributed on paper to BPD officers attending a body-camera orientation and training meeting in September 2014, just prior to the cameras being deployed in the field as part of the department's body-camera program. Twenty-nine officers returned valid responses to the paper administration, with twenty-four of those reporting that they were going to be wearing cameras during the upcoming deployment. Subsequently, a link to an electronic version of the questionnaire was emailed to the remaining officers in the department, resulting in twenty-one additional valid responses prior to the survey closing on December 22, 2014. Consequently, some of these responses were received just prior to the camera deployment (n = 29), and some were received afterward, during the first three months of the program (n = 21).

At SPD, the first survey was distributed electronically to officers via email on October 20, 2014 (about 1.5 months after the department's body-worn camera program began) and closed on December 22, 2014. Ninety-eight officers returned valid responses during this two-month period, with twenty-one respondents (21%) reporting they were already wearing cameras, and another sixty-five (66%) reporting they expected to wear one in the future during the ongoing deployment.

The initial questionnaire contained thirty-one questions, although some matrix questions contained multiple rows, resulting in a total number of requested response items of forty-six to forty-eight depending on responses to certain demographic questions. Three of these questions asked for qualitative written answers, and the rest were presented in the form of multiple-choice questions or as five-point Likert scales. Roughly four of the survey questions related to public disclosure of body-worn camera footage, and a number of additional questions asked about other privacy-related issues. The questionnaire did not ask respondents for their names, and the electronic version did not track IP addresses. In total, 148 valid responses were received for Survey 1 across both departments.

The second survey (Survey 2), which was a modified and expanded version of the first, was administered entirely online in both departments. It was available from May 23, 2015, to June 29, 2015. Officers were emailed a link to the questionnaire and were asked to participate in the follow-up survey, regardless of whether they had taken the first one. The questionnaire included most of the questions from the first one (to facilitate some longitudinal comparison) as well as some additional questions that had emerged during the qualitative fieldwork or to seek information about how officers had used the cameras (for those who had) during the intervening months between the surveys.

The base questionnaire included forty-three to forty-five items (for those who had not used a camera), four of which sought a qualitative response, with an additional twelve items asked only of those officers who had previously been assigned a camera. One new question related to public disclosure was added. The questionnaire, like the first, did not ask respondents for their names and did not track IP addresses. In total, 133 valid responses were received for Survey 2, 49 from BPD (41% of whom reported having previously used a body-worn camera) and 84 from SPD (42% having previously used a body-worn camera).

The third survey (Survey 3) was also largely based on the earlier questionnaires but included some modifications (again, building on additional issues of interest that had emerged from the qualitative research). Survey 3 was available from June 1, 2016, to June 30, 2016. Officers were emailed a link to the questionnaire and were asked to participate in a follow-up survey, regardless of whether they had taken either of the previous surveys. In addition to questions from the earlier surveys, this questionnaire also included some additional questions based on legislative developments in the interim and designed to elicit more specific responses to questions about how (or whether) officers inform civilians about the presence of the cameras and the attendant public disclosure risks, how officers perceive citizens react to the presence of the cameras, and use of cameras in medical facilities or to record victim or witness statements, as well as to gauge officer reactions to recent changes in state public disclosure law.

The base questionnaire included fifty-seven to fifty-nine items (for those who had not used a camera), four of which sought a qualitative response, with an additional eighteen items asked only of those officers who indicated they had previously been (or currently were) assigned a camera. The questionnaire, like the first two, did not ask respondents for their names and did not track IP addresses. In total, 126 valid responses were received for Survey 3, 56 from BPD (68% reporting having used a body-worn camera) and 70 from SPD (73% reporting body-worn camera use).

As well as adding items (questions), the format of some of the Likert-scale response items was also modified; whereas the first two surveys had included neutral responses as the fifth and final response choice (generally labeled "unsure" or "neutral"), the neutral response option for these questions on the third survey was presented as the median (e.g., third of five) response choice (and was labeled, e.g., "neither agree nor disagree" or "neither a positive nor a negative development"). The choice to alter the format of these Likert-scale items was made to enable additional comparison between the results from Survey 3 and recently reported results presented by other researchers studying officer attitudes in other police agencies.[2] However, the movement of the neutral option from position five to position three, and the change in label, do complicate (and compromise, to some extent) the validity of internal comparisons between the first two surveys and Survey 3. In fact, in Survey 3, the neutral response choice was often selected more frequently per question than in the first two surveys, indicating that the earlier placement had the effect of forcing respondents to commit to a more polarized position in the first two surveys. Thus, when the neutral choice was selected more frequently, the percentages of respondents indicating, for example, that they agreed or disagreed with a particular statement fell. This methodological limitation should be considered when interpreting the results presented here.

The fourth survey, essentially a copy of the third, was distributed to BPD officers electronically in the summer of 2017. Due to a request from the SPD administration, the questionnaire was not distributed at SPD until December 2017 and was open until mid-January 2018.

In all four surveys, officers were asked qualitative and quantitative questions designed to elicit their attitudes and concerns about the use of body-worn cameras, bystanders recording them while they work, and the dissemination of these recordings online. Data analysis involved multiple rounds of emergent coding of the qualitative data alongside the exploration of descriptive statistics based on the quantitative response items from the surveys. As the analysis progressed, the initial codes were consolidated and organized into general categories as themes emerged from both the interviews and qualitative survey response data. All qualitative data were then recoded against a final coding manual.

Most respondents and interviewees were male (84% to 93% across surveys) and white (84% to 88% across surveys), and most also reported having worked in a law enforcement capacity for more than ten years (69% to 80% across surveys), with only a very small number of respondents reporting fewer than five years of professional law enforcement experience (3% to 10%). Potential limitations to the study's findings include the limited sampling of newer, nonmale, and nonwhite officers in both the ride-alongs and survey responses (although the samples generally reflect the overall demographic composition of the two departments, at least in terms of sex and race). Future research should do more to understand how the perceptions of newer recruits, female, or nonwhite officers might differ from their more senior, male, or white colleagues.

Across the four surveys, regular (patrol, traffic, etc.) officers constituted between 45 and 63 percent of all respondents. Between 24 and 30 percent of respondents in each survey reported serving in higher ranking, mostly supervisory, positions. Additionally, between 8 and 10 percent of respondents reported being detectives or investigators. Ride-alongs were conducted primarily with regular patrol officers but also included three sergeants, two corporals, and one crime scene investigator. Additional interviews and informal conversations were conducted with higher ranking members of the departments' command staff, civilian staff, and additional patrol officers.

In addition to the surveys just described, I also conducted ride-alongs with officers in both departments—and while doing so observed the officers throughout the course of their shifts and conducted informal interviews with them. Some additional data were collected during short, informal conversations with other officers inside the police stations or when small groups of officers gathered for breaks or meals. The introduction to this article is one example of the analysis generated by this qualitative work. I was generally announced to officers during shift briefing meetings (roll call) or by email before a shift and was often able to approach officers on my own (either in person or via email) and request to ride with particular officers. In some cases, and especially in the early stages of the research, a supervisor would email a set of officers who were wearing cameras and ask them to accommodate me as a rider during a shift. Most officers who responded to my requests were willing to allow me to accompany them. Over time, some officers recognized me when I showed up at the station, and this recognition also led to additional requests for rides (and subsequent rides) with a number of officers. At a late stage in the project, two graduate students also completed ride-alongs (using the same general methodology) and contributed to the project. In total, the project encompassed forty ride-alongs with twenty-nine different officers, ranging from a few hours to entire ten-hour-and-forty-minute shifts, as well as numerous informal discussions with other officers and department administrators. In all cases, we made simple field notes during breaks or downtimes during a shift, which we developed further and expanded after a shift had ended (generally within a few hours).

LEGAL RESEARCH

Doctrinal legal research is the study and analysis of legal texts (e.g., statutes and judicial decisions) and rules with the aim of developing and understanding legal doctrine.[3] It involves "a synthesis of various rules, principles, norms, interpretive guidelines and values."[4] However, knowing doctrine itself does not provide a complete picture of the law; that requires application of legal rules and doctrine "to the particular facts of the situation under consideration."[5] Doctrinal legal research has long dominated the legal academy—of which it is the "core legal research method"—but "until relatively recently there has been no necessity to explain or classify it within any broader cross-disciplinary research framework."[6] Relatedly, very little academic legal research contains any methodological description, and when it does—typically when the research is interdisciplinary, it involves empirical data collection or is comparative—an article's methods section only describes the social scientific methodologies employed (e.g., sampling, case selection). As stated by Hutchinson and Duncan, "the doctrinal method is often so implicit and so tacit that many working within the legal paradigm consider that it is unnecessary to verbalise the process."[7] That is not to say the method should not be described in any detail, but merely to situate the method within its real-world context: well-utilized and practiced by lawyers and legal academics, but undertheorized and undercritiqued within and outside the discipline.

In the instant study, I conducted legal research into the regulation of the use of body-worn camera technologies by law enforcement agencies in Washington State, including state constitutional law, statutory law, decisions by Washington State courts, and federal case law related to the First and Fourth Amendments to the United States Constitution. To this end, I searched Washington law using Westlaw®, and I also conducted general Google and Google Scholar (case law) searches to identify other relevant issues and sources. For comparison, I also conducted searches of Westlaw's legal database and referred to various state legislature websites and news sources to determine whether legislatures in other states had proposed or adopted statutory laws regulating body-worn camera use (or public access to footage) in their jurisdictions. In Westlaw, I searched for statutes and cases using the following search string: "body worn camera!" OR "body worn video" OR "body camera!" OR "on-officer camera!" OR "on-officer video"

FRAMING

As I see it, this current research fits well into the tradition of the law and society movement, active for the past few decades in the United States, and is informed by movements within legal and sociolegal philosophy that privilege an empirical account of law. This study's qualitative and interdisciplinary focus draws inspiration from the philosophy embedded in new legal realism (NLR), which privileges an interdisciplinary and multimethod approach to understanding law in a broader social context and is related in many ways to Tamanaha's proposals for a social theory of law based in pragmatism and realist thought.[8] NLR is a form of sociolegal research that "is ultimately optimistic, maintaining that law is a world of action and our responsibility is to participate in it."[9]

As a point of clarity, the NLR movement itself is not entirely homogenous. Nourse and Shaffer have divided NLR into three camps of researchers: behaviorists, contextualists, and institutionalists.[10] The research presented in this book fits most clearly within the contextualist account of NLR, which broadly encompasses most of the law and society movement (as opposed to the predominantly quantitative ELS and to other sociolegal approaches primarily initiated outside the legal academy, for example within sociology or anthropology).

NLR is an emerging philosophical tradition in legal philosophy. It extends and modifies "old" legal realist thought, from a top-down focus on courts, judges, and legal institutions to a bottom-up approach that seeks to understand the law first by focusing on the impact and everyday interactions of laypersons with the law.[11] Despite its bottom-up focus, NLR also values the integrated study of "law on the books," legal practice, legal institutions, and the lawmaking process. NLR also espouses an interdisciplinary, empirical approach to legal scholarship that combines both quantitative and qualitative methods to achieve a better understanding of the human experience and the dilemmas facing the rule of law and legal institutions. In this sense, it fits within postpositivistic empiricism and also contains aspects of certain types of pragmatism, or the blending of practical and theoretical accounts of law in society.

Competing traditions within sociolegal studies have prioritized either quantitative (positivist) or qualitative (interpretivist) methodologies in studying law and its role and impact in society, reflecting the differing epistemological positions claimed by these movements. This study attempts to balance the weaknesses and strengths of these opposing views by pragmatically prioritizing "what works" to uncover "what is" (facts or truth, though not necessarily absolute) and how my participants (that is, police officers) ascribe meaning (and what that meaning is, as best as I can tell based on my perception of it) to the world of variables (legal and otherwise) that surround the use of body-worn cameras. This approach is generally aligned with the contextualist account of NLR and Tamanaha's pragmatic and realistic social theory of law.[12]

Based on these methodological and epistemological commitments, the data collection methods (field observations, interviews, surveys, legal research) and methods of analysis (grounded theory and doctrinal legal analysis) employed in this project have been conducted iteratively throughout the project. For example, earlier interviews and survey responses informed changes to the focus areas of subsequent interviews and survey questions. The purpose of the multiple surveys over time was not purely to collect quantitative data for longitudinal comparison, but also to inform the other forms of data collection occurring at the same time (and vice versa regarding other methods). This iterative and reflective approach to data collection was designed to complement and inform the different stages of coding and data analysis (grounded theory) that developed as the project progressed.

LIMITATIONS

This study is not without limitations. First, the research reported here draws from data collection within just two police departments in the same state. However, the findings from this study converge with the existing studies of police officer adoption of body-worn cameras, suggesting that the themes drawn here may be indicative of concerns officers feel outside these specific jurisdictions. Additionally, the combination of qualitative and quantitative methodologies chosen, and the specific questions asked, carry with them their own unique set of benefits and concerns. Other in-depth research with these or other agencies might reveal more nuanced findings, and broader, more focused quantitative studies with multiple agencies might also contribute to a better understanding of how these concerns might play out, or be experienced, differently in diverse policing contexts. Future research could also focus more directly on the dynamics of encounters between police officers and recording bystanders, either through qualitative fieldwork or the analysis of actual bystander videos uploaded to online platforms like YouTube. It would also be valuable to have research that interrogates how bystander videos and body-worn camera videos are handled and processed by those who post them online (the bystanders, or "copwatchers" themselves). In terms of understanding the evolving information politics of surveillance and visibility within modern-day policing, concerns about bystander video and body-worn camera adoption are only two pieces in a much larger puzzle. Other forms of surveillance, such as social media monitoring and the use of unmanned aerial vehicles (amid many others) also warrant additional investigation, as do existing and historical public disclosure laws and policies.

APPENDIX A

Tables

TABLE 2 OFFICER RESPONSES TO QUESTION OF WHETHER ADOPTION OF BODY CAMERAS WAS POSITIVE OR NEGATIVE DEVELOPMENT

Sample	Survey	Rank	n	Positive (%)	Negative (%)	Neutral (%)	Change + (%)	Change – (%)
SPD	1	Supervisor	24	83.3	8.3	8.3	—	—
		Officer	62	59.7	12.9	27.4	—	—
		Unknown	12	75.0	16.7	8.3	—	—
		Total	98	67.3	12.2	20.4	—	—
	2	Supervisor	23	87.0	4.3	8.7	3.6	(4.0)
		Officer	40	62.5	25.0	12.5	2.8	12.1
		Unknown	20	70.0	5.0	25.0	(5.0)	(11.7)
		Total	83	71.1	14.5	14.5	3.7	2.2
	3	Supervisor	23	82.6	13.0	4.3	(4.3)	8.7
		Officer	30	86.7	6.7	6.7	24.2	(18.3)
		Unknown	17	76.5	11.8	11.8	6.5	6.8
		Total	70	82.9	10.0	7.1	11.8	(4.5)
	4	Supervisor	18	88.9	5.6	5.6	6.3	(7.5)
		Officer	31	64.5	22.6	12.9	(22.2)	15.9
		Unknown	19	57.9	26.3	15.8	(18.6)	14.6
		Total	68	69.1	19.1	11.8	(13.7)	9.1
BPD	1	Supervisor	11	90.9	—	9.1	—	—
		Officer	32	53.1	21.9	25.0	—	—
		Unknown	6	66.7	16.7	16.7	—	—
		Total	49	63.3	16.3	20.4	—	—
	2	Supervisor	12	91.7	—	8.3	0.8	—
		Officer	24	75.0	12.5	12.5	21.9	(9.4)
		Unknown	13	76.9	—	23.1	10.3	(16.7)
		Total	49	79.6	6.1	14.3	16.3	(10.2)
	3	Supervisor	14	92.9	—	7.1	1.2	—
		Officer	30	63.3	20.0	16.7	(11.7)	7.5
		Unknown	12	66.7	8.3	25.0	(10.3)	8.3
		Total	56	71.4	12.5	16.1	(8.2)	6.4
	4	Supervisor	13	92.3	—	7.7	(0.5)	—
		Officer	15	86.7	—	13.3	23.3	(20.0)
		Unknown	6	100.0	—	—	33.3	8.3)
		Total	34	91.2	—	8.8	19.7	(12.5)

Parentheses indicate negative change.

All numbers have been rounded to the nearest tenth, and some rows may not add up to 100%. Non-responses are omitted.

TABLE 3 OFFICERS' RESPONSES TO QUESTION ABOUT APPROPRIATENESS OF OFFICERS USING BODY-WORN CAMERAS

Sample	Survey	Rank	n	Positive (%)	Negative (%)	Neutral (%)	Change + (%)	Change – (%)
SPD	1	Supervisor	24	87.5	12.5	—	—	—
		Officer	62	72.6	22.6	4.8	—	—
		Unknown	12	75.0	25.0	—	—	—
		Total	98	76.5	20.4	3.1	—	—
	2	Supervisor	24	95.8	4.2	—	8.3	(8.3)
		Officer	40	77.5	20.0	2.5	4.9	(2.6)
		Unknown	20	85.0	15.0	—	10.0	(10.0)
		Total	84	84.5	14.3	1.2	8.0	(6.1)
	3	Supervisor	23	87.0	8.7	4.3	(8.9)	4.5
		Officer	30	80.0	6.7	13.3	2.5	(13.3)
		Unknown	17	88.2	5.9	5.9	3.2	(9.1)
		Total	70	84.3	7.1	8.6	(0.2)	(7.1)
	4	Supervisor	18	100.0	—	—	13.0	(8.7)
		Officer	31	67.7	19.4	12.9	(12.3)	12.7
		Unknown	19	55.6	16.9	22.2	(32.7)	11.0
		Total	67	73.1	14.9	11.9	(11.2)	7.8
BPD	1	Supervisor	11	100.0	—	—	—	—
		Officer	32	87.5	9.4	3.1	—	—
		Unknown	7	71.4	28.6	—	—	—
		Total	50	88.0	10.0	2.0	—	—
	2	Supervisor	12	83.3	16.7	—	(16.7)	16.7
		Officer	24	70.8	25.0	4.2	(16.7)	15.6
		Unknown	13	76.9	15.4	7.7	5.5	(13.2)
		Total	49	75.5	20.4	4.1	(12.5)	10.4
	3	Supervisor	14	100.0	—	—	16.7	(16.7)
		Officer	30	83.3	6.7	10.0	12.5	(18.3)
		Unknown	12	75.0	8.3	16.7	(1.9)	(7.1)
		Total	56	85.7	5.4	8.9	10.2	(15.1)
	4	Supervisor	13	100.0	—	—	—	—
		Officer	15	86.7	—	13.3	3.3	(6.7)
		Unknown	6	100.0	—	—	25.0	(8.3)
		Total	34	94.1	—	5.9	8.4	(5.4)

Parentheses indicate negative change.

All numbers have been rounded to the nearest tenth, and some rows may not add up to 100%. Non-responses are omitted.

TABLE 4 OFFICER RESPONSES TO QUESTION OF HOW USEFUL BODY CAMERAS ARE FOR ACHIEVING LAW ENFORCEMENT OBJECTIVES

Sample	Survey	Rank	n	Positive (%)	Negative (%)	Neutral (%)	Change + (%)	Change − (%)
SPD	1	Supervisor	24	100.0	—	—	—	—
		Officer	62	77.4	19.4	3.2	—	—
		Unknown	12	75.0	25.0	—	—	—
		Total	98	82.7	15.3	2.0	—	—
	2	Supervisor	24	100.0	—	—	—	—
		Officer	40	90.0	7.5	2.5	12.6	(11.9)
		Unknown	20	100.0	—	—	25.0	(25.0)
		Total	84	95.2	3.6	1.2	12.5	(11.7)
	3	Supervisor	23	82.6	4.3	13.0	(17.4)	4.3
		Officer	30	86.7	6.7	6.7	(3.3)	(0.8)
		Unknown	17	88.2	—	11.8	(11.8)	—
		Total	70	85.7	4.3	10.0	(9.5)	0.7
	4	Supervisor	18	94.4	5.6	—	11.8	1.2
		Officer	31	74.2	12.9	6.5	(12.5)	6.2
		Unknown	19	57.9	12.7	31.6	(30.3)	19.8
		Total	68	75.0	13.2	11.8	(10.7)	8.9
BPD	1	Supervisor	11	100.0	—	—	—	—
		Officer	32	65.6	31.3	3.1	—	—
		Unknown	7	100.0	—	—	—	—
		Total	50	78.0	20.0	2.0	—	—
	2	Supervisor	12	91.7	—	8.3	(8.3)	—
		Officer	23	73.9	21.7	4.3	8.3	(9.5)
		Unknown	13	92.3	—	7.7	(7.7)	—
		Total	48	83.3	10.4	6.3	5.3	(9.6)
	3	Supervisor	14	100.0	—	—	8.3	—
		Officer	30	76.7	3.3	20.0	2.8	(18.4)
		Unknown	12	83.3	—	16.7	(9.0)	—
		Total	56	83.9	1.8	14.3	0.6	(8.6)
	4	Supervisor	13	100.0	—	—	—	—
		Officer	15	86.7	—	13.3	10.0	(3.3)
		Unknown	6	100.0	—	—	16.7	—
		Total	34	94.1	—	5.9	10.2	(1.8)

Positive responses indicate camera use was at least "somewhat useful"; negative responses indicate use was at least "generally not useful."

Parentheses indicate negative change.

All numbers have been rounded to the nearest tenth, and some rows may not add up to 100%. Non-responses are omitted.

TABLE 5 OFFICER RESPONSES TO QUESTION ABOUT HOW COMFORTABLE THEY ARE WITH IDEA OF WEARING CAMERA

Sample	Survey	Rank	n	Positive (%)	Negative (%)	Neutral (%)	Change + (%)	Change – (%)
SPD	1	Supervisor	24	75.0	20.8	4.2	—	—
		Officer	61	68.9	29.5	1.6	—	—
		Unknown	12	66.7	33.3	—	—	—
		Total	98	70.1	27.8	2.1	—	—
	2	Supervisor	24	83.3	16.7	—	8.3	(4.2)
		Officer	40	55.0	45.0	—	(13.9)	15.5
		Unknown	20	55.0	40.0	5.0	(11.7)	6.7
		Total	84	63.1	35.7	1.2	(7.0)	(7.9)
	3	Supervisor	23	78.3	8.7	13.0	(5.1)	(8.0)
		Officer	30	83.3	13.3	3.3	28.3	(31.7)
		Unknown	17	64.7	11.8	23.5	9.7	(28.2)
		Total	70	77.1	11.4	11.4	14.0	(24.3)
	4	Supervisor	18	94.4	—	5.6	16.2	(8.7)
		Officer	31	71.0	25.8	3.2	(12.4)	12.5
		Unknown	19	36.8	36.8	26.3	(27.9)	25.1
		Total	68	67.6	22.1	10.3	(9.5)	(10.6)
BPD	1	Supervisor	11	81.8	18.2	—	—	—
		Officer	32	53.1	46.9	—	—	—
		Unknown	7	71.4	28.6	—	—	—
		Total	50	62.0	38.0	—	—	—
	2	Supervisor	12	100.0	—	—	18.2	(18.2)
		Officer	24	66.7	25.0	8.3	13.5	(21.9)
		Unknown	13	84.6	7.7	7.7	13.2	(20.9)
		Total	49	69.2	27.8	3.0	7.2	(10.2)
	3	Supervisor	14	85.7	7.1	7.1	(14.3)	7.1
		Officer	30	56.7	33.3	10.0	(10.0)	8.3
		Unknown	12	75.0	16.7	8.3	(9.6)	9.0
		Total	56	67.9	23.2	8.9	(1.3)	(4.6)
	4	Supervisor	13	84.6	15.4	—	(1.1)	8.2
		Officer	15	86.7	—	13.3	30.0	(33.3)
		Unknown	6	100.0	—	—	25.0	(16.7)
		Total	34	88.2	5.9	5.9	20.4	(17.3)

Positive responses indicate camera use was at least "somewhat comfortable"; negative responses indicate use was at least "somewhat uncomfortable."

Parentheses indicate negative change. All numbers have been rounded to the nearest tenth, and some rows may not add up to 100%. Nonresponses are omitted.

TABLE 6 OFFICERS' RESPONSES TO QUESTION ASKING THEM TO RATE THEIR EXPERIENCE WITH WEARING BODY CAMERA

Sample	Survey	n	Positive (%)	Negative (%)	Neutral (%)	Change + (%)	Change – (%)
SPD	1	20	80.0	20.0	—	—	—
	2	35	74.3	8.6	17.1	(5.7)	(11.4)
	3	51	68.6	7.8	23.5	(5.7)	(0.8)
	4	52	61.5	21.2	17.3	(7.1)	13.4
BPD	1	10	80.0	10.0	10.0	—	—
	2	20	90.0	10.0	—	10.0	—
	3	36	63.9	11.1	25.0	(26.1)	1.1
	4	30	73.3	—	26.7	9.4	(11.1)

Responses range from "very positive" to "very negative."

Parentheses indicate negative change. All numbers have been rounded to the nearest tenth, and some rows may not add up to 100%.

TABLE 7 RATES OF AGREEMENT/DISAGREEMENT WITH STATEMENT THAT WEARING BODY CAMERA WOULD MAKE OFFICERS MORE CAUTIOUS WHEN INTERACTING WITH CIVILIANS

Department	Survey	Agree (%)	Neutral (%)	Disagree (%)
BPD	1	66.0	2.0	32.0
	2	71.4	4.1	24.5
	3	57.1	21.4	21.4
	4	52.9	23.5	23.5
SPD	1	61.2	5.1	33.7
	2	57.1	2.4	40.5
	3	45.7	27.1	27.1
	4	55.9	23.5	20.6

Numbers are rounded to the nearest tenth, and some rows may not add up to 100%.

APPENDIX B

Figures

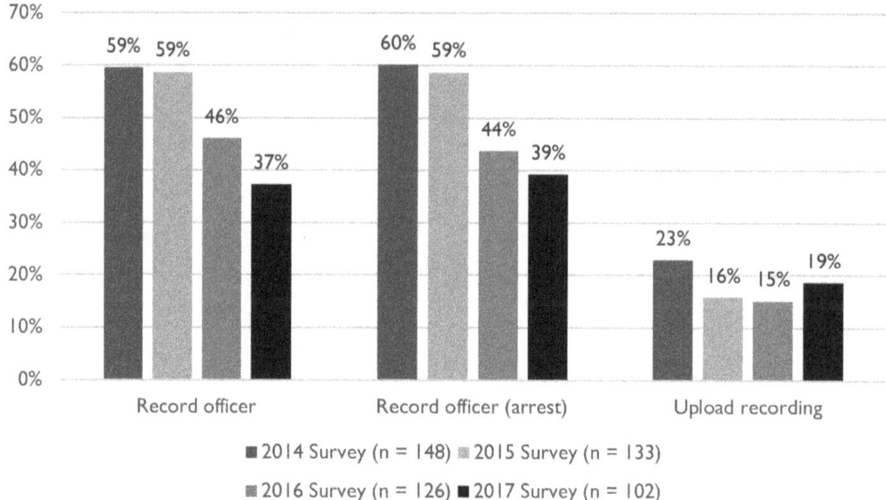

FIGURE 1. Percentages reporting that recording an officer—in general and during an arrest—or uploading a recording is appropriate (combining "very appropriate" or "somewhat appropriate" responses), by survey. Percentages are rounded and do not necessarily add up to 100.

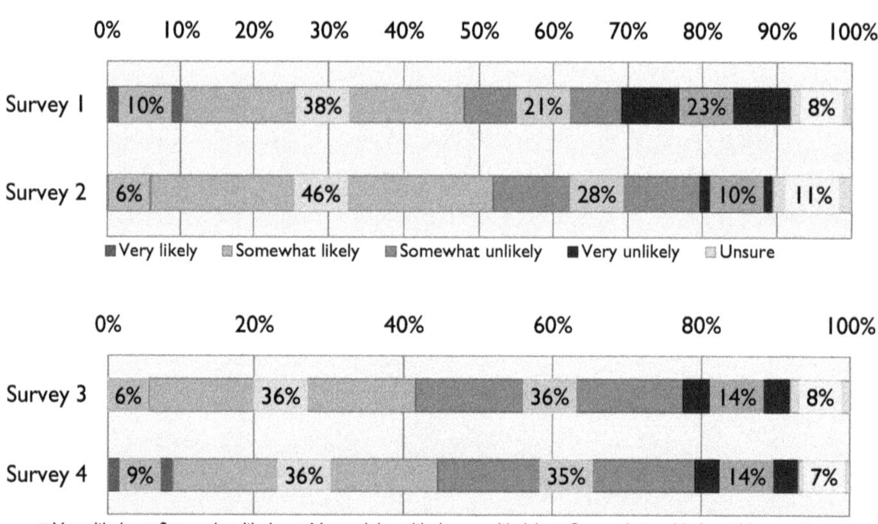

FIGURE 2. Rates of responses to the question: How likely is it that body camera use will lead to better behavior by police officers? Percentages are rounded and do not necessarily add up to 100.

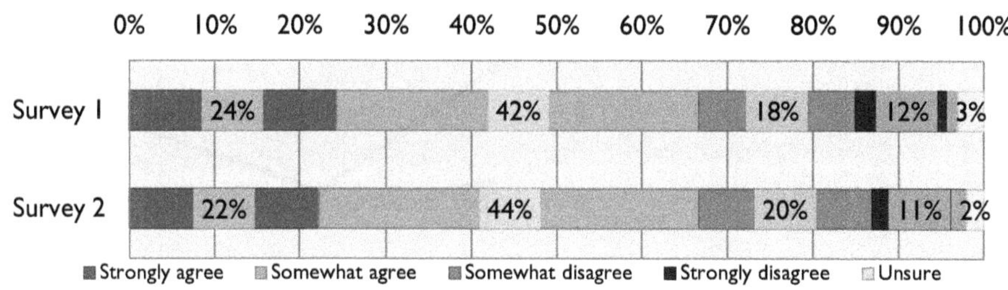

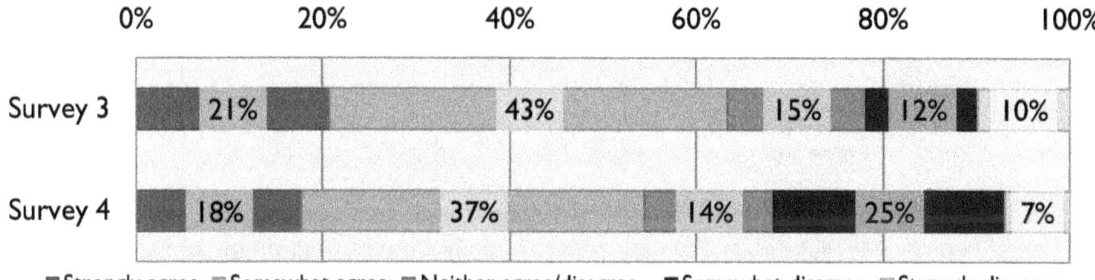

FIGURE 3. Rates of agreement with the proposition that wearing a body camera would decrease officers' willingness to use force, even when force was justified. Percentages are rounded.

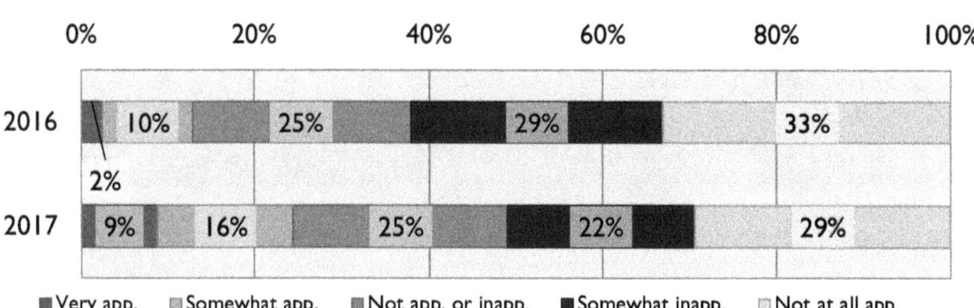

FIGURE 4. Rates of responses to the question: How appropriate is it for citizens to gain access to recordings made by an officer's body-worn video unit? Percentages are rounded and do not necessarily add up to 100.

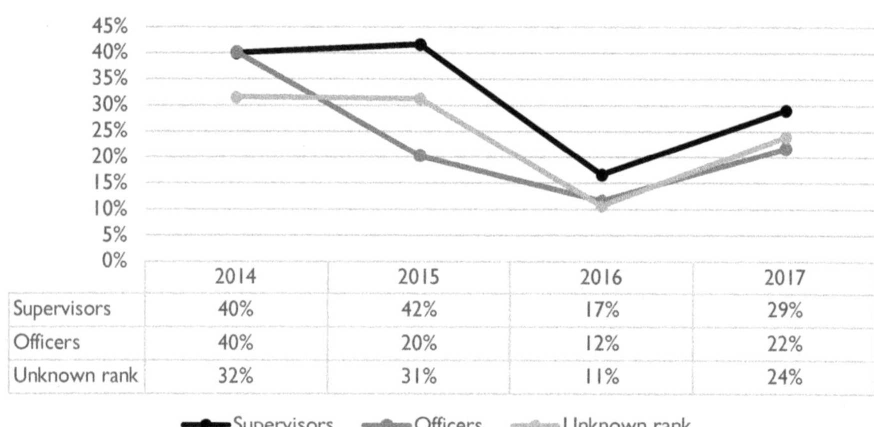

	2014	2015	2016	2017
Supervisors	40%	42%	17%	29%
Officers	40%	20%	12%	22%
Unknown rank	32%	31%	11%	24%

FIGURE 5. Percentages of respondents reporting it was "very appropriate" or "somewhat appropriate" for citizens to gain access to body camera recordings, by rank. Percentages are rounded and do not necessarily add up to 100.

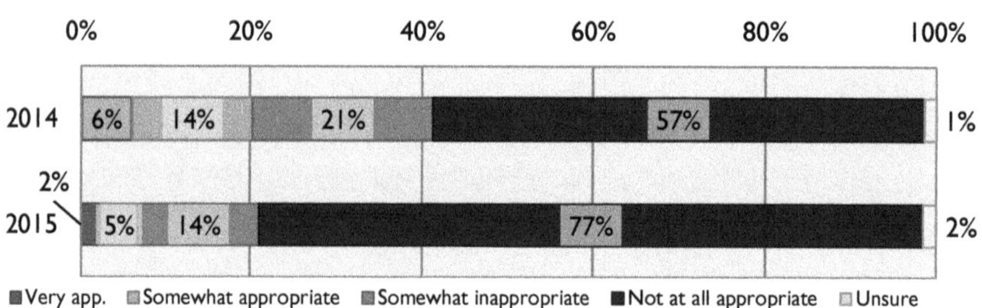

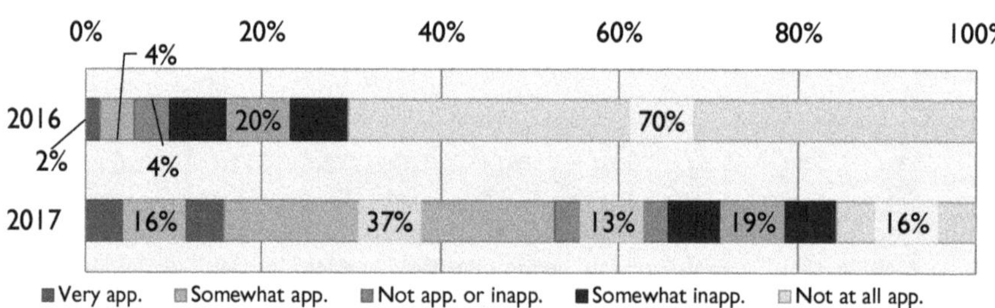

FIGURE 6. Level of agreement that body-worn camera footage should be accessible to all members of the public under public disclosure (FOI) law. Percentages are rounded and do not necessarily add up to 100.

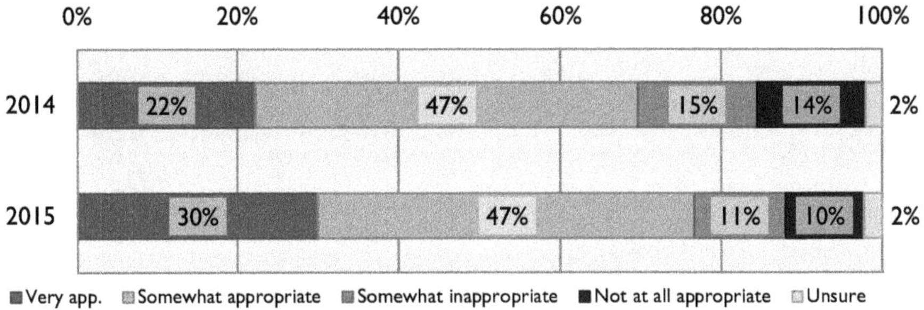

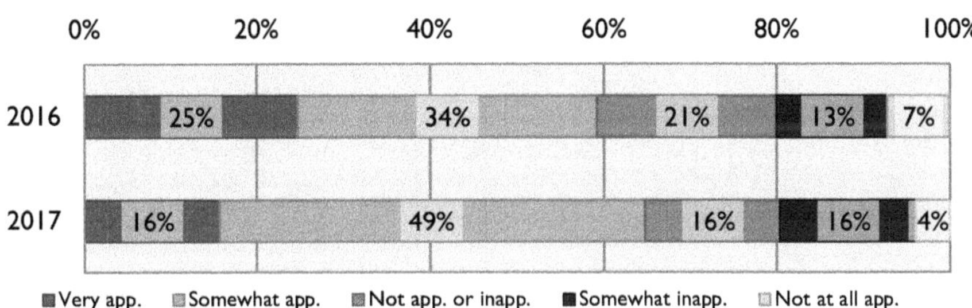

FIGURE 7. Level of agreement that body-worn camera footage should be accessible to those members of the public captured on the requested footage. Percentages are rounded and do not necessarily add up to 100.

Notes

INTRODUCTION

1. Jay Stanley, "Police Body-Mounted Cameras: With Right Policies in Place, a Win for All (Version 2.0)," American Civil Liberties Union, 4–5, March 2015, www.aclu.org/sites/default/files/assets/police_body-mounted_cameras-v2.pdf.

2. I choose to use *bystander* rather than *citizen* because the latter discounts and marginalizes the reality that noncitizens (including individuals present in a community without proper legal documentation) might also participate in these practices.

3. Rosa Squillacote and Leonard Feldman, "Police Abuse and Democratic Accountability: Agonistic Surveillance of the Administrative State," in *Police Abuse in Contemporary Democracies*, ed. Michelle D. Bonner et al. (Cham, Switzerland: Palgrave Macmillan, 2018), 136.

4. Kelly Gates, "The Work of Wearing Cameras: Body-Worn Devices and Police Media Labor," in *The Routledge Companion to Labor and Media*, ed. Richard Maxwell (New York/Oxon: Routledge, 2017), 252.

5. Gates, "Work of Wearing Cameras," 252–53.

6. Gates, "Work of Wearing Cameras," 253.

7. Andrew John Goldsmith, "Policing's New Visibility," *British Journal of Criminology* 50, no. 5 (2010): 915.

8. See Egon Bittner, *Aspects of Police Work* (Boston: Northeastern University Press, 1990), 36.

9. *Sousveillance* refers to the practice of watching from below, as in civilians watching those in power, such as the state. The term is explained in greater depth in chapter 1.

10. Philip Pettit, "Freedom as Antipower," *Ethics* 106, no. 3 (1996): 576–604.

11. Pettit, "Freedom as Antipower," 576–77.

12. Frank Lovett and Philip Pettit, "Neorepublicanism: A Normative and Institutional Research Program," *Annual Review of Political Science* 12 (2009): 11.

13. Andrew Roberts, "A Republican Account of the Value of Privacy," *European Journal of Political Theory* 14, no. 3 (2015): 327.

14. Pettit, "Freedom as Antipower," 589.

15. See, for example, Sander Flight, *Focus: Evaluatie Pilot Bodycams Politie Eenheid Amsterdam 2017–2018* (report of the Politie & Wetenschap and Sander Flight Onderzoek & Advies, 2019), 11–12.

16. Patricia Paperman, "Surveillance Underground: The Uniform as an Interactive Device," *Ethnography* 4, no. 3 (2003): 397–419.

17. Rob C. Mawby, *Policing Images: Policing, Communication and Legitimacy* (Portland, OR: Willan, 2002), 5.

18. Mawby, *Policing Images*, 2.

19. Chris Greer and Eugene McLaughlin, "We Predict a Riot? Public Order Policing, New Media Environments and the Rise of the Citizen Journalist," *British Journal of Criminology* 50, no. 6 (2010): 1041–59.

20. Goldsmith, "Policing's New Visibility," 915, citing John B. Thompson, "The New Visibility," *Theory, Culture and Society* 22, no. 6 (2005): 31–51.

21. Gary T. Marx, "Surveillance and Society," in *Encyclopedia of Social Theory*, ed. George Ritzer (Thousand Oaks, CA: SAGE Publications, 2005).

22. Tyler Wall and Travis Linnemann, "Staring Down the State: Police Power, Visual Economies, and the 'War on Cameras,'" *Crime, Media and Culture* 10, no. 2 (2014): 133–49 (re: "war on cameras"); and Mary D. Fan, *Camera Power: Proof, Policing, Privacy, and Audiovisual Big Data* (Cambridge, UK: Cambridge University Press, 2019), 12 (re: "peaceful weapons of resistance").

23. Goldsmith, "Policing's New Visibility," 915; and Bryce Clayton Newell, "Collateral Visibility: A Socio-Legal Study of Police Body Camera Adoption, Privacy, and Public Disclosure in Washington State," *Indiana Law Journal* 92, no. 4 (2017): 1339.

24. Karen Levy and Solon Barocas, "Refractive Surveillance: Monitoring Customers to Manage Workers," *International Journal of Communication* 12 (2018): 1166.

25. Bert-Jaap Koops et al., "The Reasonableness of Remaining Unobserved: A Comparative Analysis of Visual Surveillance and Voyeurism in Criminal Law," *Law & Social Inquiry* 43, no. 4 (2018): 1219.

26. Koops et al., "Reasonableness of Remaining Unobserved," 1211.

27. Koops et al., "Reasonableness of Remaining Unobserved," 1219 (internal citations omitted).

28. Emmeline Taylor and Murray Lee, "Points of View: Arrestees' Perspectives on Police Body-Worn Cameras and Their Perceived Impact on Police–Citizen Interactions," *British Journal of Criminology* 59, no. 4 (July 2019): 965; Emmeline Taylor and Murray Lee, "Off the Record? Arrestee Concerns about the Manipulation, Modification, and Misrepresentation of Police Body-Worn Camera Footage," *Surveillance & Society* 17, nos. 3/4 (2019): 477; Murray Lee, Emmeline Taylor, and Matthew Willis, "Being Held to Account: Detainees' Perceptions of Police Body-Worn Cameras," *Australian & New Zealand Journal of Criminology* 52, no. 2 (2019): 182; Tom Ellis, Craig Jenkins, and Paul Smith,

Evaluation of the Introduction of Personal Issue Body Worn Video Cameras (Operation Hyperion) on the Isle of Wight (final report to Hampshire Constabulary; University of Portsmouth, 2015); Jon Maskaly et al., "The Effects of Body-Worn Cameras (BWCs) on Police and Citizen Outcomes: A State-of-the-Art Review," *Policing: An International Journal of Police Strategies & Management* 40, no. 4 (2017): 672–88; and William H. Sousa, Terance D. Miethe, and Mari Sakiyama, "Inconsistencies in Public Opinion of Body-Worn Cameras on Police: Transparency, Trust, and Improved Police–Citizen Relationships," *Policing* 12, no 1 (2018): 100–108.

29. Alex S. Vitale, *The End of Policing* (London: Verso, 2017), 17.

30. Tjerk Timan, "The Body-Worn Camera as a Transitional Technology," *Surveillance & Society* 14, no. 1 (2016): 145; and Flight, *Focus*, 12.

31. Janet B. L. Chan, "The Technological Game: How Information Technology Is Transforming Police Practice," *Criminal Justice* 1, no. 2 (2001): 140.

32. Bert-Jaap Koops, "Criteria for Normative Technology: An Essay on the Acceptability of 'Code as Law' in Light of Democratic and Constitutional Values," in *Regulating Technologies*, ed. Roger Brownsword and Karen Yeung (Oxford: Hart Publishing, 2008), 158.

33. Ronald Leenes, "Framing Techno-Regulation: An Exploration of State and Non-state Regulation by Technology," *Legisprudence* 5, no. 2 (2011): 149.

34. Justin T. Ready and Jacob T. N. Young, "The Impact of On-Officer Video Cameras on Police-Citizen Contacts: Findings from a Controlled Experiment in Mesa, AZ," *Journal of Experimental Criminology* 11, no. 3 (2015): 445–58.

35. See Barak Ariel, William A. Farrar, and Alex Sutherland, "The Effect of Police Body-Worn Cameras on Use of Force and Citizens' Complaints against the Police: A Randomized Controlled Trial," *Journal of Quantitative Criminology* 31, no. 3 (2015): 509–35 (re: decreased use of force by officers); Barak Ariel et al., "Report: Increases in Police Use of Force in the Presence of Body-Worn Cameras Are Driven by Officer Discretion: A Protocol-Based Subgroup Analysis of Ten Randomized Experiments," *Journal of Experimental Criminology* 12, no. 3 (2016): 453–63 (re: discretion about when to turn cameras on); and Barak Ariel et al., "Wearing Body Cameras Increases Assaults against Officers and Does Not Reduce Police Use of Force: Results from a Global Multi-Site Experiment," *European Journal of Criminology* 13, no. 6 (2016): 744–55 (re: the risk of assaults on officers by civilians).

36. Paul T. Jaeger, "Information Policy, Information Access, and Democratic Participation: The National and International Implications of the Bush Administration's Information Policies," *Government Information Quarterly* 24, no. 4 (2007): 851 (re: "the manipulation of information access for political gain"); and Manuel Castells, *Communication Power* (Oxford: Oxford University Press, 2009), 197 (re: "decisive tool of power-making").

37. Paul T. Jaeger and Natalie Greene Taylor, *Foundations of Information Policy* (Chicago: ALA Neal-Schuman, 2019), 3.

38. Andrea Brighenti, "Visibility: A Category for the Social Sciences," *Current Sociology* 55, no. 3 (2007): 328–29.

39. Jodi Dean, *Publicity's Secret: How Technoculture Capitalizes on Democracy* (Ithaca, NY: Cornell University Press, 2002), 15–16.

40. Sandra Braman, *Change of State: Information, Policy, and Power* (Cambridge, MA: MIT Press, 2006), 1.

41. Kevin D. Haggerty, "Tear Down the Walls: On Demolishing the Panopticon," in *Theorizing Surveillance: The Panopticon and Beyond*, ed. David Lyon (Cullompton, UK: Willan Publishing, 2006), 30.

42. Dean, *Publicity's Secret*, 3.

43. Stuart Allan and Chris Peters, "Visual Truths of Citizen Reportage: Four Research Problematics," *Information, Communication & Society* 18, no. 11 (2015): 1349–50; see also Alberto Hermida and Víctor Hernández-Santaolalla, "Twitter and Video Activism as Tools for Countersurveillance: The Case of Social Protests in Spain," *Information, Communication & Society* 21, no. 3 (2018): 416–33; Mary Angela Bock, "Film the Police! Cop-Watching and Its Embodied Narratives," *Journal of Communication* 66, no. 1 (2016): 13–34; Gregory R. Brown, "The Blue Line on Thin Ice: Police Use of Force Modifications in the Era of Cameraphones and YouTube," *British Journal of Criminology* 56, no. 2 (2016): 293–312; Ben Brucato, "Standing by Police Violence: On the Constitution of the Ideal Citizen as Sousveiller," *American Studies Journal* 61 (2016), art. 6, www.asjournal.org/61–2016/standing-police-violence-constitution-ideal-citizen-sousveiller; Ashley K. Farmer and Ivan Y. Sun, "Citizen Journalism and Police Legitimacy: Does Recording the Police Make a Difference?," in *The Politics of Policing: Between Force and Legitimacy*, ed. Mathieu Deflem (Bingley, UK: Emerald Group Publishing, 2016), 239–56; Ajay Sandhu, "Camera-Friendly Policing: How the Police Respond to Cameras and Photographers," *Surveillance & Society* 14, no. 1 (2016): 78–89; Kevin D. Haggerty and Ajay Sandhu, "The Police Crisis of Visibility," *IEEE Technology and Society Magazine* 2014 (Summer): 9–12; Mary Grace Antony and Ryan J. Thomas, "'This Is Citizen Journalism at Its Finest': YouTube and the Public Sphere in the Oscar Grant Shooting Incident," *New Media & Society* 12, no. 8 (2010): 1280–96; Greer and McLaughlan, "We Predict a Riot?"; Dean Wilson and Tanya Serisier, "Video Activism and the Ambiguities of Counter-Surveillance," *Surveillance & Society* 8, no. 2 (2010): 166–80; and Laura Huey, Kevin Walby, and Aaron Doyle, "Cop Watching in the Downtown Eastside: Exploring the Use of (Counter) Surveillance as a Tool of Resistance," in *Surveillance and Security: Technological Politics and Power in Everyday Life*, ed. Torin Monahan (New York: Routledge, 2006), 149–65.

44. Bryce Clayton Newell, "Transparent Lives and the Surveillance State: Policing, New Visibility, and Information Policy" (PhD diss., University of Washington, 2015); Bryce Clayton Newell, "Technopolicing, Surveillance, and Citizen Oversight: A Neorepublican Theory of Liberty and Information Control," *Government Information Quarterly* 31, no. 3 (2014): 421–31; Wilson and Serisier, "Video Activism"; Huey, Walby, and Doyle, "Cop Watching"; Marx, "Surveillance and Society" (re: inverse or reciprocal surveillance); Steve Mann, Jason Nolan, and Barry Wellman, "Sousveillance: Inventing and Using Wearable Computing Devices for Data Collection in Surveillance Environments," *Surveillance & Society* 1, no. 3 (2003): 331–55 (re: sousveillance); and Manuel Castells, "Communication, Power and Counter-Power in the

Network Society," *International Journal of Communication* 1 (2007): 239 (re: "counter-power").

45. Thomas Mathiesen, "The Viewer Society: Michel Foucault's 'Panopticon' Revisited," *Theoretical Criminology* 1, no. 2 (1997): 215–34; and Ajay Sandhu and Kevin D. Haggerty, "Policing on Camera," *Theoretical Criminology* 21, no. 1 (2017): 78–95.

46. Goldsmith, "Policing's New Visibility," 915, quoting Keith Tester, Introduction to *The Flâneur*, ed. Keith Tester (London: Routledge, 1994), 5.

47. Sandra Braman, "Defining Information Policy," *Journal of Information Policy* 1, no. 1 (2011): 3.

48. Braman, *Change of State*, xviii, 41.

49. See Samantha Besson and Jose Luis Marti, "Law and Republicanism: Mapping the Issues," in *Legal Republicanism: National and International Perspectives*, ed. Samantha Besson and Jose Luis Marti (Oxford: Oxford University Press, 2009), 3–36.

50. Newell, "Technopolicing, Surveillance, and Citizen Oversight."

51. Vitale, *End of Policing*, 30.

52. Pettit, "Freedom as Antipower," 589.

CHAPTER 1. VISIBILITY, SURVEILLANCE, AND THE POLICE

1. David Correia and Tyler Wall, *Police: A Field Guide* (London: Verso, 2018), 66.

2. See, for example, Correia and Wall, *Police: A Field Guide*.

3. Correia and Wall, *Police: A Field Guide*, 2.

4. Alex S. Vitale, *The End of Policing* (London: Verso, 2017), 4.

5. Correia and Wall, *Police: A Field Guide*, 5.

6. Correia and Wall, *Police: A Field Guide*, 5.

7. Vitale, *End of Policing*; and Mary D. Fan, *Camera Power: Proof, Policing, Privacy, and Audiovisual Big Data* (Cambridge, UK: Cambridge University Press, 2019), 23.

8. Tyler Wall and Travis Linnemann, "Staring Down the State: Police Power, Visual Economies, and the 'War on Cameras,'" *Crime, Media and Culture* 10, no. 2 (2014): 136; and Mark Neocleous, *The Fabrication of Social Order: A Critical Theory of Police Power* (London: Pluto Press, 2000).

9. Andrew Goldsmith, "Police Reform and the Problem of Trust," *Theoretical Criminology* 9, no. 4 (2005): 444.

10. Mark Neocleous, *Critique of Security* (Edinburgh: Edinburgh University Press, 2008).

11. Ben Brucato, "Fabricating the Color Line in a White Democracy: From Slave Catchers to Petty Sovereigns," *Theoria: A Journal of Social and Political Theory* 61, no. 141 (2014): 31.

12. Brucato, "Fabricating the Color Line," 31; see also Vitale, *End of Policing*, 2–4, 14.

13. Seth Stoughton, "Law Enforcement's 'Warrior' Problem," *Harvard Law Review Forum* 128 (2015): 226; Vitale, *End of Policing*, 3; and Sue Rahr and

Stephen K. Rice, "From Warriors to Guardians: Recommitting American Police Culture to Democratic Ideals," *New Perspectives in Policing Bulletin* (April 2015): 1–14.

14. Vitale, *End of Policing*, 1.

15. Rahr and Rice, "From Warriors to Guardians," 2.

16. Stoughton, "Law Enforcement's 'Warrior' Problem," 225–26.

17. Vitale, *End of Policing*, 3.

18. David Lyon, *Surveillance Studies: An Overview* (Cambridge, UK: Polity Press, 2007), 14.

19. Kevin D. Haggerty and Richard V. Ericson, "The New Politics of Surveillance and Visibility," in *The New Politics of Surveillance and Visibility*, ed. Kevin D. Haggerty and Richard V. Ericson (Toronto: University of Toronto Press, 2006), 3.

20. Lyon, *Surveillance Studies*, 49.

21. Stanley Cohen, *Visions of Social Control: Crime, Punishment and Classification* (Cambridge, UK: Polity, 1985); and Lyon, *Surveillance Studies*, 49.

22. Lyon, *Surveillance Studies*, 49.

23. Lyon, *Surveillance Studies*, 52–53.

24. Kevin D. Haggerty, "Tear Down the Walls: On Demolishing the Panopticon," in *Theorizing Surveillance: The Panopticon and Beyond*, ed. David Lyon (Cullompton, UK: Willan Publishing, 2006)," 23.

25. See Haggerty, "Tear Down the Walls," 23; and Lyon, *Surveillance Studies*, 47, 57.

26. Lyon, *Surveillance Studies*, 59.

27. Thomas Mathiesen, "The Viewer Society: Michel Foucault's 'Panopticon' Revisited," *Theoretical Criminology* 1, no. 2 (1997): 215–34.

28. Mathiesen, "Viewer Society," 219 (emphasis in original).

29. Steve Mann and Joseph Ferenbok, "New Media and the Power Politics of Sousveillance in a Surveillance Dominated World," *Surveillance & Society* 11, nos. 1/2 (2013): 18–34; and Steve Mann, Jason Nolan, and Barry Wellman, "Sousveillance: Inventing and Using Wearable Computing Devices for Data Collection in Surveillance Environments," *Surveillance & Society* 1, no. 3 (2003): 331–55 (re: "sousveillance"); Torin Monahan, "Counter-Surveillance as Political Intervention?," *Social Semiotics* 16, no. 4 (2006): 515–34 (re: "counter-surveillance"); and Manuel DeLanda, *War in the Age of Intelligent Machines* (New York: Zone, 1991); and Karl Palmås, "Predicting What You'll Do Tomorrow: Panspectric Surveillance and the Contemporary Corporation," *Surveillance & Society* 8, no. 3 (2011): 338–54 (re: "panspectron").

30. Monahan, "Counter-Surveillance as Political Intervention?," 516.

31. Kevin D. Haggerty and Richard V. Ericson, "The Surveillant Assemblage," *British Journal of Sociology* 51, no. 4 (2000): 605–22 (re: "surveillant assemblages":); and Daniel J. Solove, *The Digital Person: Technology and Privacy in the Information Age* (New York: New York University Press, 2004) (re: "digital dossiers").

32. Gary T. Marx, "Surveillance and Society," in *Encyclopedia of Social Theory*, ed. George Ritzer (Thousand Oaks, CA: SAGE, 2005).

33. Haggerty and Ericson, "Surveillant Assemblage"; and Haggerty and Ericson, "New Politics of Surveillance," 4–5.

34. C. William R. Webster, "CCTV Policy in the UK: Reconsidering the Evidence Base," *Surveillance & Society* 6, no. 1 (2009): 10–22; and Martin Gill and Angela Spriggs, *Home Office Research Study 292: Assessing the Impact of CCTV*, The Home Office (UK), February 2005.

35. Ann Rudinow Sætnan, Heidi Mork Lomell, and Carsten Wiecek, "Controlling CCTV in Public Spaces: Is Privacy the (Only) Issue? Reflections on Norwegian and Danish Observations," *Surveillance and Society* 2, nos. 2/3 (2004): 396–414.

36. Heidi Mork Lomell, "Targeting the Unwanted: Video Surveillance and Categorical Exclusion in Oslo, Norway," *Surveillance & Society* 2, nos. 2/3 (2004): 346–60 (re: "purification"/"commercialization"); and David Lyon, ed., *Surveillance as Social Sorting: Privacy, Risk, and Digital Discrimination* (London: Routledge, 2003) (re: "surveillance as social sorting").

37. Lomell, "Targeting the Unwanted."

38. Lomell, "Targeting the Unwanted"; Clive Norris and Gary Armstrong, *The Maximum Surveillance Society: The Rise of CCTV* (Oxford: Berg, 1999); and Michael McCahill, *The Surveillance Web: The Rise of Visual Surveillance in an English City* (Portland, OR: Willan Publishing, 2002).

39. See Lyon, *Surveillance as Social Sorting* (variety of settings).

40. Lomell, "Targeting the Unwanted"; and Sætnan, Lomell, and Wiecek, "Controlling CCTV in Public Spaces."

41. Elia Zureik, "Theorizing Surveillance: The Case of the Workplace," in *Surveillance as Social Sorting: Privacy, Risk, and Digital Discrimination*, ed. David Lyon (London: Routledge, 2003), 31–56; Kirstie Ball, "Categorizing the Workers: Electronic Surveillance and Social Ordering in the Call Center," in Lyon, *Surveillance as Social Sorting*, 201–25; Sherri Coultrup and Patrick D. Fountain, "Effects of Electronic Monitoring and Surveillance on the Psychological Contract of Employees: An Exploratory Study," *Proceedings of the American Society of Business and Behavioral Sciences* 19, no. 1 (2012): 219–35; Anna Johnston and Myra Cheng, "Electronic Surveillance in the Workplace: Concerns for Employees and Challenges for Privacy Advocates" (paper delivered at the International Conference on Personal Data Protection, November 28, 2002, Seoul, Korea); and Adam D. Moore, "Employee Monitoring and Computer Technology: Evaluative Surveillance v. Privacy," *Business Ethics Quarterly* 10, no. 3 (2000): 697–709.

42. Felix Stalder and David Lyon, "Electronic Identity Cards and Social Classification," in Lyon, *Surveillance as Social Sorting*, 77–93.

43. Colin Bennett, Charles Raab, and Priscilla Regan, "People and Place: Patterns of Individual Identification within Intelligent Transportation Systems," in Lyon, *Surveillance as Social Sorting*, 153–75.

44. Dorothy Nelkin and Lori Andrews, "Surveillance Creep in the Genetic Age," in Lyon, *Surveillance as Social Sorting*, 94–110.

45. Jennifer Poudrier, "'Racial' Categories and Health Risks: Epidemiological Surveillance Among Canadian First Nations," in Lyon, *Surveillance as Social Sorting*, 111–34.

46. Lomell, "Targeting the Unwanted"; and Sætnan, Lomell, and Wiecek, "Controlling CCTV."

47. Haggerty, "Tear Down the Walls," 29.

48. Haggerty, "Tear Down the Walls," 29.

49. Haggerty and Ericson, "New Politics of Surveillance," 5.

50. Haggerty, "Tear Down the Walls," 41.

51. See Barak Ariel, William A. Farrar, and Alex Sutherland, "The Effect of Police Body-Worn Cameras on Use of Force and Citizens' Complaints against the Police: A Randomized Controlled Trial," *Journal of Quantitative Criminology* 31, no. 3 (2015): 509–35.

52. See Michel Foucault, *Discipline and Punish: The Birth of the Prison*, trans. Alan Sheridan (Hammondsworth, UK: Penguin, 1979); and Lyon, *Surveillance Studies*, 59.

53. Lyon, "Search for Surveillance Theories," 4.

54. Lyon, "Search for Surveillance Theories," 12.

55. Andrew John Goldsmith, "Policing's New Visibility," *British Journal of Criminology* 50, no. 5 (2010): 914.

56. Richard V. Ericson and Kevin D. Haggerty, *Policing the Risk Society* (Toronto: University of Toronto Press, 1997), 35, 139.

57. Bryce Clayton Newell, "Crossing Lenses: Policing's New Visibility and the Role of 'Smartphone Journalism' as a Form of Freedom-Preserving Reciprocal Surveillance," *Journal of Law, Technology & Policy* 2014, no. 1 (2014): 63.

58. Ajay Sandhu and Kevin D. Haggerty, "Policing on Camera," *Theoretical Criminology* 21, no. 1 (2017): 79.

59. Fan, *Camera Power*, 3–5.

60. Vitale, *End of Policing*, 23.

61. Jay Stanley, "Police Body-Mounted Cameras: With Right Policies in Place, a Win for All," American Civil Liberties Union, October 2013, www.aclu.org/files/assets/police_body-mounted_cameras.pdf; and Jay Stanley, "Police Body-Mounted Cameras: With Right Policies in Place, a Win for All (Version 2.0)," American Civil Liberties Union, 4–5, March 2015, www.aclu.org/sites/default/files/assets/police_body-mounted_cameras-v2.pdf.

62. Fan, *Camera Power*, 9, 12–13.

63. Fan, *Camera Power*, 13.

64. Vitale, *End of Policing*, 222.

65. Vitale, *End of Policing*, 24.

66. Bert-Jaap Koops et al., "The Reasonableness of Remaining Unobserved: A Comparative Analysis of Visual Surveillance and Voyeurism in Criminal Law," *Law & Social Inquiry* 43, no. 4 (2018): 1211.

67. Lyon, *Surveillance Studies*, 48.

68. Stéphane Leman-Langlois, Afterword to *Technocrime: Technology, Crime and Social Control*, ed. Stéphane Leman-Langlois (Portland, OR: Willan, 2008), 244.

69. Karen Levy and Solon Barocas, "Refractive Surveillance: Monitoring Customers to Manage Workers," *International Journal of Communication* 12 (2018): 1166.

70. By *adequate*, I mean the existing law doesn't provide clear and satisfactory legal guidance to agencies, individual officers tasked with using the technology, courts, or the public as to how the surveillance technology at issue should (or should not) be used or regulated within the context of the broader legal framework into which the technology has been, or will be, deployed.

71. Brenda L. Berkelaar and Millie A. Harrison, "Information Visibility," in *Oxford Research Encyclopedia of Communication* (Oxford: Oxford University Press, 2019), doi:10.1093/acrefore/9780190228613.013.12; and Cynthia Stohl, Michael Stohl, and Paul M. Leonardi, "Managing Opacity: Information Visibility and the Paradox of Transparency in the Digital Age," *International Journal of Communication* 10 (2016): 123–37.

72. Berkelaar and Harrison, "Information Visibility"; Stohl, Stohl, and Leonardi, "Managing Opacity" (re: ideological baggage); and Clare Birchall, "Radical Transparency?," *Cultural Studies ↔ Critical Methodologies* 14, no. 1 (2014): 77 (re: "a trust-building alternative to secrecy").

73. Birchall, "Radical Transparency?," 77.

74. Bryce Clayton Newell, "Collateral Visibility: A Socio-legal Study of Police Body Camera Adoption, Privacy, and Public Disclosure in Washington State," *Indiana Law Journal* 92, no. 4 (2017): 1365–70; and Mary D. Fan, "Privacy, Public Disclosure, Police Body Cameras: Policy Splits," *Alabama Law Review* 68, no. 2 (2016): 413–17.

75. Ajay Sandhu, "Camera-Friendly Policing: How the Police Respond to Cameras and Photographers," *Surveillance & Society* 14, no. 1 (2016): 78.

76. Wall and Linnemann, "Staring Down the State," 137.

77. Goldsmith, "Policing's New Visibility," 915.

78. See Newell, "Crossing Lenses"; and Bryce Clayton Newell, "Technopolicing, Surveillance, and Citizen Oversight: A Neorepublican Theory of Liberty and Information Control," *Government Information Quarterly* 31, no. 3 (2014): 421–31.

79. Goldsmith, "Policing's New Visibility," 915.

80. Sandra Braman, *Change of State: Information, Policy, and Power* (Cambridge, MA: MIT Press, 2006), 19.

81. Paul T. Jaeger, "Information Policy, Information Access, and Democratic Participation: The National and International Implications of the Bush Administration's Information Policies," *Government Information Quarterly* 24, no. 4 (2007): 851.

82. Braman, *Change of State*, 6.

83. Braman, *Change of State*, 26.

84. See Bert-Jaap Koops et al., "A Typology of Privacy," *University of Pennsylvania Journal of International Law* 38 (2017): 566–69.

85. Rebecca Wexler, "Technology's Continuum: Body Cameras, Data Collection and Constitutional Searches," in *Visual Imagery and Human Rights Practice*, ed. Sandra Ristovska and Monroe Price (Cham, Switzerland: Palgrave Macmillan, 2018), 91.

86. See Daniel J. Solove, "Access and Aggregation: Privacy, Public Records, and the Constitution," *Minnesota Law Review* 86 (2002): 1137–1209.

87. Solove, "Access and Aggregation."

88. Braman, *Change of State*, 1.

89. Craig Forcese and Aaron Freeman, *The Laws of Government: The Legal Foundations of Canadian Democracy* (Toronto: Irwin Law, 2005), 481–84.

90. Forcese and Freeman, *Laws of Government*, 481–84.

91. Mann, Nolan, and Wellman, "Sousveillance" (re: inverse surveillance); and Marx, "Surveillance and Society"; Haggerty and Ericson, "New Politics of Surveillance," 10 (re: reciprocal surveillance).

CHAPTER 2. PRIVACY, SPEECH, AND ACCESS TO INFORMATION

1. Department of Justice v. Reporters Committee for Freedom of the Press, 489 U.S. 749, 779 (1989).

2. *Reporters Committee for Freedom of the Press*, 489 U.S. at 764.

3. Woodrow Hartzog and Frederic Stutzman, "The Case for Online Obscurity," *California Law Review* 101, no. 1 (2013): 21.

4. Hartzog and Stutzman, "Case for Online Obscurity," 21.

5. See, for example, Jeremy Travis, "Invisible Punishment: An Instrument of Social Exclusion," in *Invisible Punishment: The Collateral Consequences of Mass Imprisonment*, ed. Marc Mauer and Meda Chesney-Lind (New York: New Press, 2002), 15–36; John Hagan and Ronit Dinovitzer, "Collateral Consequences of Imprisonment for Children, Communities, and Prisoners," *Crime and Justice* 26 (1999): 121–62; and Forrest Stuart, "Becoming 'Copwise': Policing, Culture, and the Collateral Consequences of Street-Level Criminalization," *Law & Society Review* 50, no. 2 (2016): 279–313.

6. Stuart, "Becoming Copwise," 280–81 (emphasis omitted) (citations omitted).

7. S.B. 6408, 65th Leg., 2018 Reg. Sess. (Wa. 2018).

8. RCW § 42.56.240(14)(a)(i)–(vii) (individual quotations omitted for readability).

9. RCW § 42.56.240(18).

10. RCW § 42.56.240(14)(f)(i).

11. RCW § 42.56.240(14)(f)(ii).

12. See Bryce Clayton Newell, "Collateral Visibility: A Socio-legal Study of Police Body Camera Adoption, Privacy, and Public Disclosure in Washington State," *Indiana Law Journal* 92, no. 4 (2017): 1329–99.

13. See Eugene Volokh, "Freedom of Speech and Information Privacy: The Troubling Implications of a Right to Stop People from Speaking about You," *Stanford Law Review* 52 (2000): 1049–1124.

14. Alexander Meiklejohn, *Free Speech and its Relation to Self-Government* (New York: Harper, 1948); Alexander Meiklejohn, *Political Freedom: The Constitutional Powers of the People* (New York: Harper, 1960); and Alexander Meiklejohn, "The First Amendment Is an Absolute," *Supreme Court Review* 1961 (1961): 245–66.

15. Cass R. Sunstein, *Democracy and the Problem of Free Speech* (New York: The Free Press, 1993), 257.

16. Meiklejohn, "First Amendment Is an Absolute," 257.

17. Meiklejohn, "First Amendment Is an Absolute," 255.

18. Meiklejohn, "First Amendment Is an Absolute," 263.

19. Jack M. Balkin, "The Future of Free Expression in a Digital Age," *Pepperdine Law Review* 36 (2009): 438.

20. Jack M. Balkin, "Digital Speech and Democratic Culture: A Theory of Freedom of Expression for the Information Society," *New York University Law Review* 79, no. 1 (2004): 3.

21. Martin H. Reddish, *The Adversary First Amendment* (Stanford, CA: Stanford University Press, 2013); and Martin H. Reddish and Abby Marie Mollen, "Understanding Post's and Meiklejohn's Mistakes: The Central Role of Adversary Democracy in the Theory of Free Expression," *Northwestern University Law Review* 103, no. 3 (2009): 1303–70.+

22. See Daniel J. Solove, "A Taxonomy of Privacy," *University of Pennsylvania Law Review* 154 (2006): 477–564.

23. Julie E. Cohen, "What Privacy Is For," *Harvard Law Review* 126 (2013): 1904.

24. Adam D. Moore, *Privacy Rights: Moral and Legal Foundations* (University Park: Pennsylvania State University Press, 2010), 14–16.

25. See Bert-Jaap Koops et al., "A Typology of Privacy," *University of Pennsylvania Journal of International Law* 38 (2017): 483–575 (re: different types of privacy); and Solove, "Taxonomy of Privacy," 488–91 (re: privacy harms).

26. Koops et al., "Typology of Privacy."

27. Adam D. Moore, "Privacy, Speech, and the Law," *Journal of Information Ethics* 22, no. 1 (2013): 21–43; and Moore, *Privacy Rights*.

28. Cohen, "What Privacy Is For," 1904–33.

29. Moore, "Privacy, Speech, and the Law," 21–43.

30. Alan F. Westin, *Privacy and Freedom* (New York: Atheneum, 1967), 21–22.

31. Cohen, "What Privacy Is For," 1905; see also Andrew Roberts, "A Republican Account of the Value of Privacy," *European Journal of Political Theory* 14, no. 3 (2015): 320–44.

32. Westin, *Privacy and Freedom*, 11.

33. Westin, *Privacy and Freedom*, 21.

34. Roberts, "Republican Account," 321.

35. *See* Julie E. Cohen, *Configuring the Networked Self: Law, Code, and the Play of Everyday Practice* (New Haven: Yale University Press, 2012), 6; see also Jack M. Balkin, "Room for Maneuver: Julie Cohen's Theory of Freedom in the Information State," *Jerusalem Review of Legal Studies* 6, no. 1 (2012): 81.

36. Cohen, *Configuring the Networked Self*, 6 (emphasis added); *see also* Balkin, "Room for Maneuver," 81.

37. Cohen, *Configuring the Networked Self*, 224.

38. Balkin, "Room for Maneuver," 81, quoting Cohen, *Configuring the Networked Self*, 234, 239.

39. Michael L. Rich, "Limits on the Perfect Preventative State," *Connecticut Law Review* 46 (2014): 928 (re: "gaps and imperfections"); and Kevin Miller, "Total Surveillance, Big Data, and Predictive Crime Technology: Privacy's Perfect Storm," *Journal of Technology Law & Policy* 19 (2014): 134 (re: "disorganization").

40. Rich, "Limits on the Perfect Preventative State," 928 (re: "perfect preventive state"). These aspects of Cohen's theory come into fairly direct conflict with Etzioni's communitarian position, which would prioritize public safety as an important common good. Indeed, Cohen herself directly tackles the liberal communitarian position when she states, "Privacy's goal, simply put, is to ensure that the development of subjectivity and the development of communal values do not proceed in lockstep." Cohen, *Configuring the Networked Self*, 150; and Cohen, "What Privacy Is For," 1911.

41. Cohen, *Configuring the Networked Self*, 6.

42. Roberts, "Republican Account," 335.

43. Daniel J. Solove, *The Digital Person: Technology and Privacy in the Information Age* (New York: New York University Press, 2004), 47–48.

44. Philip Pettit, "Freedom as Antipower," *Ethics* 106, no. 3 (1996): 588.

45. Pettit, "Freedom as Antipower," 588.

46. Pettit, "Freedom as Antipower," 589.

47. Paul T. Jaeger, "Information Policy, Information Access, and Democratic Participation: The National and International Implications of the Bush Administration's Information Policies," *Government Information Quarterly* 24, no. 4 (2007): 843.

48. Jaeger, "Information Policy," 843.

49. Egon Bittner, *Aspects of Police Work* (Boston: Northeastern University Press, 1990), 94–97.

50. Michael Buckland, "Information as Thing," *Journal of the American Society of Information Science* 42, no. 5 (1991): 351–60.

51. Buckland, "Information as Thing," 351.

52. See Bittner, *Aspects of Police Work*, 97.

53. Steve Herbert, "Tangled Up in Blue: The Elusive Quest for Police Legitimacy," *Theoretical Criminology* 10, no. 4 (2006): 482.

54. Herbert, "Tangled Up in Blue," 482.

55. Samuel Walker, *Police Accountability: The Role of Citizen Oversight* (Belmont, CA: Wadsworth Thompson Learning, 2000), 7.

56. Andrew John Goldsmith, "Policing's New Visibility," *British Journal of Criminology* 50, no. 5 (2010): 915 (internal citations omitted).

57. Herbert, "Tangled Up in Blue," 489.

58. Herbert, "Tangled Up in Blue," 489.

59. Peter K. Manning, *The Narc's Game: Organizational and Informational Limits on Drug Law Enforcement* (Cambridge, MA: MIT Press, 1980), 55.

60. See Bittner, *Aspects of Police Work*, 48.

61. Bittner, *Aspects of Police Work*, 37.

62. Bittner, *Aspects of Police Work*, 33; and Herbert, "Tangled Up in Blue," 481–82.

CHAPTER 3. BYSTANDER VIDEO AND "THE RIGHT TO RECORD"

1. See "Wife's Cellphone Video Shows Police Shooting of Keith Lamont Scott," *Washington Post*, September 23, 2016, www.washingtonpost.com/video

/national/wifes-cellphone-video-shows-police-shooting-of-keith-lamont-scott/2016/09/23/301813fa-81b3-11e6-9578-558cc125c7ba_video.html.

2. Mary D. Fan, *Camera Power: Proof, Policing, Privacy, and Audiovisual Big Data* (Cambridge, UK: Cambridge University Press, 2019), 18 (re: "regulation by information"); and Tyler Wall and Travis Linnemann, "Staring Down the State: Police Power, Visual Economies, and the 'War on Cameras,'" *Crime, Media and Culture* 10, no. 2 (2014): 137 (re: "interests of the state").

3. Jonathan Finn, "Seeing Surveillantly: Surveillance as Social Practice," in *Eyes Everywhere: The Global Growth of Camera Surveillance*, ed. Aaron Doyle, Randy Lippert, and David Lyon, (Abingdon, UK: Routledge, 2012), 77 (re: "passive or hidden observation"); Seth F. Kreimer, "Pervasive Image Capture and the First Amendment: Memory, Discourse, and the Right to Record," *University of Pennsylvania Law Review* 159, no. 2 (2011): 344 (re: "spontaneous image capture"); and Finn, "Seeing Surveillantly," 77; Kreimer, "Pervasive Image Capture," 344–347 (re: "a form of civic engagement or duty").

4. Stuart Allan, *Citizen Witnessing: Revisioning Journalism in Times of Crisis* (Cambridge, UK: Polity Press, 2013), 76.

5. Kevin D. Haggerty and Ajay Sandhu, "The Police Crisis of Visibility," *IEEE Technology and Society Magazine* 2014 (Summer): 11.

6. Howard M. Wasserman, "Police Misconduct, Video Recording, and Procedural Barriers to Rights Enforcement," *North Carolina Law Review* 96 (2018): 1314.

7. See Justin Fenton, "Claim: Woman Arrested, Camera Destroyed after Recording Baltimore Police," *Baltimore Sun*, May 15, 2013, http://articles.baltimoresun.com/2013-05-15/news/bal-claim-woman-arrested-camera-destroyed-after-recording-baltimore-police-20130515_1_christopher-sharp-camera-phone-wbal-tv.

8. See, for example, J.A. v. Miranda, Civil Action No. PX 16-3953 (D.C. MD. September 1, 2017); State v. Russo, 407 P.3d 137, 192–93 (Hawaii 2017); and Gerskovich v. Iocco, 15 Civ. 7280 (RMB) (S.D.N.Y., July 17, 2017).

9. Gillan and Quinton v. The United Kingdom, (2010) 50 E.H.R.R. 45 (ECtHR, 2010).

10. Smith v. City of Cumming, 212 F.3d 1332, 1333 (11th Cir. 2000).

11. See, for example, Blackston v. Alabama, 30 F.3d 117, 120 (11th Cir. 1994); Iacobucci v. Boulter, 1997; Thompson v. City of Clio, 765 F.Supp. 1066, 1070–71 (M.D.Ala. 1991) (re: film public meetings); Fordyce v. City of Seattle, 55 F.3d 436, 439 (9th Cir. 1995) (re: matters of public interest); and United States v. Hastings, 695 F.2d 1278, 1281 (11th Cir.1983); Lambert v. Polk County, 723 F.Supp. 128, 133 (S.D.Iowa, 1989) (re: greater right to document or access information).

12. Glik v. Cunniffe, 655 F.3d 78, 85 (1st Cir. 2011).

13. *Glik*, 655 F.3d at 85.

14. ACLU of Illinois v. Alvarez, 679 F.3d 583, 586–87 (7th Cir. 2012).

15. Sharp v. Baltimore City Police et al., DOJ Statement of Interest, CA 11–2888 (D.Md. Jan. 10, 2012).

16. Gericke v. Begin, 753 F.3d 1 (1st Cir. 2014).

17. Bowens v. Superintendent of Miami South Beach Police Dept., 557 Fed. Appx. 857 (11th Cir. 2014).

18. Fields v. City of Philadelphia, 862 F.3d 353, 360 (3rd Cir. 2017) (internal citations omitted).

19. *Fields*, 862 F.3d at 360.

20. *Fields*, 862 F.3d at 359.

21. *Fields*, 862 F.3d at 360 (internal citations omitted).

22. *Russo*, 407 P.3d 137.

23. Gerskovich v. Iocco, 15 Civ. 7280 (RMB) (S.D.N.Y., July 17, 2017).

24. Margaret Kohn, "Unblinking: Citizens and Subjects in the Age of Video Surveillance," *Constellations* 17 (2010): 572–88.

25. Mocek v. City of Albuquerque, 3 F.Supp.3d 1002, 1074–76 (D.N.M., 2014); and Mocek v. City of Albuquerque, No. CIV 11–1009 JB/KBM (D.N.M., January 14, 2013).

26. King v. City of Indianapolis, 969 F.Supp.2d 1085, 1092 (S.D. Ind., 2013).

27. Sandberg v. Englewood, Colorado, 727 Fed.Appx. 950, 963 (10th Cir. 2018).

28. Kelly v. Borough of Carlisle, 622 F.3d 248, 262 (3rd Cir. 2010).

29. But Lichtenberg and Smith found evidence that "police homicides and assaults were found to be very infrequent occurrences during traffic encounters," casting "doubt . . . on the United States Supreme Court's reliance on an assumption of danger during the routine police–citizen traffic encounter." Illya D. Lichtenberg and Alisa Smith, "How Dangerous Are Routine Police–citizen Traffic Stops? A Research Note," *Journal of Criminal Justice* 29, no. 5 (2001): 419, 426.

30. Fleck v. Trustees of University of Pennsylvania, 995 F.Supp.2d 390, 397–98 (E.D.Pa., 2014).

31. State v. Roden, 179 Wash.2d 893, 900 (Wash. 2014) (internal citations omitted); see also State v. Kipp, 179 Wash.2d 718, 729 (Wash. 2014).

32. *Fordyce*, 55 F.3d 436.

33. State v. Flora, 68 Wash.App. 802, 806 (Wash. Ct. App. 1992).

34. *Flora*, 68 Wash.App. at 808.

35. See, for example, *Roden*, 179 Wash.2d at 899–900; and Johnson v. Hawe, 388 F.3d 676 (9th Cir. 2004).

36. State v. D.J.W., 76 Wash.App. 135, 140 (Wash. App. 1994); Kadoranian v. Bellingham Police Dept., 119 Wash.2d 178, 190 (Wash. 1992); *Flora*, 68 Wash.App. at 806; and *Johnson*, 388 F.3d at 683.

37. Alford v. Haner, 333 F.3d 972, 976 (9th Cir. 2003).

38. *Johnson*, 388 F.3d at 684.

39. State v. Modica, 136 Wash.App. 434, 449 (Wash. App. 2006); see also State v. Townsend, 147 Wash.2d 666, 675 (Wash. 2002); and In re Marriage of Farr, 87 Wash.App. 177, 184 (Wash. App. 1997).

40. RCW § 9.73.030(3).

41. *Modica*, 136 Wash.App. 434; State v. Pejsa, 75 Wash.App. 139 (Wash. App. 1994) (re: telephone conversations); *Townsend*, 147 Wash.2d 666 (re: emails); and *In re Marriage of Farr*, 87 Wash.App. 177 (re: voicemail messages).

42. State v. Caliguri, 99 Wash.2d 501 (Wash. 1983) (re: commit murder); and State v. Williams, 94 Wash.2d 531 (Wash. 1980); RCW § 9.73.030(2)(b) (re: extortion/blackmail or unlawful requests).

43. State v. Bonilla, 23 Wash.App. 869 (Wash. App., 1979); RCW § 9.73.030(2)(a) (re: police and fire stations); RCW § 9.73.030(2)(c) (re: "at an extremely inconvenient hour"); and *Pejsa*, 75 Wash.App. 139; RCW § 9.73.030(2)(d) (re: hostage takers or barricaded persons).

44. Kevin D. Haggerty, "Tear Down the Walls: On Demolishing the Panopticon," in *Theorizing Surveillance: The Panopticon and Beyond*, ed. David Lyon (Cullompton, UK: Willan Publishing, 2006), 30.

45. Charles Goodwin, "Professional Vision," *American Anthropologist* 96, no. 3 (1994): 606, 615–16.

46. Ajay Sandhu and Kevin D. Haggerty, "Policing on Camera," *Theoretical Criminology* 21, no. 1 (2017): 89.

47. Richard V. Ericson, "The News Media and Account Ability in Criminal Justice," in *Accountability for Criminal Justice: Selected Essays*, ed. Philip C. Stenning (Toronto: University of Toronto Press, 1995), 137.

48. Richard V. Ericson, Patricia M. Baranek, and Janet B. L. Chan, *Negotiating Control: A Study of News Sources* (Toronto: University of Toronto Press, 1989).

49. Laura Huey, Kevin Walby, and Aaron Doyle, "Cop Watching in the Downtown Eastside: Exploring the Use of (Counter) Surveillance as a Tool of Resistance," in *Surveillance and Security: Technological Politics and Power in Everyday Life*, ed. Torin Monahan (New York: Routledge, 2006), 155.

50. Wall and Linnemann, "Staring Down the State: Police Power, Visual Economies, and the 'War on Cameras,'" *Crime, Media and Culture* 10, no. 2 (2014): 133–49 (re: "war on cameras"); and Stephanie Simon, "Suspicious Encounters: Ordinary Preemption and the Securitization of Photography," *Security Dialogue* 43, no. 2 (2012): 159–70 (re: "preemptive security" measure).

51. Simon, "Suspicious Encounters," 162.

52. Sandhu and Haggerty, "Policing on Camera," 80–81.

53. Sandhu and Haggerty, "Policing on Camera," 84–85; and Ajay Sandhu, "Camera-Friendly Policing: How the Police Respond to Cameras and Photographers," *Surveillance & Society* 14, no. 1 (2016): 82–83.

54. Sandhu and Haggerty, "Policing on Camera," 82, 84; and Sandhu, "Camera-Friendly Policing," 83.

55. Sandhu and Haggerty, "Policing on Camera," 88.

56. Ashley K. Farmer, "Copwatchers: Citizen Journalism and the Changing Police-Community Dynamic" (PhD diss., University of Delaware, 2016), 11.

57. Famer and Sun, "Citizen Journalism and Police Legitimacy," 248, 252–53; and Farmer, "Copwatchers," 105.

58. Gregory R. Brown, "The Blue Line on Thin Ice: Police Use of Force Modifications in the Era of Cameraphones and YouTube," *British Journal of Criminology* 56, no. 2 (2016): 293–312.

59. Brown, "Blue Line on Thin Ice," 302.

60. Brown, "Blue Line on Thin Ice," 304.

61. Huey, Walby, and Doyle, "Cop Watching in the Downtown Eastside."

62. Huey, Walby, and Doyle, "Cop Watching in the Downtown Eastside," 155.

63. *Russo*, 407 P.3d at 140.

64. *Russo*, 407 P.3d at 148–49, citing *Gericke*, 753 F.3d at 8.

65. Goodwin, "Professional Vision," 606.

66. Susann Wagenknecht, "Beyond Non-/Use: The Affected Bystander and Her Escalation," *New Media & Society* 20, no. 7 (2018): 2236.

67. Mitchell Dean, *Governmentality: Power and Rule in Modern Society* (London: SAGE, 2010), 17–19.

68. Dean, *Governmentality*, 19.

69. Ben Brucato, "The New Transparency: Police Violence in the Context of Ubiquitous Surveillance," *Media and Communication* 3, no. 3 (2015): 44.

70. Brucato, "New Transparency," 44.

71. This became a rallying cry for protestors seeking police video in the aftermath of the police shooting of Keith Lamont Scott in Charlotte, North Carolina, in September 2016. See Alan Yuhas and Oliver Laughland, "Charlotte Police Release Footage of Fatal Keith Scott Shooting," *Guardian*, September 25, 2016, www.theguardian.com/us-news/2016/sep/24/video-keith-scott-shooting-charlotte-police.

72. See, for example, Rémi Boivin et al., "The Body-Worn Camera Perspective Bias," *Journal of Experimental Criminology* 13, no. 1 (2017): 125–42.

73. Goodwin, "Professional Vision," 606.

CHAPTER 4. POLICING AS (MONITORED) PERFORMANCE

1. See Michael D. White, Janne E. Gaub, and Natalie Todak, "Exploring the Potential for Body-Worn Cameras to Reduce Violence in Police–Citizen Encounters," *Policing* 12, no. 1 (2018): 66–76.

2. White, Gaub, and Todak, "Exploring the Potential for Body-Worn Cameras," n7.

3. Baris Cayli, Charlotte Hargreaves, and Philip Hodgson, "Body-Worn Cameras: Determining the Democratic Habitus of Policing," *Safer Communities* 17, no. 4 (2018): 216–18.

4. Cayli, Hargreaves, and Hodgson, "Body-Worn Cameras," 219.

5. Cayli, Hargreaves, and Hodgson, "Body-Worn Cameras," 220.

6. Cayli, Hargreaves, and Hodgson, "Body-Worn Cameras," 217.

7. Cayli, Hargreaves, and Hodgson, "Body-Worn Cameras," 217.

8. Cayli, Hargreaves, and Hodgson, "Body-Worn Cameras," 218–20.

9. Cayli, Hargreaves, and Hodgson, "Body-Worn Cameras," 218.

10. Edmonton Police Service, *Body Worn Video: Considering the Evidence* (final report of the Edmonton Police Service Body Worn Video Pilot Project, June 2015), 27.

11. Barak Ariel, "Police Body Cameras in Large Police Departments," *Journal of Criminal Law & Criminology* 106, no. 4 (2016): 753.

12. Ariel, "Police Body Cameras in Large Police Departments," 753.

13. Michael D. White, Natalie Todak, and Janne E. Gaub, "Examining Body-Worn Camera Integration and Acceptance among Police Officers, Citizens, and External Stakeholders," *Criminology & Public Policy* 17, no. 3 (2018): 660.

14. White, Todak, and Gaub, "Examining Body-Worn Camera Integration," 660.

15. White, Todak, and Gaub, "Examining Body-Worn Camera Integration," 660.

16. Jessica Huff, Charles M. Katz, and Vincent J. Webb, "Understanding Police Officer Resistance to Body-Worn Cameras," *Policing: An International Journal* 41, no. 4 (2018): 489.

17. Huff, Katz, and Webb, "Understanding Police Officer Resistance," 491.

18. Sander Flight, *Focus: Evaluatie pilot bodycams Politie Eenheid Amsterdam 2017–2018* (report of the Politie & Wetenschap and Sander Flight Onderzoek & Advies, 2019), 132–33.

19. Max Goetschel and Jon M. Peha, "Police Perceptions of Body-Worn Cameras," *American Journal of Criminal Justice* 42 (2017): 705.

20. John Ortiz Smykla et al., "Police Body-Worn Cameras: Perceptions of Law Enforcement Leadership," *American Journal of Criminal Justice* 41 (2016): 434–35.

21. Ian Adams and Sharon Mastracci, "Police Body-Worn Cameras: Effects on Officers' Burnout and Perceived Organizational Support," *Police Quarterly* 22, no. 1 (2019): 15.

22. Adams and Mastracci, "Police Body-Worn Cameras," 14.

23. Barak Ariel, William A. Farrar, and Alex Sutherland, "The Effect of Police Body-Worn Cameras on Use of Force and Citizens' Complaints against the Police: A Randomized Controlled Trial," *Journal of Quantitative Criminology* 31, no. 3 (2015): 524.

24. Anthony A. Braga et al., "The Effects of Body-Worn Cameras on Police Activity and Police-Citizen Encounters: A Randomized Controlled Trial," *Journal of Criminal Law & Criminology* 108, no. 3 (2018): 533–34.

25. Ariel, "Police Body Cameras in Large Police Departments," 756.

26. Braga et al., "Effects of Body-Worn Cameras," 535.

27. David Yokum, Anita Ravishankar, and Alexander Coppock, "Evaluating the Effects of Police Body-Worn Cameras: A Randomized Controlled Trial" (report [working paper] of The Lab @ DC, Office of the City Administrator, Executive Office of the Mayor, Washington, DC, October 20, 2017), https://bwc.thelab.dc.gov/TheLabDC_MPD_BWC_Working_Paper_10.20.17.pdf.

28. Kristen Drew, "Bellingham Police Now Equipped with Body Cameras," *KOMO News*, October 3, 2014, https://web.archive.org/web/20201112033850/https://komonews.com/news/local/bellingham-police-now-equipped-with-body-cameras.

29. Rebecca Wexler, "Technology's Continuum: Body Cameras, Data Collection and Constitutional Searches," in *Visual Imagery and Human Rights Practice*, ed. Sandra Ristovska and Monroe Price (Cham, Switzerland: Palgrave Macmillan, 2018), 91, 93–94.

30. Wexler, "Technology's Continuum," 91–92, 102.

31. Ajay Sandhu and Kevin D. Haggerty, "Policing on Camera," *Theoretical Criminology* 21, no. 1 (2017): 89 (re: "ability to control the accounts of what happened on the street"); and Richard V. Ericson, "The News Media and Account Ability in Criminal Justice," in *Accountability for Criminal Justice: Selected Essays*, ed. Philip C. Stenning (Toronto: University of Toronto Press, 1995), 137 (re: "satisfy the rights and obligations of accountability"; emphasis in original).

32. Richard V. Ericson, Patricia M. Baranek, and Janet B. L. Chan, *Negotiating Control: A Study of News Sources* (Toronto: University of Toronto Press, 1989).

33. Steve Herbert, *Citizens, Cops, and Power* (Chicago: University of Chicago Press, 2006); and Steve Herbert, "Tangled Up in Blue: The Elusive Quest for Police Legitimacy," *Theoretical Criminology* 10, no. 4 (2006): 481–504.

34. Herbert, "Tangled Up in Blue," 482, 487–88.

35. Herbert, "Tangled Up in Blue," 487–88.

36. Herbert, "Tangled Up in Blue," 488.

37. Ariel, Farrar, and Sutherland, "Effect of Police Body-Worn Cameras," 509–35.

38. Herbert, "Tangled Up in Blue," 491.

39. Herbert, *Citizens, Cops, and Power*; and Herbert, "Tangled Up in Blue."

CHAPTER 5. THE (TECHNO-)REGULATION OF POLICE WORK

1. Jon McKenzie, *Perform or Else: From Discipline to Performance* (New York: Routledge, 2001).

2. Louise Amoore and Alexandra Hall, "Border Theatre: On the Arts of Security and Resistance," *Cultural Geographies* 17, no. 3 (2010): 303.

3. Baris Cayli, Charlotte Hargreaves, and Philip Hodgson, "Body-Worn Cameras: Determining the Democratic Habitus of Policing," *Safer Communities* 17, no. 4 (2018): 217 (re: aware of their own behavior); Michael D. White, Natalie Todak, and Janne E. Gaub, "Examining Body-Worn Camera Integration and Acceptance among Police Officers, Citizens, and External Stakeholders," *Criminology & Public Policy* 17, no. 3 (2018): 660 (re: perceptions may wane over time); and Jessica Huff, Charles M. Katz, and Vincent J. Webb, "Understanding Police Officer Resistance to Body-Worn Cameras," *Policing: An International Journal* 41, no. 4 (2018): 489 (re: characteristics of individual officers).

4. Barak Ariel, "Police Body Cameras in Large Police Departments," *Journal of Criminal Law & Criminology* 106, no. 4 (2016): 752 (re: *decrease* the likelihood that officers will make an arrest); Anthony A. Braga et al., "The Effects of Body-Worn Cameras on Police Activity and Police-Citizen Encounters: A Randomized Controlled Trial," *Journal of Criminal Law & Criminology* 108, no. 3 (2018): 532 (re: *increase* the likelihood that officers will issue citations and make arrests): and Justin T. Ready and Jacob T. N. Young, "The Impact of On-Officer Video Cameras on Police-Citizen Contacts: Findings from a Controlled Experiment in Mesa, AZ," *Journal of Experimental Criminology* 11, no. 3 (2015): 451–52 (re: not more or less likely to make arrests).

5. Braga et al., "Effects of Body-Worn Cameras," 533–35; and Barak Ariel, William A. Farrar, and Alex Sutherland, "The Effect of Police Body-Worn Cameras on Use of Force and Citizens' Complaints against the Police: A Randomized Controlled Trial," *Journal of Quantitative Criminology* 31, no. 3 (2015): 523–24.

6. David Yokum, Anita Ravishankar, and Alexander Coppock, "Evaluating the Effects of Police Body-Worn Cameras: A Randomized Controlled Trial" (Report [Working Paper] of The Lab @ DC, Office of the City Administrator, Executive Office of the Mayor, Washington, DC, October 20, 2017, https://bwc.thelab.dc.gov/TheLabDC_MPD_BWC_Working_Paper_10.20.17.pdf (re: impact on overall use of force); and Ariel, "Police Body Cameras in Large Police Departments," 756 (re: reports filed by officers did increase significantly).

7. Yokum, Ravishankar, and Coppock, "Evaluating the Effects of Police Body-Worn Cameras," 22.

8. Cayli, Hargreaves, and Hodgson, "Body-Worn Cameras," 218–220; and Ariel, "Police Body Cameras in Large Police Departments," 752–53.

9. Ariel, "Police Body Cameras in Large Police Departments," 753.

10. Julia Black, "What Is Regulatory Innovation?," in *Regulatory Innovation*, ed. Julia Black, Martin Lodge, and Mark Thatcher (Cheltenham, UK: Edward Elgar, 2005), 11.

11. Ronald Leenes, "Framing Techno-Regulation: An Exploration of State and Non-State Regulation by Technology," *Legisprudence* 5, no. 2 (2011): 149.

12. Peter Manning, "Technology, Law and Policing," in *Comparative Policing from a Legal Perspective*, ed. Monica den Boer (Cheltenham, UK: Edward Elgar Publishing, 2018), 305.

13. State v. Creegan, 123 Wn. App. 718, 722 (Wash. App. 2004).

14. Bob Ferguson, "Video and Audio Recording of Communications between Citizens and Law Enforcement Officers Using Body Cameras Attached to Police Uniforms," Washington State Office of the Attorney General, opinion no. 8, Nov. 24, 2014, www.atg.wa.gov/ago-opinions/video-and-audio-recording-communications-between-citizens-and-law-enforcement-officers.

15. Rebecca Wexler, "Technology's Continuum: Body Cameras, Data Collection and Constitutional Searches," in *Visual Imagery and Human Rights Practice*, ed. Sandra Ristovska and Monroe Price (Cham, Switzerland: Palgrave Macmillan, 2018), 91, 93–94.

16. Wexler, "Technology's Continuum," 91–92, 102.

17. Lawrence Lessig, *Code and Other Laws of Cyberspace* (New York: Basic Books, 1999), 53.

18. Howard W. Odum, "Notes on the Technicways in Contemporary Society," *American Sociological Review* 2, no. 3 (1937): 336; and *Oxford Dictionaries*, s.v. "Folkways," accessed November 14, 2019, https://en.oxforddictionaries.com/definition/folkways.

19. Manning, "Technology, Law and Policing," 290.

20. Manning, "Technology, Law and Policing," 290.

21. danah boyd, *It's Complicated: The Social Lives of Networked Teens* (New Haven, CT: Yale University Press, 2014), 10.

22. boyd, *It's Complicated*, 10–11.

23. Ryan Calo, "Can Americans Resist Surveillance?," *University of Chicago Law Review* 83 (2016): 24 (internal quotations omitted).

24. boyd, *It's Complicated*, 11.

25. Scottish Government (UK), *The Effectiveness of Public Space CCTV: A Review of Recent Published Evidence Regarding the Impact of CCTV on Crime* (report of the Justice Analytical Services, Police and Community Safety Directorate, Edinburgh, Scottish Government, 2009, 4.

26. See, for example, Rachel Armitage, "To CCTV or Not to CCTV? A Review of Current Research into the Effectiveness of CCTV Systems in Reducing Crime," NACRO, May 2002, www.epic.org/privacy/surveillance/spotlight/0505/nacro02.pdf.

27. Steve Miletich, "Seattle Police Sergeant Demoted for Retaliating against Man Angry about Being Towed," *Seattle Times*, December 7, 2018, www.seattletimes.com/seattle-news/crime/seattle-police-sergeant-disciplined-demoted-for-sitting-outside-workplace-of-man-who-cursed-him/.

28. *Oxford Dictionaries*, s.v. "civility," accessed November 14, 2019, https://en.oxforddictionaries.com/definition/civility.

29. Steve Herbert, "Tangled Up in Blue: The Elusive Quest for Police Legitimacy," *Theoretical Criminology* 10, no. 4 (2006): 489 (re: "create the social reality that they police"); and Peter K. Manning, *The Narc's Game: Organizational and Informational Limits on Drug Law Enforcement* (Cambridge, MA: MIT Press, 1980), 55 (re: environment in which officers act).

30. Barak Ariel et al., "Wearing Body Cameras Increases Assaults against Officers and Does Not Reduce Police Use of Force: Results from a Global Multi-Site Experiment," *European Journal of Criminology* 13, no. 6 (2016): 744–55.

31. Ariel, "Police Body Cameras in Large Police Departments," 753.

32. Vanita Gupta, foreword to *The Illusion of Accuracy: How Body-Worn Camera Footage Can Distort Evidence* (report from Upturn and The Leadership Conference on Civil & Human Rights, November 2017), https://www.upturn.org/reports/2017/the-illusion-of-accuracy/.

33. Gupta, foreword; Upturn, *Illusion of Accuracy*; see also Leadership Conference & Upturn, *Police Body Worn Cameras: A Policy Scorecard* (The Leadership Conference on Civil & Human Rights and Upturn, November 2017), https://www.bwcscorecard.org/.

34. Upturn, *Illusion of Accuracy*.

35. Upturn, *Illusion of Accuracy*.

36. Brennan Center, "Police Body-Worn Camera Policies," Brennan Center, July 19, 2019, www.brennancenter.org/our-work/research-reports/police-body-worn-camera-policies.

37. Gupta, foreword; and Upturn, *Illusion of Accuracy*.

38. Sander Flight, *Focus: Evaluatie pilot bodycams Politie Eenheid Amsterdam 2017–2018* (report of the Politie & Wetenschap and Sander Flight Onderzoek & Advies, 2019), 133–34.

39. Steve Herbert, *Citizens, Cops, and Power* (Chicago: University of Chicago Press, 2006); and Herbert, "Tangled Up in Blue."

CHAPTER 6. PUBLIC DISCLOSURE AS "DIRECT TO YOUTUBE" ALTERNATIVE

1. See Lee Rankin, "End of Program Evaluation/Recommendations: On-Officer Body Camera System," Mesa Police Department, 2013, 5, 12–13. http://issuu.com/leerankin6/docs/final_axon_flex_evaluation_12-3-13-.

2. Karen Levy and Solon Barocas, "Refractive Surveillance: Monitoring Customers to Manage Workers," *International Journal of Communication* 12 (2018): 1166.

3. See Jessica Glenza, "Seattle Police Post Blurry Body-camera Videos to YouTube in Transparency Bid," *Guardian*, March 9, 2015, http://www.theguardian.com/us-news/2015/mar/09/seattle-police-posting-body-camera-footage-youtube-transparency.

4. One important note regarding this question's modified format on Survey 3 should be made here, as neutral responses increased dramatically on this question, from below 5 percent on the first survey to almost 25 percent on the third survey. It appears likely that the placement of the neutral response choice in the middle of the five-point spectrum influenced the frequency with which respondents chose this option.

5. However, we also see neutral responses increasing sharply on Survey 3, suggesting that this decline in positive responses may (or may not) be attributable to the changed placement of the neutral response choice in the Likert scale, rather than to any meaningful change in respondent attitudes. Regardless, the results clearly indicate a much stronger level of agreement with limited public access than with more liberal access policies.

6. Importantly, the 2016 legislation, which was proposed and enacted after some of the fieldwork was conducted, provided for a categorical exemption for the statements of victims of sexual assault or domestic violence. See Revised Code of Washington § 42.56.240(14)(a)(vi)–(vii).

CONCLUSION

1. Peter K. Manning, *The Narc's Game: Organizational and Informational Limits on Drug Law Enforcement* (Cambridge, MA: MIT Press, 1980), 55.

2. Paul T. Jaeger, "Information Policy, Information Access, and Democratic Participation: The National and International Implications of the Bush Administration's Information Policies," *Government Information Quarterly* 24, no. 4 (2007): 842.

3. Daniel J. Solove, "Access and Aggregation: Privacy, Public Records, and the Constitution," *Minnesota Law Review* 86 (2002): 1138.

4. Daniel J. Solove, "Privacy and Power: Computer Databases and Metaphors for Information Privacy," *Stanford Law Review* 53 (2001): 1393–1462; Solove, "Access and Aggregation" (re: "database problem"); and Kevin D. Haggerty and Richard V. Ericson, "The Surveillant Assemblage," *British Journal of Sociology* 51, no. 4 (2000): 605–22 (re: "surveillant assemblage").

5. Andrew Roberts, "A Republican Account of the Value of Privacy," *European Journal of Political Theory* 14, no. 3 (2015): 329.

6. Roberts, "Republican Account," 322.

7. M. Ryan Calo, "The Boundaries of Privacy Harm," *Indiana Law Journal* 86 (2011): 1143.

8. Julie E. Cohen, *Configuring the Networked Self: Law, Code, and the Play of Everyday Practice* (New Haven, CT: Yale University Press, 2012), 6.

9. Philip Pettit, "Freedom as Antipower," *Ethics* 106, no. 3 (1996): 578.

10. Pettit, "Freedom as Antipower," 584.

11. Julie E. Cohen, "What Privacy Is For," *Harvard Law Review* 126 (2013): 1905 (re: "informed and reflective citizenship); and Michael L. Rich, "Limits on the Perfect Preventative State," *Connecticut Law Review* 46 (2014): 928 (re: "gaps . . . in systems").

12. Alan Westin, *Privacy and Freedom* (New York: Atheneum, 1967), 21–22.

13. Cohen, "What Privacy Is For," 1905.

14. Roberts, "Republican Account," 339.

15. Manuel Castells, *Communication Power* (Oxford: Oxford University Press, 2009), 197.

16. Jonah Bossewitch and Aram Sinnreich, "The End of Forgetting: Strategic Agency Beyond the Panopticon," *New Media & Society* 15, no. 2 (2012): 225.

17. Steve Herbert, "Tangled Up in Blue: The Elusive Quest for Police Legitimacy," *Theoretical Criminology* 10, no. 4 (2006): 489 (re: local communities); and Manning, *Narc's Game*, 55 (re: "act in accord with, and reify").

METHODOLOGICAL NOTE

1. The timing of the survey distributions was impacted by a number of considerations, including finalizing access to the departments for purposes of the research. It would have been ideal to administer the first questionnaire prior to any deployment by each department, but it was not possible to do so for the SPD.

2. See, for example, Wesley G. Jennings, Lorie A. Fridell, and Mathew D. Lynch, "Cops and Cameras: Officer Perceptions of the Use of Body-Worn Cameras in Law Enforcement," *Journal of Criminal Justice* 42, no. 6 (2014): 549–56.

3. See Paul Chynoweth, "Legal Research," in *Advanced Research Methods in the Built Environment*, ed. Andrew Knight and Les Ruddock (Oxford: Blackwell Publishing, 2008), 28, 29.

4. Terry Hutchinson and Nigel Duncan, "Defining and Describing What We Do: Doctrinal Legal Research," *Deakin Law Review* 17, no. 1 (2012): 84.

5. Chynoweth, "Legal Research."

6. Hutchinson and Duncan, "Defining and Describing What We Do," 85.

7. Hutchinson and Duncan, "Defining and Describing What We Do," 99.

8. Brian Z. Tamanaha, *Realistic Socio-legal Theory: Pragmatism and a Social Theory of Law* (Oxford: Clarendon Press, 1997), 26–57.

9. Victoria Nourse and Gregory Shaffer, "Varieties of New Legal Realism: Can a New World Order Prompt a New Legal Theory?," *Cornell Law Review* 95 (2009): 61–137.

10. Nourse and Shaffer, "Varieties of New Legal Realism," 70.

11. Nourse and Shaffer, "Varieties of New Legal Realism," 70.

12. Nourse and Shaffer, "Varieties of New Legal Realism," 79–85 (account of NLR); and Tamanaha, *Realistic Socio-legal Theory*.

Bibliography

Adams, Ian, and Sharon Mastracci. "Police Body-Worn Cameras: Effects on Officers' Burnout and Perceived Organizational Support." *Police Quarterly* 22, no. 1 (2019): 5–30.

Allan, Stuart. *Citizen Witnessing: Revisioning Journalism in Times of Crisis.* Cambridge, UK: Polity Press, 2013.

Allan, Stuart, and Chris Peters. "Visual Truths of Citizen Reportage: Four Research Problematics." *Information, Communication & Society* 18, no. 11 (2015): 1348–61.

Amoore, Louise, and Alexandra Hall. "Border Theatre: On the Arts of Security and Resistance." *Cultural Geographies* 17, no. 3 (2010): 299–319.

Antony, Mary Grace, and Ryan J. Thomas. "'This Is Citizen Journalism at Its Finest': YouTube and the Public Sphere in the Oscar Grant Shooting Incident." *New Media & Society* 12, no. 8 (2010): 1280–96.

Ariel, Barak. "Police Body Cameras in Large Police Departments." *Journal of Criminal Law & Criminology* 106, no. 4 (2016): 729–68.

Ariel, Barak, William A. Farrar, and Alex Sutherland. "The Effect of Police Body-Worn Cameras on Use of Force and Citizens' Complaints against the Police: A Randomized Controlled Trial." *Journal of Quantitative Criminology* 31, no. 3 (2015): 509–35.

Ariel, Barak, Alex Sutherland, Darren Henstock, Josh Young, Paul Drover, Jayne Sykes, Simon Megicks, and Ryan Henderson. "Report: Increases in Police Use of Force in the Presence of Body-Worn Cameras Are Driven by Officer Discretion: A Protocol-Based Subgroup Analysis of Ten Randomized Experiments." *Journal of Experimental Criminology* 12, no. 3 (2016): 453–63.

———. "Wearing Body Cameras Increases Assaults against Officers and Does Not Reduce Police Use of Force: Results from a Global Multi-Site Experiment." *European Journal of Criminology* 13, no. 6 (2016): 744–55.

Armitage, Rachel. "To CCTV or Not to CCTV? A Review of Current Research into the Effectiveness of CCTV Systems in Reducing Crime." NACRO, May 2002. www.epic.org/privacy/surveillance/spotlight/0505/nacro02.pdf.

Balkin, Jack M. "Digital Speech and Democratic Culture: A Theory of Freedom of Expression for the Information Society." *New York University Law Review* 79, no. 1 (2004): 1–58.

———. "The Future of Free Expression in a Digital Age." *Pepperdine Law Review* 36 (2009): 427–44.

———. "Room for Maneuver: Julie Cohen's Theory of Freedom in the Information State." *Jerusalem Review of Legal Studies* 6, no. 1 (2012): 79–95.

Ball, Kirstie. "Categorizing the Workers: Electronic Surveillance and Social Ordering in the Call Center." In *Surveillance as Social Sorting: Privacy, Risk and Digital Discrimination*, edited by David Lyon, 201–25. London: Routledge, 2003.

Bennett, Colin, Charles Raab, and Priscilla Regan. "People and Place: Patterns of Individual Identification within Intelligent Transportation Systems." In *Surveillance as Social Sorting: Privacy, Risk and Digital Discrimination*, edited by David Lyon, 153–75. London: Routledge, 2003.

Berkelaar, Brenda L., and Millie A. Harrison. "Information Visibility." In *Oxford Research Encyclopedia of Communication*. Oxford: Oxford University Press, 2019. doi:10.1093/acrefore/9780190228613.013.12.

Besson, Samantha, and Jose Luis Marti. "Law and Republicanism: Mapping the Issues." In *Legal Republicanism: National and International Perspectives*, edited by Samantha Besson and Jose Luis Marti, 3–36. Oxford: Oxford University Press, 2009.

Birchall, Clare. "Radical Transparency?" *Cultural Studies ↔ Critical Methodologies* 14, no. 1 (2014): 77–88.

Bittner, Egon. *Aspects of Police Work*. Boston: Northeastern University Press, 1990.

Black, Julia. "What Is Regulatory Innovation?" In *Regulatory Innovation*, edited by Julia Black, Martin Lodge, and Mark Thatcher, 1–15. Cheltenham, UK: Edward Elgar, 2005.

Bock, Mary Angela. "Film the Police! Cop-Watching and Its Embodied Narratives." *Journal of Communication* 66, no. 1 (2016): 13–34.

Boivin, Rémi, Annie Gendron, Camille Faubert, and Bruno Poulin. "The Body-Worn Camera Perspective Bias." *Journal of Experimental Criminology* 13, no. 1 (2017): 125–42.

Bossewitch, Jonah, and Aram Sinnreich. "The End of Forgetting: Strategic Agency beyond the Panopticon." *New Media & Society* 15, no. 2 (2012): 224–42.

boyd, danah. *It's Complicated: The Social Lives of Networked Teens*. New Haven, CT: Yale University Press, 2014.

Braga, Anthony A., William H. Sousa, James R. Coldren Jr., and Denise Rodriguez. "The Effects of Body-Worn Cameras on Police Activity and Police-Citizen Encounters: A Randomized Controlled Trial." *Journal of Criminal Law & Criminology* 108, no. 3 (2018): 511–38.

Braman, Sandra. *Change of State: Information, Policy, and Power*. Cambridge, MA: MIT Press, 2006.

———. "Defining Information Policy." *Journal of Information Policy* 1, no. 1 (2011): 1–5.

Brennan Center. "Police Body-Worn Camera Policies." Brennan Center "Resource," July 19, 2019. www.brennancenter.org/our-work/research-reports/police-body-worn-camera-policies.

Brighenti, Andrea. "Visibility: A Category for the Social Sciences." *Current Sociology* 55, no. 3 (2007): 323–42.

Brown, Gregory R. "The Blue Line on Thin Ice: Police Use of Force Modifications in the Era of Cameraphones and YouTube." *British Journal of Criminology* 56, no. 2 (2016): 293–312.

Brucato, Ben. "Fabricating the Color Line in a White Democracy: From Slave Catchers to Petty Sovereigns." *Theoria: A Journal of Social and Political Theory* 61, no. 141 (2014): 30–54.

———. "The New Transparency: Police Violence in the Context of Ubiquitous Surveillance." *Media and Communication* 3, no. 3 (2015): 39–55.

———. "Standing by Police Violence: On the Constitution of the Ideal Citizen as Sousveiller." *American Studies Journal* 61 (2016): art. 6. www.asjournal.org/61–2016/standing-police-violence-constitution-ideal-citizen-sousveiller.

Buckland, Michael. "Information as Thing." *Journal of the American Society of Information Science* 42, no. 5 (1991): 351–60.

Calo, M. Ryan. "The Boundaries of Privacy Harm." *Indiana Law Journal* 86 (2011): 1131–62.

Calo, Ryan. "Can Americans Resist Surveillance?" *University of Chicago Law Review* 83 (2016): 23–43.

Castells, Manuel. *Communication Power*. Oxford: Oxford University Press, 2009.

———. "Communication, Power and Counter-Power in the Network Society." *International Journal of Communication* 1 (2007): 238–66.

Cayli, Baris, Charlotte Hargreaves, and Philip Hodgson. "Body-Worn Cameras: Determining the Democratic Habitus of Policing." *Safer Communities* 17, no. 4 (2018): 213–23.

Chan, Janet B. L. "The Technological Game: How Information Technology Is Transforming Police Practice." *Criminal Justice* 1, no. 2 (2001): 139–59.

Chynoweth, Paul. "Legal Research." In *Advanced Research Methods in the Built Environment*, edited by Andrew Knight and Les Ruddock, 28–38. Oxford: Blackwell Publishing, 2008.

Cohen, Julie E. *Configuring the Networked Self: Law, Code, and the Play of Everyday Practice*. New Haven, CT: Yale University Press, 2012.

Cohen, Julie E. *Configuring the Networked Self: Law, Code, and the Play of Everyday Practice*. New Haven, CT: Yale University Press, 2012.

———. "What Privacy Is For." *Harvard Law Review* 126 (2013): 1904–33.

Cohen, Stanley. *Visions of Social Control: Crime, Punishment and Classification*. Cambridge, UK: Polity, 1985.

Correia, David, and Tyler Wall, *Police: A Field Guide*. London: Verso, 2018.

Coultrup, Sherri, and Patrick D. Fountain. "Effects of Electronic Monitoring and Surveillance on the Psychological Contract of Employees: An Exploratory Study." *Proceedings of the American Society of Business and Behavioral Sciences* 19, no. 1 (2012): 219–35.

Dean, Jodi. *Publicity's Secret: How Technoculture Capitalizes on Democracy*. Ithaca, NY: Cornell University Press, 2002.

Dean, Mitchell. *Governmentality: Power and Rule in Modern Society*. London: SAGE, 2010.

DeLanda, Manuel. *War in the Age of Intelligent Machines*. New York: Zone, 1991.

Drew, Kristen. "Bellingham Police Now Equipped with Body Cameras." *KOMO News*, October 3, 2014. https://web.archive.org/web/20201112033850/https://komonews.com/news/local/bellingham-police-now-equipped-with-body-cameras.

Edmonton Police Service. *Body Worn Video: Considering the Evidence*. Final Report of the Edmonton Police Service Body Worn Video Pilot Project, June 2015.

Eikenberry, Kenneth O., and Nancy Thygesen Day. "Recording Conversations—Emergencies—Central Dispatch." Opinion of the Washington Attorney General No. 11 (May 20, 1988).

Ellis, Tom, Craig Jenkins, and Paul Smith. *Evaluation of the Introduction of Personal Issue Body Worn Video Cameras (Operation Hyperion) on the Isle of Wight*. Final Report to Hampshire Constabulary. University of Portsmouth, 2015.

Ericson, Richard V. "The News Media and Account Ability in Criminal Justice." In *Accountability for Criminal Justice: Selected Essays*, edited by Philip C. Stenning, 135–61. Toronto: University of Toronto Press, 1995.

Ericson, Richard V., Patricia M. Baranek, and Janet B. L. Chan. *Negotiating Control: A Study of News Sources*. Toronto: University of Toronto Press, 1989.

Ericson, Richard V., and Kevin D. Haggerty. *Policing the Risk Society*. Toronto: University of Toronto Press, 1997.

Etzioni, Amitai. "A Cyber Age Privacy Doctrine: A Liberal Communitarian Approach." *I/S: A Journal of Law and Policy for the Information Society* 10, no. 2 (2014): 641–69.

———. *The Limits of Privacy*. New York: Basic Books, 1999.

———. *Privacy in a Cyber Age: Policy and Practice*. New York: Palgrave Macmillan, 2015.

Fan, Mary D. *Camera Power: Proof, Policing, Privacy, and Audiovisual Big Data*. Cambridge, UK: Cambridge University Press, 2019.

———. "Privacy, Public Disclosure, Police Body Cameras: Policy Splits." *Alabama Law Review* 68, no. 2 (2016): 395–444.

Farmer, Ashley K. "Copwatchers: Citizen Journalism and the Changing Police-Community Dynamic." PhD diss., University of Delaware, 2016.

Farmer, Ashley K., and Ivan Y. Sun. "Citizen Journalism and Police Legitimacy: Does Recording the Police Make a Difference?" In *The Politics of Policing: Between Force and Legitimacy*, edited by Mathieu Deflem, 239–56. Bingley, UK: Emerald Group Publishing, 2016.

Fenton, Justin. "Claim: Woman Arrested, Camera Destroyed after Recording Baltimore Police." *Baltimore Sun*, May 15, 2013. http://articles.baltimoresun.com/2013-05-15/news/bal-claim-woman-arrested-camera-destroyed-after-recording-baltimore-police-20130515_1_christopher-sharp-camera-phone-wbal-tv.

Ferguson, Bob. "Video and Audio Recording of Communications between Citizens and Law Enforcement Officers Using Body Cameras Attached to Police Uniforms." Washington State Office of the Attorney General, opinion no. 8 (November 24, 2014). www.atg.wa.gov/ago-opinions/video-and-audio-recording-communications-between-citizens-and-law-enforcement-officers.

Finn, Jonathan. "Seeing Surveillantly: Surveillance as Social Practice." In *Eyes Everywhere: The Global Growth of Camera Surveillance*, edited by Aaron Doyle, Randy Lippert, and David Lyon, 67–80. Abingdon, UK: Routledge, 2012.

Flight, Sander. *Focus: Evaluatie pilot bodycams Politie Eenheid Amsterdam 2017–2018*. Report of the Politie & Wetenschap, Den Haag, and Sander Flight Onderzoek & Advies, 2019.

Forcese, Craig, and Aaron Freeman. *The Laws of Government: The Legal Foundations of Canadian Democracy*. Toronto: Irwin Law, 2005.

Foucault, Michel. *Discipline and Punish: The Birth of the Prison*. Translated by Alan Sheridan. Hammondsworth, UK: Penguin, 1979.

Gates, Kelly. "The Work of Wearing Cameras: Body-Worn Devices and Police Media Labor." In *The Routledge Companion to Labor and Media*, edited by Richard Maxwell, 252–64. New York: Routledge, 2017.

Gill, Martin, and Angela Spriggs. *Home Office Research Study 292: Assessing the Impact of CCTV*. The Home Office (UK), February 2005.

Glenza, Jessica. "Seattle Police Post Blurry Body-Camera Videos to YouTube in Transparency Bid." *Guardian*, March 9, 2015. www.theguardian.com/us-news/2015/mar/09/seattle-police-posting-body-camera-footage-youtube-transparency.

Goetschel, Max, and Jon M. Peha. "Police Perceptions of Body-Worn Cameras." *American Journal of Criminal Justice* 42 (2017): 698–726.

Goldsmith, Andrew. "Police Reform and the Problem of Trust." *Theoretical Criminology* 9, no. 4 (2005): 443–70.

Goldsmith, Andrew John. "Policing's New Visibility." *British Journal of Criminology* 50, no. 5 (2010): 914–34.

Goodwin, Charles. "Professional Vision." *American Anthropologist* 96, no. 3 (1994): 606–33.

Greer, Chris, and Eugene McLaughlin. "We Predict a Riot? Public Order Policing, New Media Environments and the Rise of the Citizen Journalist." *British Journal of Criminology* 50, no. 6 (2010): 1041–59.

Gupta, Vanita. Foreword to *The Illusion of Accuracy: How Body-Worn Camera Footage Can Distort Evidence*. Report from Upturn and The Leadership Conference on Civil & Human Rights, November 2017. www.upturn.org/reports/2017/the-illusion-of-accuracy/.

Hagan, John, and Ronit Dinovitzer. "Collateral Consequences of Imprisonment for Children, Communities, and Prisoners." *Crime and Justice* 26 (1999): 121–62.

Haggerty, Kevin D. "Tear Down the Walls: On Demolishing the Panopticon." In *Theorizing Surveillance: The Panopticon and Beyond*, edited by David Lyon, 23–45. Cullompton, UK: Willan Publishing, 2006.

Haggerty, Kevin D., and Richard V. Ericson. "The New Politics of Surveillance and Visibility." In *The New Politics of Surveillance and Visibility*, edited by Kevin D. Haggerty and Richard V. Ericson, 3–25. Toronto: University of Toronto Press, 2006.

———. "The Surveillant Assemblage." *British Journal of Sociology* 51, no. 4 (2000): 605–22.

Haggerty, Kevin D., and Ajay Sandhu. "The Police Crisis of Visibility." *IEEE Technology and Society Magazine*, Summer 2014, 9–12.

Hartzog, Woodrow, and Frederic Stutzman. "The Case for Online Obscurity." *California Law Review* 101, no. 1 (2013): 1–49.

Herbert, Steve. *Citizens, Cops, and Power*. Chicago: University of Chicago Press, 2006.

———. "Tangled Up in Blue: The Elusive Quest for Police Legitimacy." *Theoretical Criminology* 10, no. 4 (2006): 481–504.

Hermida, Alberto, and Víctor Hernández-Santaolalla. "Twitter and Video Activism as Tools for Countersurveillance: The Case of Social Protests in Spain." *Information, Communication & Society* 21, no. 3 (2018): 416–33.

Huey, Laura, Kevin Walby, and Aaron Doyle. "Cop Watching in the Downtown Eastside: Exploring the Use of (Counter) Surveillance as a Tool of Resistance." In *Surveillance and Security: Technological Politics and Power in Everyday Life*, edited by Torin Monahan, 149–65. New York: Routledge, 2006.

Huff, Jessica, Charles M. Katz, and Vincent J. Webb. "Understanding Police Officer Resistance to Body-Worn Cameras." *Policing: An International Journal* 41, no. 4 (2018): 482–95.

Hutchinson, Terry, and Nigel Duncan. "Defining and Describing What We Do: Doctrinal Legal Research." *Deakin Law Review* 17, no. 1 (2012): 83–119.

Jaeger, Paul T. "Information Policy, Information Access, and Democratic Participation: The National and International Implications of the Bush Administration's Information Policies." *Government Information Quarterly* 24, no. 4 (2007): 840–59.

Jaeger, Paul T., and Natalie Greene Taylor. *Foundations of Information Policy*. Chicago: ALA Neal-Schuman, 2019.

Jennings, Wesley G., Lorie A. Fridell, and Mathew D. Lynch. "Cops and Cameras: Officer Perceptions of the Use of Body-Worn Cameras in Law Enforcement." *Journal of Criminal Justice* 42, no. 6 (2014): 549–56.

Johnston, Anna, and Myra Cheng. "Electronic Surveillance in the Workplace: Concerns for Employees and Challenges for Privacy Advocates." Paper delivered at the International Conference on Personal Data Protection, November 28, 2002, Seoul, Korea.

Kohn, Margaret. "Unblinking: Citizens and Subjects in the Age of Video Surveillance." *Constellations* 17 (2010): 572–88.

Koops, Bert-Jaap. "Criteria for Normative Technology: An Essay on the Acceptability of 'Code as Law' in Light of Democratic and Constitutional Values."

In *Regulating Technologies*, edited by Roger Brownsword and Karen Yeung, 157–74. Oxford: Hart Publishing, 2008.

Koops, Bert-Jaap, Bryce Clayton Newell, Andrew Roberts, Ivan Skorvánek, and Maša Galič. "The Reasonableness of Remaining Unobserved: A Comparative Analysis of Visual Surveillance and Voyeurism in Criminal Law." *Law & Social Inquiry* 43, no. 4 (2018): 1210–35.

Koops, Bert-Jaap, Bryce Clayton Newell, Tjerk Timan, Ivan Škorvánek, Tomislav Chokrevski, and Maša Galič. "A Typology of Privacy." *University of Pennsylvania Journal of International Law* 38 (2017): 483–575.

Kreimer, Seth F. "Pervasive Image Capture and the First Amendment: Memory, Discourse, and the Right to Record." *University of Pennsylvania Law Review* 159, no. 2 (2011): 335–409.

Leadership Conference & Upturn, *Police Body Worn Cameras: A Policy Scorecard*. The Leadership Conference on Civil & Human Rights and Upturn, November 2017. https://www.bwcscorecard.org/.

Lee, Murray, Emmeline Taylor, and Matthew Willis. "Being Held to Account: Detainees' Perceptions of Police Body-Worn Cameras." *Australian & New Zealand Journal of Criminology* 52, no. 2 (2019): 174–92.

Leenes, Ronald. "Framing Techno-Regulation: An Exploration of State and Non-State Regulation by Technology." *Legisprudence* 5, no. 2 (2011): 143–69.

Leman-Langlois, Stéphane. Afterword to *Technocrime: Technology, Crime and Social Control*, edited by Stéphane Leman-Langlois, 243–46. Portland, OR: Willan, 2008.

Lessig, Lawrence. *Code and Other Laws of Cyberspace*. New York: Basic Books, 1999.

Levy, Karen, and Solon Barocas. "Refractive Surveillance: Monitoring Customers to Manage Workers." *International Journal of Communication* 12 (2018): 1166–88.

Lichtenberg, Illya D., and Alisa Smith. "How Dangerous Are Routine Police–Citizen Traffic Stops? A Research Note." *Journal of Criminal Justice* 29, no. 5 (2001): 419–28.

Lomell, Heidi Mork. "Targeting the Unwanted: Video Surveillance and Categorical Exclusion in Oslo, Norway." *Surveillance & Society* 2, nos. 2/3 (2004): 346–60.

Lovett, Frank, and Philip Pettit. "Neorepublicanism: A Normative and Institutional Research Program." *Annual Review of Political Science* 12 (2009): 11–30.

Lyon, David. "The Search for Surveillance Theories." In *Theorizing Surveillance: The Panopticon and Beyond*, edited by David Lyon, 3–20. Cullompten, UK: Willan Publishing, 2006.

———, ed. *Surveillance as Social Sorting: Privacy, Risk, and Digital Discrimination*. London: Routledge, 2003.

———. *Surveillance Studies: An Overview*. Cambridge, UK: Polity Press, 2007.

Mann, Steve, and Joseph Ferenbok. "New Media and the Power Politics of Sousveillance in a Surveillance Dominated World." *Surveillance & Society* 11, nos. 1/2 (2013): 18–34.

Mann, Steve, Jason Nolan, and Barry Wellman. "Sousveillance: Inventing and Using Wearable Computing Devices for Data Collection in Surveillance Environments." *Surveillance & Society* 1, no. 3 (2003): 331–55.
Manning, Peter K. *The Narc's Game: Organizational and Informational Limits on Drug Law Enforcement*. Cambridge, MA: MIT Press, 1980.
———. "Technology, Law and Policing." In *Comparative Policing from a Legal Perspective*, edited by Monica den Boer, 290–305. Cheltenham, UK: Edward Elgar Publishing, 2018.
Marx, Gary T. "Surveillance and Society." In *Encyclopedia of Social Theory*, edited by George Ritzer, 816–21. Thousand Oaks, CA: SAGE, 2005.
Maskaly, Jon, Christopher Donner, Wesley G. Jennings, Barak Ariel, and Alex Sutherland. "The Effects of Body-Worn Cameras (BWCs) on Police and Citizen Outcomes: A State-of-the-Art Review." *Policing: An International Journal of Police Strategies & Management* 40, no 4 (2017): 672–88.
Mathiesen, Thomas. "The Viewer Society: Michel Foucault's 'Panopticon' Revisited." *Theoretical Criminology* 1, no. 2 (1997): 215–34.
Mawby, Rob C. *Policing Images: Policing, Communication and Legitimacy*. Portland, OR: Willan Publishing, 2002.
McCahill, Michael. *The Surveillance Web: The Rise of Visual Surveillance in an English City*. Portland, OR: Willan Publishing, 2002.
McKenzie, Jon. *Perform or Else: From Discipline to Performance*. New York: Routledge, 2001.
Meiklejohn, Alexander. "The First Amendment Is an Absolute." *Supreme Court Review* 1961 (1961): 245–66.
———. *Free Speech and Its Relation to Self-Government*. New York: Harper, 1948.
———. *Political Freedom: The Constitutional Powers of the People*. New York: Harper, 1960.
Milan, Stefania, and Lonneke van der Velden. "The Alternative Epistemologies of Data Activism." *Digital Culture and Society* 2, no. 2 (2016): 57–74.
Miletich, Steve. "Seattle Police Sergeant Demoted for Retaliating against Man Angry about Being Towed." *Seattle Times*, December 7, 2018. www.seattletimes.com/seattle-news/crime/seattle-police-sergeant-disciplined-demoted-for-sitting-outside-workplace-of-man-who-cursed-him/.
Miller, Kevin. "Total Surveillance, Big Data, and Predictive Crime Technology: Privacy's Perfect Storm." *Journal of Technology Law & Policy* 19 (2014): 105–46.
Monahan, Torin. "Counter-Surveillance as Political Intervention?" *Social Semiotics* 16, no. 4 (2006): 515–34.
Moore, Adam D. "Employee Monitoring and Computer Technology: Evaluative Surveillance v. Privacy." *Business Ethics Quarterly* 10, no. 3 (2000): 697–709.
———. *Privacy Rights: Moral and Legal Foundations*. University Park: Pennsylvania State University Press, 2010.
———. "Privacy, Speech, and the Law." *Journal of Information Ethics* 22, no. 1 (2013): 21–43.
Murakami Wood, David, and C. William R. Webster. "Living in Surveillance Societies: The Normalisation of Surveillance in Europe and the Threat of

Britain's Bad Example." *Journal of Contemporary European Research* 5, no. 2 (2009): 259–73.

Nelkin, Dorothy, and Lori Andrews. "Surveillance Creep in the Genetic Age." In *Surveillance as Social Sorting: Privacy, Risk and Digital Discrimination*, edited by David Lyon, 94–110. London: Routledge, 2003.

Neocleous, Mark. *Critique of Security*. Edinburgh: Edinburgh University Press, 2008.

———. *The Fabrication of Social Order: A Critical Theory of Police Power*. London: Pluto Press, 2000.

Newell, Bryce Clayton. "Collateral Visibility: A Socio-legal Study of Police Body-Camera Adoption, Privacy, and Public Disclosure in Washington State." *Indiana Law Journal* 92, no. 4 (2017): 1329–99.

———. "Crossing Lenses: Policing's New Visibility and the Role of 'Smartphone Journalism' as a Form of Freedom-Preserving Reciprocal Surveillance." *Journal of Law, Technology & Policy* 2014, no. 1 (2014): 59–104.

———. "The Massive Metadata Machine: Liberty, Power, and Secret Mass Surveillance in the U.S. and Europe." *I/S: A Journal of Law and Policy for the Information Society* 10, no. 2 (2014): 481–522.

———. "Technopolicing, Surveillance, and Citizen Oversight: A Neorepublican Theory of Liberty and Information Control." *Government Information Quarterly* 31, no. 3 (2014): 421–31.

———. "Transparent Lives and the Surveillance State: Policing, New Visibility, and Information Policy." PhD diss., University of Washington, 2015.

Norris, Clive, and Gary Armstrong. *The Maximum Surveillance Society: The Rise of CCTV*. Oxford: Berg, 1999.

Nourse, Victoria, and Gregory Shaffer. "Varieties of New Legal Realism: Can a New World Order Prompt a New Legal Theory?" *Cornell Law Review* 95 (2009): 61–137.

Odum, Howard W. "Notes on the Technicways in Contemporary Society." *American Sociological Review* 2, no. 3 (1937): 336–46.

Palmås, Karl. "Predicting What You'll Do Tomorrow: Panspectric Surveillance and the Contemporary Corporation." *Surveillance & Society* 8, no. 3 (2011): 338–54.

Paperman, Patricia. "Surveillance Underground: The Uniform as an Interactive Device." *Ethnography* 4, no 3 (2003): 397–419.

Pettit, Philip. "Freedom as Antipower." *Ethics* 106, no. 3 (1996): 576–604.

Poudrier, Jennifer. "'Racial' Categories and Health Risks: Epidemiological Surveillance among Canadian First Nations." In *Surveillance as Social Sorting: Privacy, Risk and Digital Discrimination*, edited by David Lyon, 111–34. London: Routledge, 2003.

Rahr, Sue, and Stephen K. Rice. "From Warriors to Guardians: Recommitting American Police Culture to Democratic Ideals." *New Perspectives in Policing Bulletin* (April 2015): 1–14. NCJ 248654.

Rankin, Lee. 2013. "End of Program Evaluation/Recommendations: On-Officer Body Camera System." Mesa Police Department, 2013. http://issuu.com/leerankin6/docs/final_axon_flex_evaluation_12-3-13-.

Ready, Justin T., and Jacob T. N. Young. "The Impact of On-Officer Video Cameras on Police-Citizen Contacts: Findings from a Controlled Experiment in Mesa, AZ." *Journal of Experimental Criminology* 11, no. 3 (2015): 445–58.

Reddish, Martin H. *The Adversary First Amendment*. Stanford, CA: Stanford University Press, 2013.

Reddish, Martin H., and Abby Marie Mollen. "Understanding Post's and Meiklejohn's Mistakes: The Central Role of Adversary Democracy in the Theory of Free Expression." *Northwestern University Law Review* 103, no. 3 (2009): 1303–70.

Reiner, Robert. "The Dialectics of Dixon: The Changing Image of the TV Cop." In *Police Force, Police Service: Care and Control in Britain*, ed. Mike Stephens and Saul Becker, 11–32. London: Macmillan, 1994.

Rich, Michael L. "Limits on the Perfect Preventative State." *Connecticut Law Review* 46 (2014): 883–935.

Roberts, Andrew. "A Republican Account of the Value of Privacy." *European Journal of Political Theory* 14, no. 3 (2015): 320–44.

Sætnan, Ann Rudinow, Heidi Mork Lomell, and Carsten Wiecek. "Controlling CCTV in Public Spaces: Is Privacy the (Only) Issue? Reflections on Norwegian and Danish Observations." *Surveillance and Society* 2, nos. 2/3 (2004): 396–414.

Sandhu, Ajay. "Camera-Friendly Policing: How the Police Respond to Cameras and Photographers." *Surveillance & Society* 14, no. 1 (2016): 78–89.

Sandhu, Ajay, and Kevin D. Haggerty. "Policing on Camera." *Theoretical Criminology* 21, no. 1 (2017): 78–95.

Scottish Government (UK). *The Effectiveness of Public Space CCTV: A Review of Recent Published Evidence Regarding the Impact of CCTV on Crime.* Justice Analytical Services, Police and Community Safety Directorate. Edinburgh: Scottish Government, 2009.

Simon, Stephanie. "Suspicious Encounters: Ordinary Preemption and the Securitization of Photography." *Security Dialogue* 43, no. 2 (2012): 157–73.

Smykla, John Ortiz, Matthew S. Crow, Vaughn J. Crichlow, and Jamie A. Snyder. "Police Body-Worn Cameras: Perceptions of Law Enforcement Leadership." *American Journal of Criminal Justice* 41 (2016): 424–43.

Solove, Daniel J. "Access and Aggregation: Privacy, Public Records, and the Constitution." *Minnesota Law Review* 86 (2002): 1137–1209.

———. *The Digital Person: Technology and Privacy in the Information Age.* New York: New York University Press, 2004.

———. "Privacy and Power: Computer Databases and Metaphors for Information Privacy." *Stanford Law Review* 53 (2001): 1393–1462.

———. "A Taxonomy of Privacy." *University of Pennsylvania Law Review* 154 (2006): 477–564.

Sousa, William H., Terance D. Miethe, and Mari Sakiyama. "Inconsistencies in Public Opinion of Body-Worn Cameras on Police: Transparency, Trust, and Improved Police–Citizen Relationships." *Policing* 12, no. 1 (2018): 100–108.

Squillacote, Rosa, and Leonard Feldman. "Police Abuse and Democratic Accountability: Agonistic Surveillance of the Administrative State." In *Police*

Abuse in Contemporary Democracies, edited by Michelle D. Bonner, Guillermina Seri, Mary Rose Kubal, and Michael Kempa, 135–64. Cham, Switzerland: Palgrave Macmillan, 2018.

Stalder, Felix, and David Lyon. "Electronic Identity Cards and Social Classification." In *Surveillance as Social Sorting: Privacy, Risk and Digital Discrimination*, edited by David Lyon, 77–93. London: Routledge, 2003.

Stanley, Jay. "Police Body-Mounted Cameras: With Right Policies in Place, a Win for All." American Civil Liberties Union, 2013. www.aclu.org/files/assets/police_body-mounted_cameras.pdf.

———. "Police Body-Mounted Cameras: With Right Policies in Place, a Win for All (Version 2.0)." American Civil Liberties Union, March 2015. www.aclu.org/sites/default/files/assets/police_body-mounted_cameras-v2.pdf.

Stohl, Cynthia, Michael Stohl, and Paul M. Leonardi. "Managing Opacity: Information Visibility and the Paradox of Transparency in the Digital Age." *International Journal of Communication* 10 (2016): 123–37.

Stoughton, Seth. "Law Enforcement's 'Warrior' Problem." *Harvard Law Review Forum* 128 (2015): 225–34.

Stuart, Forrest. "Becoming 'Copwise': Policing, Culture, and the Collateral Consequences of Street-Level Criminalization." *Law & Society Review* 50, no. 2 (2016): 279–313.

Sunstein, Cass R. *Democracy and the Problem of Free Speech*. New York: Free Press, 1993.

Tamanaha, Brian Z. *Realistic Socio-legal Theory: Pragmatism and a Social Theory of Law*. Oxford: Clarendon Press, 1997.

Taylor, Emmeline, and Murray Lee. "Off the Record? Arrestee Concerns about the Manipulation, Modification, and Misrepresentation of Police Body-Worn Camera Footage." *Surveillance & Society* 17, nos. 3/4 (2019): 473–83.

———. "Points of View: Arrestees' Perspectives on Police Body-Worn Cameras and Their Perceived Impact on Police–Citizen Interactions." *British Journal of Criminology* 59, no. 4 (July 2019): 958–78.

Ten, C. L. "Mill on Self-Regarding Actions." *Philosophy* 43 (1968): 29–37.

Tester, Keith. Introduction to *The Flâneur*, edited by Keith Tester, 1–21. London: Routledge, 1994.

Thompson, John B. "The New Visibility." *Theory, Culture and Society* 22, no. 6 (2005): 31–51.

Timan, Tjerk. "The Body-Worn Camera as a Transitional Technology." *Surveillance & Society* 14, no. 1 (2016): 145–49.

Travis, Jeremy. "Invisible Punishment: An Instrument of Social Exclusion." In *Invisible Punishment: The Collateral Consequences of Mass Imprisonment*, edited by Marc Mauer and Meda Chesney-Lind, 15–36. New York: New Press, 2002.

Upturn. *The Illusion of Accuracy: How Body-Worn Camera Footage Can Distort Evidence*. Upturn and The Leadership Conference on Civil & Human Rights, November 2017. www.upturn.org/reports/2017/the-illusion-of-accuracy/.

Vitale, Alex S. *The End of Policing*. London: Verso, 2017.

Volokh, Eugene. "Freedom of Speech and Information Privacy: The Troubling Implications of a Right to Stop People from Speaking about You." *Stanford Law Review* 52 (2000): 1049–1124.

Wagenknecht, Susann. "Beyond Non-/Use: The Affected Bystander and Her Escalation." *New Media & Society* 20, no. 7 (2018): 2235–51.

Walker, Samuel. *Police Accountability: The Role of Citizen Oversight*. Belmont, CA: Wadsworth Thompson Learning, 2000.

Wall, Tyler, and Travis Linnemann. "Staring Down the State: Police Power, Visual Economies, and the 'War on Cameras.'" *Crime, Media and Culture* 10, no. 2 (2014): 133–49.

Washington Post. "Wife's Cellphone Video Shows Police Shooting of Keith Lamont Scott." September 23, 2016. www.washingtonpost.com/video/national/wifes-cellphone-video-shows-police-shooting-of-keith-lamont-scott/2016/09/23/301813fa-81b3-11e6-9578-558cc125c7ba_video.html.

Wasserman, Howard M. "Police Misconduct, Video Recording, and Procedural Barriers to Rights Enforcement." *North Carolina Law Review* 96 (2018): 1313–62.

Webster, C. William R. "CCTV Policy in the UK: Reconsidering the Evidence Base." *Surveillance & Society* 6, no. 1 (2009): 10–22.

Westin, Alan F. *Privacy and Freedom*. New York: Atheneum, 1967.

Wexler, Rebecca. "Technology's Continuum: Body Cameras, Data Collection and Constitutional Searches." In *Visual Imagery and Human Rights Practice*, edited by Sandra Ristovska and Monroe Price, 89–105. Cham, Switzerland: Palgrave Macmillan, 2018.

Whitaker, Reg. *The End of Privacy: How Total Surveillance Is Becoming a Reality*. New York: New Press, 1999.

White, Michael D., Janne E. Gaub, and Natalie Todak. "Exploring the Potential for Body-Worn Cameras to Reduce Violence in Police–Citizen Encounters." *Policing* 12, no. 1 (2018): 66–76.

White, Michael D., Natalie Todak, and Janne E. Gaub. "Examining Body-Worn Camera Integration and Acceptance among Police Officers, Citizens, and External Stakeholders." *Criminology & Public Policy* 17, no. 3 (2018): 649–77.

Wilson, Dean, and Tanya Serisier. "Video Activism and the Ambiguities of Counter-Surveillance." *Surveillance & Society* 8, no. 2 (2010): 166–80.

Yokum, David, Anita Ravishankar, and Alexander Coppock. "Evaluating the Effects of Police Body-Worn Cameras: A Randomized Controlled Trial." Report (Working Paper) of The Lab @ DC, Office of the City Administrator, Executive Office of the Mayor, Washington, DC, October 20, 2017. https://bwc.thelab.dc.gov/TheLabDC_MPD_BWC_Working_Paper_10.20.17.pdf.

Yuhas, Alan, and Oliver Laughland, "Charlotte Police Release Footage of Fatal Keith Scott Shooting." *Guardian*, September 25, 2016. www.theguardian.com/us-news/2016/sep/24/video-keith-scott-shooting-charlotte-police.

Zureik, Elia. "Theorizing Surveillance: The Case of the Workplace." In *Surveillance as Social Sorting: Privacy, Risk and Digital Discrimination*, edited by David Lyon, 31–56. London: Routledge, 2003.

CASES

ACLU of Illinois v. Alvarez, 679 F.3d 583 (7th Cir. 2012).
Alford v. Haner, 333 F.3d 972 (9th Cir. 2003).
Blackston v. Alabama, 30 F.3d 117 (11th Cir. 1994).
Bowens v. Superintendent of Miami South Beach Police Dept., 557 Fed.Appx. 857 (11th Cir. 2014).
Department of Justice v. Reporters Committee for Freedom of the Press, 489 U.S. 749 (1989).
Fields v. City of Philadelphia, 862 F.3d 353 (3rd Cir. 2017).
Fleck v. Trustees of University of Pennsylvania, 995 F.Supp.2d 390 (E.D.Pa., 2014).
Fordyce v. City of Seattle, 55 F.3d 436 (9th Cir. 1995).
Gericke v. Begin, 753 F.3d 1 (1st Cir. 2014).
Gerskovich v. Iocco, 15 Civ. 7280 (RMB) (S.D.N.Y., July 17, 2017).
Gillan and Quinton v. The United Kingdom, (2010) 50 E.H.R.R. 45 (ECtHR, 2010).
Glik v. Cunniffe, 655 F.3d 78 (1st Cir. 2011).
Iacobucci v. Boulter, No. CIV.A. 94-10531 (D.Mass, Mar. 26, 1997).
In re Marriage of Farr, 87 Wash.App. 177 (Wash. App. 1997).
J.A. v. Miranda, Civil Action No. PX 16-3953 (D.C. MD. September 1, 2017).
Johnson v. Hawe, 388 F.3d 676 (9th Cir. 2004).
Kadoranian v. Bellingham Police Dept., 119 Wash.2d 178 (Wash. 1992).
Kelly v. Borough of Carlisle, 622 F.3d 248 (3rd Cir. 2010).
King v. City of Indianapolis, 969 F.Supp.2d 1085 (S.D. Ind., 2013).
Lambert v. Polk County, 723 F.Supp. 128 (S.D.Iowa, 1989).
Lewis v. State, Dept. of Licensing, 157 Wash.2d 446 (Wash. 2006).
Mocek v. City of Albuquerque, No. CIV 11–1009 JB/KBM (D.N.M., January 14, 2013).
Mocek v. City of Albuquerque, 3 F.Supp.3d 1002 (D.N.M., 2014).
Sandberg v. Englewood, 727 Fed.Appx. 950 (10th Cir. 2018).
Sharp v. Baltimore City Police et al., DOJ Statement of Interest, CA 11–2888 (D.Md. Jan. 10, 2012).
Smith v. City of Cumming, 212 F.3d 1332 (11th Cir. 2000).
State v. Bonilla, 23 Wash.App. 869 (Wash. App., 1979).
State v. Caliguri, 99 Wash.2d 501 (Wash. 1983).
State v. Creegan, 123 Wash. App. 718 (Wash. App. 2004).
State v. D.J.W., 76 Wash.App. 135 (Wash. App. 1994).
State v. Flora, 68 Wash.App. 802 (Wash. Ct. App. 1992).
State v. Kipp, 179 Wash.2d 718 (Wash. 2014).
State v. Modica, 136 Wash.App. 434 (Wash. App. 2006).
State v. Pejsa, 75 Wash.App. 139 (Wash. App. 1994).
State v. Roden, 179 Wash.2d 893 (Wash. 2014).
State v. Russo, 407 P.3d 137 (Hawaii 2017).
State v. Townsend, 147 Wash.2d 666 (Wash. 2002).
State v. Williams, 94 Wash.2d 531 (Wash. 1980).

Thompson v. City of Clio, 765 F.Supp. 1066 (M.D.Ala. 1991).
United States v. Hastings, 695 F.2d 1278 (11th Cir.1983).

STATUTES AND OTHER LEGISLATION

Revised Code of Washington § 9.73.030, *et seq.*
Revised Code of Washington § 42.56, *et seq.*
Senate Bill 6408, 65th Legislature, 2018 Regular Session (Washington, 2018).

Index

Note: BPD refers to Bellingham Police Department and SPD refers to Spokane Police Department

Founded in 1893,
UNIVERSITY OF CALIFORNIA PRESS
publishes bold, progressive books and journals on topics in the arts, humanities, social sciences, and natural sciences—with a focus on social justice issues—that inspire thought and action among readers worldwide.

The UC PRESS FOUNDATION
raises funds to uphold the press's vital role as an independent, nonprofit publisher, and receives philanthropic support from a wide range of individuals and institutions—and from committed readers like you. To learn more, visit ucpress.edu/supportus.

Milton Keynes UK
Ingram Content Group UK Ltd.
UKHW012255080124
435686UK00007B/546